Islam, a Challenge to Faith; Studies on the
Mohammedan Religion and the Needs and
Opportunities of the Mohammedan World
From the Standpoint of Christian Missions

ISLAM: A CHALLENGE TO FAITH

Peter J. Zwemer

Hon. Ion Keith Falconer

Karl G. Pfander

Bishop Valpy French

C. V. A. Van Dyck

Kamil Abdel Messiah

Henry Martyn

Benjamin W. Labaree

PIONEERS IN MOSLEM LANDS

ISLAM

A CHALLENGE TO FAITH

STUDIES ON THE MOHAMMEDAN RELIGION
AND THE NEEDS AND OPPORTUNITIES OF
THE MOHAMMEDAN WORLD FROM THE
STANDPOINT OF CHRISTIAN MISSIONS

BY

SAMUEL M. ZWEMER, F.R.G.S.

SECRETARY, STUDENT VOLUNTEER MOVEMENT
MISSIONARY IN ARABIA

NEW YORK
STUDENT VOLUNTEER MOVEMENT
FOR FOREIGN MISSIONS
1907

TO MY WIFE

συγκοινωνή μου ἐν τῇ θλίψει καὶ ἐν τῇ
βασιλείᾳ καὶ ὑπομονῇ Ἰησοῦ Χριστοῦ

"There are comparative religions, but Christianity is not one of them."—*Joseph Parker.*

"To talk, as some do, as if the religion of the prophet of Arabia were well suited to the Semites, or to the Mogul and Turkish races, or, again, to the Negro, is merely to show oneself culpably ignorant at once of human nature, of Christian truth, and even of Islam itself. Such platitudes will never satisfy anyone who has at heart the highest interests of his fellowmen.

"Just as was the case at Rome at the close of one of the great æons in the world's history, so now among ourselves there are men, priding themselves on their enlightenment and liberality of sentiment, who—as their prototypes worshipped Isis and Serapis, or, again, followed Epicurus or Plato, according as the varying fashion of the day might impel them—are ready to call themselves now Agnostics, now Buddhists, and now Mohammedans, as the fancy may strike them. Such men may, perhaps, bolster up Islam for a time, and thus, for a time, retard its inevitable downfall. But, in spite of their utmost efforts, the true nature of this religious system will become generally known, and will then be seen to be indefensible. Mohammed is, in every way, unfitted to be the ideal of a single human being In spite, therefore, of its many half-truths borrowed from other systems, it is not too much to say that Islam has preserved, in the life and character of its founder, an enduring and ever active principle of degradation and decay."—*W. St. Clair Tisdall.*

PREFACE

The churches of Christendom are at last awaking to the fact that one of the great unsolved missionary problems of the Twentieth Century is the evangelization of the Mohammedan world. The Cairo Conference reports, the Haystack Centennial volume, the organization of new missionary societies for work among Moslems, and the recent statements concerning the Moslem peril in West Africa and the Soudan, all carry this message to the churches and the student-world of Christendom. The Cairo Conference appeal, voicing the opinion of many leading missionaries from every Moslem land, was primarily a call for trained men from the universities and professional schools. And this appeal, in the words of Mr. John R. Mott, "has laid upon students as never before the responsibility of reaching the Mohammedan world."

But if we are to reach that world with the gospel of Christ we must first know of it and know it. There is no lack of literature on Mohammed and Islam, as is evident from the very extensive bibliography of the subject in all the languages of Europe, not to speak of the literature written by Moslems themselves. But at the same time there is great ignorance even among cultured people of the real character of Mohammed and the real doctrine and moral value of Islam, as well as of its widespread aggressive power as a missionary religion. To present the subject anew, therefore, needs no apology, especially since much of the best literature on Islam is inaccessible to most readers, being in a foreign language.

This book lays no claim to originality save in the form in which the results of the labors of others in this wide field are presented. The bibliographies given for each chapter show the sources of information. The purpose of the book is to present Islam as a challenge to the faith and enterprise of the church. It has a message for those who believe the Gospel and believe that the Gospel is the power of God unto salvation to every one that believeth—to the Mohammedan no less than to the heathen.

Its argument, following the order of the chapters, can be expressed in a single sentence: Islam, the greatest of all the non-Christian religions is not of divine but of human origin (I and II), altho so widely extended (III), and it is wholly inadequate, in spite of much that is true, to meet man's needs intellectually (IV), spiritually (V), or morally (VI), as proved by its own history (VII); therefore the present condition of Moslem lands with their unprecedented opportunities and crises (VIII), and the work which has already been accomplished (IX and X), are a challenge to evangelize the whole Mohammedan world in this generation (XI and XII).

Whether the facts presented and the authorities quoted prove the truth of the argument is left to the candid judgment of the reader.

New York, October, 1907.

CONTENTS

ix

CHAPTER III

THE SPREAD OF ISLAM

CHAPTER IV

THE FAITH OF ISLAM

Scope of the chapter—The relation of Moslem faith to practice —The six articles of their creed—Sources of this belief.

1 *The Moslem Idea of God*—His Unity—His character—The opinion of Hauri—Of James Freeman Clarke—How distinguished from Judaic and Christian monotheism.

2 *The Doctrine of Angels*—Three species of spiritual beings: (a) Angels—Classification—The four archangels—Recording angels—Avenging angels—Guardian angels.

CHAPTER VI

THE ETHICS OF ISLAM

CHAPTER IX

MISSIONS TO MOSLEMS

CHAPTER X

METHODS AND RESULTS

CHAPTER XI

THE PROBLEM AND THE PERIL

CHAPTER XII

A CHALLENGE TO FAITH

MAPS

TABLES

APPENDICES

ILLUSTRATIONS

"Islam—the mightiest system of monotheism the world has ever known, 'shadowing with wings' the three continents of Asia and Africa, having, in its progress, stamped out of existence tens of thousands of Christian churches and riveted upon 200,000,000 of men its doctrines, polity, ceremonial, and code of laws, and imbedded itself in the Arabic language like the nummulite fossils in the ledges of Jebel Mokattam, until it stands to-day like a towering mountain range whose summits are gilded with the light of the great truths of God's existence and unity, and whose foothills run down into the sloughs of polygamy and oppression and degradation of women."—*H. H. Jessup.*

THE ORIGIN AND SOURCES OF ISLAM

"The epigraphic evidence which Dr. Glaser has presented to us shows that the rise of Mohammedanism was not the strange and unique phenomenon it has hitherto been thought to be. It had been prepared for centuries previously. Arabia had for ages been the home of culture and the art of writing, and for about two hundred years before the birth of Mohammed his countrymen had been brought into close contact with the Jewish faith Future research will doubtless explain fully how great was his debt to the Jewish masters of Mecca and the Sabean kingdom of Southern Arabia."—*Professor A. H. Sayce,* in the *Independent.*

I

THE ORIGIN AND SOURCES OF ISLAM

Importance of the Subject.—In order to understand the genesis of Islam, the mightiest.of the non-Christian faiths, we must know something of the condition of Arabia before the birth of Mohammed. Then, perhaps, we shall be able to discover the factors that influenced the hero-prophet, the environment that stirred his genius, and the allied forces which made it possible for him so powerfully to sway the destinies of his own generation and change the current of the empire of all Western Asia and Northern Africa.

To the student of history the wonderful rise and rapid spread of Islam is an epoch in the records of the past; to the diplomat and the statesman Islam is a present-day problem of gigantic proportions and perplexing factors; to Christendom Islam is a challenge of faith that has not yet been met, and a barrier stretching from Persia to Morocco that has not yet been broken down. "To the follower of Christ, and especially to the student of Christian history, Islam possesses a melancholy interest peculiar to it among the religions of the world. It alone can claim to have met and vanquished Christianity. Islam arose in a region accessible to Christianity, for Mecca is only eight hundred miles from Jerusalem, over a road travelled by Mohammed in his youth. It arose at a time when Christianity should have evangelized Arabia, for in the six centuries by which the gospel of Christ preceded the creed of Mohammed, Christianity had spread to the borders of the Pacific, Indian and Atlantic Oceans, had revolutionized the greatest empire known to ancient history, and had created a vast literature, and a new learning. Why did it lose in Asia? What were the causes of defeat? Why was it possible for Mohammed to arise in that age of the world?"[1]

When we consider, however, the condition of paganism in Arabia before the rise of Islam, and know something of the large Jewish settlements and of early Christianity in the Peninsula, together with the strategic and unique importance of Mecca as a centre of pilgrimage and commerce long before Mohammed, some of these questions begin to receive an answer.

Mohammedan writers divide Arabian history into two periods—that before the advent of their prophet, and that after his mission. The former they name, in accordance with the practice of Mohammed himself, *Wakt-el-Jahiliya*, the "Time of Ignorance," or, perhaps better, the "Time of Barbarism"; the latter is that of Islam, of revelation and true religion. Professor Goldziher has shown that the original significance of *El Jahiliya* was not that of a time of heathen ignorance in the New Testament sense,[2] but rather a time of rude barbaric ethics in distinction to the civilized code of Islam.[3] The term was first used in an ethical sense, but later took on a general meaning.

It is not surprising that Moslem writers chose to paint the picture of pagan Arabia as dark as possible, in order

[1]William A Shedd, "Islam and the Oriental Churches," 4
[2]Acts 17.30.   [3]I. Goldziher, "Mohammedanische Studien," Vol. I, 220-228.

that "the light of God," as the Prophet is called, might appear more bright in contrast. Following these authorities Sale and others have given a somewhat wrong impression of the state of Arabia in the sixth and seventh centuries. The commonly accepted idea that Mohammed preached entirely new truth as a prophet of monotheism, and uplifted the Arabs to a higher plane of civilization, is only half true. No part of Arabia has ever reached as high a stage of material civilization under the rule of Islam as Yemen enjoyed under its Christian, Jewish or Pagan dynasties of the Himyarites, as is proved by the monuments of South Arabia. No less an authority than Fresnel has shown that the pre-Islamic Arabs were on a higher *moral* plane than the Arabs after their conversion to Islam;[1] and Perron contrasts the freedom and the legal status of woman prior to Mohammed, with her servile condition under Islam.[2]

Pagan Arabia.—During many centuries before Mohammed, the Arabs throughout the Peninsula, except in Yemen, were divided into numerous tribes and clans, bound together by no political tie, but only by a traditional sentiment of unity, which they believed (or feigned to believe) a unity of blood. Each group was a unit and was largely in competition with all the other clans.

The Arabs took delight in endless genealogies, and boasted of nothing so much as noble ancestors. In habits some were pastoral and some nomadic; others, like the clans of Mecca and Taif, were traders, and had monopolies of the caravan traffic. The immense caravan trade, which brought all the wealth of Ormuz and Ind to Egypt and the Roman Empire, crossed Arabia and left its influ-

[1]Fresnel, "Lettres sur l'Histoire des Arabes avant l'Islamisme" in *Journal Asiat.* (1849), 533.

[2]Perron, "Femmes Arabes avant et depuis l'Islamisme" (Paris, 1858),

ence. A. Sprenger adds this interesting fact at the close
of his account of the great caravan routes: "The history
of the earliest commerce is the history of incense, and
the land of incense was Arabia."[1] The three great routes
were the following: from the Persian Gulf through the
heart of Arabia to the Jauf and Damascus, with a branch
to Mecca; from the Tigris southward along Wady er
Rumma to the Jewish settlement in Khaibar; and, the
most important of all, the road from Sanaa along the
west coast through Mecca, Yathrib, Medina, and Maan
to Syria.[2] The importance of Mecca was first commercial
and then religious; together with Taif it was the halting-
place for the caravans from the south, and the depot of
the trade from the East.

The Arabs had enjoyed, for several thousand years before the Christian era, an almost absolute freedom from
foreign dominion or occupation. Neither the Egyptians,
the Assyrians, the Babylonians, the ancient Persians, nor
the Macedonians, in their march of conquest, ever subjugated or held any part of Arabia. But before the coming of the Prophet the proud freemen of the desert were
compelled to bend their necks repeatedly to the yoke of
Roman, Abyssinian, and Persian rulers. In A. D. 105
Trajan sent his general, Cornelius Palma, and subdued
the Nabathean kingdom of North Arabia. Mesopotamia
was conquered, and the eastern coast of the peninsula
was completely devastated by the Romans in A. D. 116.
Hira yielded to the monarchs of Persia, as Ghassan did
to the generals of Rome. "It is remarked, even by a Mohammedan writer," says Sir William Muir, "that the de-
cadence of the race of Ghassan was preparing the way

[1] A Sprenger, "Die Alte Geographie Arabiens," last chapter (Berne, 1875).
[2] See Map, Hubert Grimme, "Mohammed," (Munich, 1904).

for the glories of the Arabian prophet." In other words, Arabia was being invaded by foreign powers, and the Arabs were being made ready for a political leader to break these yokes and restore the old-time independence. Roman domination asserted itself, even over Mecca, not long before the Hegira. "For shortly after his accession to the throne, A. D. 610, the Emperor Heraclius nominated Othman, then a convert to Christianity, as governor of Mecca, recommending him to the Koreishites in an authoritative letter."[1] The Abyssinian wars and invasions of Arabia during the century preceding Mohammed are better known. "Their dominion in Yemen," says Ibn Ishak, "lasted seventy-two years, and they were finally driven out by the Persians, at the request of the Arabs." Arabia was thus in a condition of general political unrest just at the time when Mohammed came to manhood, and the hour was ripe for a political leader, able to unite the Arabs against the non-Arabs, whether Persians, Abyssinians or Greeks.[2]

Social Conditions.—The position of women in the "Time of Ignorance" was, in some respects, inferior; but in others far superior to that under Islam. The cruel custom of female infanticide prevailed in many parts of heathen Arabia. This was probably due, in the first instance, to poverty or famine, and afterward became a social custom, to limit population. Professor Wilken suggests, as a further reason, that wars had tended to an excess of females over males. An Arab poet tells of a niece who refused to leave her husband to whom she was assigned after her capture. Her uncle was so enraged

[1] S. W. Koelle, "Mohammed and Mohammedanism," 5.
[2] See chapter on "'Arab und 'Agam" in "Mohammedanische Studien," Vol. I, 101-147 (Halle, 1889), and A. P. Caussin de Perceval, "Essai sur L'Histoire des Arabes avant l'Islamisme," Vol. I, 214-291.

that he buried all his daughters alive, and never allowed
another one to live. Even one beautiful damsel, who had
been saved alive by her mother, was ruthlessly placed in
a grave by the father, and her cries stifled with earth.
This horrible custom, however, was not usual. We are
told of one distinguished pre-Islamic Arab, named Saa-
Saa, who tried to put down the practice of "digging a
grave by the side of the bed on which daughters were
born."[1] The use of the veil was almost unknown in Arabia before Islam, nor did the harem system prevail in the
days of idolatry. Women had rights, and were respected.
In two instances, beside that of Zenobia, we read of Arabian queens ruling over their tribes; and Freytag, in his
Arabian proverbs, gives a list of female judges who exercised their office before Islam. According to Nöldeke
and Grimme,[2] the Nabathean and South Arabian coins
and inscriptions prove that women held an independent
and honorable position; they built expensive family
graves, owned estates, and were independent traders,
as, for example, was Khadijah, the wife of Mohammed.

There is a genuine spirit of chivalry in the pre-Islamic
poetry of Arabia. A woman was never given away by
her father in an unequal match nor against her consent.
Professor G. A. Wilken has conclusively shown that
women had the right, before Mohammed's time, in every
case, to choose their own husbands, and cites the case of
Khadijah, who offered her hand to Mohammed.[3] Even
captive women were not kept in slavery, as is evident
from the verses of Hatim:

[1]Sinajet et Tarb fi Tekaddamet el Arab, (Beirut edition).
[2]Hubert Grimme, "Mohammed," Chap I
[3]G. A. Wilken, "Het Matriarchaat bij de oude Arabieren" (1884), and a
supplement to the same in answer to his critics (1885, The Hague).

"They did not give us Taites, their daughters in marriage,
But we wooed them against their will with our swords;
And with us captivity brought no abasement.
They neither toiled making bread nor made the pot boil,
But we mingled them with our women, the noblest,
And they bare us fair sons, white of face."

Polyandry and polygamy were both practised; the right of divorce belonged to the wife as well as to the husband; temporary marriages were also common. As was natural among a nomad race, the bond was quickly made and easily dissolved. But this was not the case among the Jews and Christians of Yemen and Nejran. Two kinds of marriages were in vogue. The *muta'a* was a purely personal contract between a man and a woman; no witnesses were necessary, and the woman did not leave her home or come under the authority of her husband; even the children belonged to the wife. This marriage, so frequently described in Arabic poetry, was not considered illicit, but was openly celebrated in verse, and brought no disgrace on the woman. In the other kind of marriage, called *nikah,* the woman became subject to her husband by capture or purchase. In the latter case the purchase-money was paid to the bride's kin. In later chapters of this book we will see that both these forms of marriage still obtain among the Shiah sect of Moslems.

Robertson Smith sums up the position of women in Arabia before Islam, in these words: "It is very remarkable that, in spite of Mohammed's humane ordinances, the place of women in the family, and in society, has steadily declined under his law. In ancient Arabia we find many proofs that women moved more freely and asserted themselves more strongly than in the modern East. The Arabs themselves recognized that the position of woman had fallen, and it continued still to fall under Islam, because the effect of Mohammed's legislation in favor of women was more than outweighed by the establishment of marriages of dominion as the one legitimate type, and by the gradual loosening of the principle that married women could count on their own kin to stand by them against their husbands."[1]

Pre-Islamic Literature.—The seven ancient Arabian poems, called *Muallakat* or *Muthahabat,* are proof of a golden age of literature, and doubtless are only fragments of a much larger collection. To them we owe much of our knowledge of the early Arabian life and faith. Palgrave says: "If poor in architectural, Arabia is superabundantly rich in literary monuments"; and this is true, even of the "Time of Ignorance." Zuhair, Zarafa, Imru-al Kais, Amru-bin-Kulsum, Al Harith, Antar and Labid furnished the model for later Arabian poetry, and their poems, as we have them, are remarkable for perfection of form and language.

Wellhausen mentions Adi bin Zaid, Abu Daud, Al 'Ascha, and other Christian Arabian poets, of whose poetry only fragments are left, and adds that early Arabian Christianity had a marked influence on the pre-Islamic culture through the channel of poetry. The poets were already voicing the cry of Arabia for the unknown God; they were the prophets of the new era.[2] In addition to poetry, three things were coveted by the Pagan Arabs, and were the object of pride: eloquence, horsemanship and liberal hospitality. There were large competitive contests in oratory and poetry at Okatz. Here

[1] Robertson Smith, "Kinship and Marriage in Early Arabia," 100-104. For further information on the position of women in pre-Islamic times among all the Semitic races see a valuable paper, "Woman in the Ancient Hebrew Cult," by Ismar J. Peritz, Ph D , in *The Journal of Biblical Literature* (1898), Part II.

[2] J. Wellhausen, "Reste Arabischen Heidentums," 232, 234 (Berlin, 1897).

Surah 59:2-4

Surah 48:17-22

there was also an annual market which was so large that
the line of booths stretched for ten miles between Taif
and Nachla; Wellhausen pictures the scene as described
by the poets: a crowd of traders, artisans, blacksmiths,
horse-doctors, poets, athletes, wine-sellers; a great gathering of the tribes from every quarter, and every sort of
friendly competitive contest; an agricultural fair, an
oratorical contest, and a religious camp-meeting combined.[1] An entire month was given up to these inter-
tribal, commercial and social gatherings here and at Mecca; an annual truce of God among the warlike nomads.
Mohammed was the first Arab that dared make war during the sacred months, and break the troth of Pagan
Arabia.

According to Moslem tradition, the science of writing
was not known in Mecca until introduced by Harb,
father of Abu Soofian, the great opponent of Mohammed, about A. D. 560. But this is evidently an error, for
close intercourse existed long before this between Mecca
and Yemen through caravan trade, and in Yemen writing was well known for centuries. In another tradition
Abd ul Muttalib is said to have written to Medina for
help in his younger days, i. e., about 520 A. D. Both
Jews and Christians also dwelt in the vicinity of Mecca
for two hundred years before the Hegira, and used some
form of writing. For writing-materials they had abund-
ance of reeds and palm-leaves, as well as the flat, smooth
shoulder-blades of the camel. There are many rock inscriptions in Northern Arabia and monuments in Yemen.
The seven great poems are said to have been written in
gold on Egyptian silk and suspended in the Kaaba at
Mecca.

[1] J. Wellhausen, "Reste Arabischen Heidentums," 88-91

Arabian Polytheism.—Concerning the religion of the Arabs, before Islam, the Mohammedan writer, Ash-Shahristani, says: "The Arabs of pre-Islamic times may, with reference to religion, be divided into various classes. Some of them denied the Creator, the resurrection and men's return to God, and asserted that Nature possesses in itself the power of bestowing life, but that time destroys. Others believed in a Creator and a creation produced by Him out of nothing, but yet denied the resurrection. Others believed in a Creator and a creation, but denied God's prophets and worshipped false gods, concerning whom they believed that in the next world they would become mediators between themselves and God. For these deities they undertook pilgrimages; they brought votive offerings to them, offered them sacrifices, and approached them with rites and ceremonies. Some things they held to be Divinely permitted, others prohibited."[1]

This is an admirable account, altho his silence regarding the Jews and Christians of Arabia is unaccountable. There is no doubt that Arabia, for two centuries before the Hegira, was a refuge for all sorts of religious fugitives, and each band added something to the national stock of religious ideas.

There were Sabeans, or Star-worshippers, in the Northwest along the Euphrates; Zoroastrians came to East Arabia; Jews settled at Khaibar, Medina, and in Yemen. For all Pagan Arabia Mecca was the centre many centuries before Mohammed. Here stood the Kaaba, the Arabian Pantheon, with its three hundred and sixty idols—one for each day in the year. Here the tribes of Hejaz met in annual pilgrim-

[1] See Arabic original in W. St. Clair Tisdall, "The Original Sources of the Qur'ân," 36, 37.

age, to rub and kiss the Black Stone, to circumambulate the Beit Allah or Bethel of their faith, and to hang portions of their garments on the sacred trees. At Nejran a sacred date-plant was the centre of pilgrimage. Everywhere in Arabia there were sacred stones, or stone-heaps, where the Arab devotees congregated, to obtain special blessings. The belief in jinn, or genii, was well-nigh universal, but there was a distinction between them and gods. The gods had individuality, while the jinn had not; the gods were worshipped, the jinn were only feared; the god had one form, the jinn appeared in many. All that the Moslem world believes to-day, in regard to jinn, is wholly borrowed from Arabian heathenism. The Arabs were always superstitious, and legends of all sorts cluster around every weird desert-rock, gnarled tree, or intermittent fountain in Arabia. The early Arabs, therefore, marked off such sacred territory by pillars, or cairns, and considered many things, such as shedding of blood, cutting of trees, killing game, etc., forbidden within the enclosure. This is the origin of the Moslem teaching about the *Haramain,* or sacred territories, around Mecca and Medina.

Sacrifices were common, but not by fire. The blood of the offering was smeared over the rude stone-altars, and the flesh was eaten by the worshipper. First-fruits were given to the gods, and libations were poured out; a hair-offering formed a part of the ancient pilgrimage; this also is imitated to-day. In fact the whole ceremony of the Moslem pilgrimage to Mecca is taken over from pre-Islamic practice, and is thoroughly pagan.[1]

[1] J. Wellhausen, "Reste Arabischen Heidentums," 68-101.
C Snouck Hurgronje, "Het Mekkaansche Feest." (Leyden, 1880.)
W. St Clair Tisdall, "The Original Sources of the Qur'ān," 43-47.

Our present knowledge of the Arabian gods is gained from a work of Ibn al Kelbi, written two hundred years after the Hegira, entitled *Kitab-el-Asnam,* or the Book of Idols. The work itself is no longer extant, but it is largely quoted in Jakut's "Geographical Lexicon." The principal idols of Arabia are given below; ten of them are mentioned by name in the Koran.[1]

Above all these tutelary and "mediator-gods" was the supreme deity, whom they called Allah—ὅ θέος, the God. This name occurs very frequently in pre-Islamic poetry, on the inscriptions and in proverbs and personal names. "Altho polytheism had, even in very early times,

[1]HOBAL, who was in the form of a man, had the place of honor in the Kaaba. He was termed "creator of the heavens and the earth." Dozy identifies him with Baal of Syria, the first part of the name being the Hebrew article.

WADD (signifying friendship), worshipped by the Northern Arabs at Duma, but also in the South.

SUWAH, an idol in the form of a woman and worshipped by the Hamdan tribe

YAGHUTH, in the shape of a lion.

YA'OOK, in the form of a horse, worshipped in Yemen. Bronze images of this idol are found in ancient tombs.

NASR, who was the eagle-god.

EL UZZA, identified by some scholars with Venus, worshipped at times under the form of an acacia tree. One of the daughters of Allah according to pagan ideas.

ALLAT, the chief idol of the tribe of Thakif, at Taif, who tried to compromise with Mohammed and promised to accept Islam if he would not destroy their god for three years. The name appears to be the feminine of Allah, and she was considered a daughter of Allah

MANAT, a huge stone worshipped by several tribes as a daughter of Allah.

DUWAR, the virgin's idol; young women used to go around it in procession; hence its name.

ISAF and NAILA, which stood near Mecca on the hills of Safa and Mirwa; the visitation of these popular shrines is now a part of the Moslem pilgrimage ritual.

HABHAB, a large stone on which camels were slaughtered There are also other idols and shrines mentioned, some of which have since been transformed into sacred places of Islam, each with its appropriate tradition. Wellhausen, "Reste Arabischen Heidentums," 104.

found an entrance into Arabia, yet the belief in the One True God had never entirely faded away from the minds of the people. The most binding agreements between different tribes were confirmed by an oath taken in calling on the name of God (Allah); and the expression, 'An enemy of God,' was deemed the most opprobrious that could be used."[1] Wellhausen, in speaking of the gradual disintegration and dissolution of polytheism in Arabia in the century before Mohammed, says: "In the sixth and seventh centuries of our era Allah had outgrown the other gods. This is clearly evident from the Koran itself. 'When the pagan Arabs were in real peril they turned to Allah, and not to their tribal gods,' says Mohammed. Also, for the heathen Arabs, Allah was the real possessor of Divinity, and Mohammed can only use the polemic against them that they allow idols to be partners of Deity."[2]

Ibn Hisham states, on the authority of Ibn Ishak, that the tribes of Kinanah and Koreish, when performing the ceremonies around the Kaaba, used to say: *"Labbaika, Allahuma,* we are present in Thy service, O God; Thou hast no partner, except the partner of Thy dread. Thou ownest him and whatsoever he owneth." The meaning is not clear, but the language employed shows the superior position of Allah, who had no equals. The idea of the unity of God was not introduced among the Arabs for the first time by Mohammed. Nor did Mohammed invent the word for the Supreme Deity. The idea was common, and so was the word. Mohammed's own father, who died before his son's birth, was called Abd Allah; and the Kaaba of Mecca, long before Islam, was known

---

[1] W. St. Clair Tisdall, "The Original Sources of the Qur'ân," 31-35.
[2] J. Wellhausen, "Reste Arabischen Heidentums," 217.

as Beit Allah, or House of God. The tribal worship of the ancient Arabs bears much resemblance, therefore, to the saint worship of the Greek and Roman churches, i. e., it was to their mind compatible with a knowledge and acknowledgment of the Supreme Being. Yet, as Wellhausen points out: "In worship Allah often had the last place, those gods being preferred who represented the interests of a particular circle, and fulfilled the private desires of their worshippers. Neither the fear of Allah nor their reverence for the gods had much influence. The chief practical consequence of the great feasts was the observance of a truce in the holy months; and this, in time, had become mainly an affair of pure practical convenience. In general the disposition of the heathen Arabs, if it is all truly reflected in their poetry, was profane in an unusual degree. The ancient inhabitants of Mecca practised piety essentially as a trade, just as they do now; their trade depended on the feast, and its fair on the inviolability of the Haram and on the truce of the holy months."

Not only had the old polytheism lost its force, so that the aged Abu Ubaiha wept on his deathbed at Mecca, for fear the worship of Uzza would be neglected, but the better classes of Mecca and Medina had ceased to believe anything at all.[1] The forms of religion were kept up rather for political and commercial reasons than as a matter of faith and conviction.[2] And the reason for this decline of paganism is not far to seek. "The religious decay in Arabia, shortly before Islam," says Hirschfeld, "may well be taken in a negative sense, in the sense of the tribes losing the feeling of kinship with the tribal

[1] J. Wellhausen, "Reste Arabischen Heidentums," 220.
[2] E. H. Palmer, "Translation of the Qur'ân," Intro. Vol. I, xv.

THE KAABA

The Kaaba, or Beit Allah, is the prayer-centre of the Mohammedan world and the objective point of thousands of pilgrims every year. According to Moslem writers it was first constructed in Heaven 2,000 years before the creation of the world. Adam, the first man, built the Kaaba on earth exactly under the spot occupied by its perfect model in Heaven.

14

gods. We may express this more concretely by saying that *the gods had become gradually more nebulous through the destructive influence exercised for about four hundred years by Jewish and Christian ideas upon Arabian heathenism."*[1] How did these Jewish and Christian ideas influence the Arabs of Mohammed's time, and Mohammed himself, and to what extent?

The Jews of Arabia.—The Jews came to Arabia from the earliest times. Since the days of Solomon the Red Sea was a centre of busy traffic, and the Hebrews had probably located at the trading ports. Dozy finds epigraphic and other evidence that Jews settled at Mecca as early as the time of David, and that their settlement continued until the fifth century of the Christian era.[2] But his monograph on the subject is not altogether convincing. It is certain, however, that the later conquests of Palestine by Assyrians, Babylonians, Persians, Greeks and Romans sent waves of Jewish immigration into Arabia as far as Yemen. A number of native Arab tribes also embraced Judaism, and at the time of Mohammed we find this people scattered over the peninsula in small compact colonies. Not only were they numerous, but also powerful, especially at Sanaa, Medina, Khaibar and other centres. In Mohammed's time the three large Jewish tribes, called Bni Koraiza, Bni Nadhir, and Bni Kainuka, all dwelling near Medina, were so powerful that, after his arrival there in A. D. 622, he made an offensive and defensive alliance with them. The fact that the Koran refers repeatedly to the Jews, and calls them, as well as the Christians, "People of the Book," shows that they

[1] Quoted from *The Journal of the Royal Asiatic Society* in S. M. Zwemer, "Arabia, the Cradle of Islam," 158

[2] R. Dozy, "De Israelieten te Mekka van David's tijd tot op onze tijdrekening." (Leyden, 1864, German translation, Leipsic, 1864.)

possessed and used the Old Testament, and that, doubtless, many of them could read and write. For in Surah 2:70-73, we read, in reference to the Jews: "But
there are illiterates among them, who are not acquainted
with the Book, but with lies only, and have but vague
fancies. Woe to those who, with their own hands, tran-
scribe the Book corruptly, and then say," etc. Therefore,
the others could read.

These Jewish colonies, with their teachers and their
Talmud, had, for centuries, exerted a strong educational
influence toward monotheism. And it is evident, not only
from the Koran, but from the earliest Moslem biographies of Mohammed, that he was greatly indebted to
Judaism, both for his doctrines and narratives. How
early in his life Mohammed came in touch with Jewish
teaching, or teachers, is uncertain, but that he obtained
his knowledge of Old Testament history from Jews well
versed in Talmudic lore is admitted by all students of
Islam, and was conclusively shown by Rabbi Abraham
Geiger, in his prize essay on the subject.[1] The fact that
the Jews at Mecca and Medina possessed inspired books,
and were undoubtedly descendants of Abraham, whom
the Koreish and other tribes claimed as their ancestor,
gave them great weight and influence. Native Arabian
legends would be made to fit in with Jewish patriarchal
stories, and so, as Muir remarks: "By a summary ad-
justment the story of Palestine became the story of the
Hejaz, the precincts of the Kaaba were hallowed as the
scene of Hagar's distress, and the sacred well—Zemzem
—as the source of her relief. The pilgrims hastened to

[1]"Was hat Mohammed aus dem Judentum aufgenommen?" (Wiesbaden,
1833.) English translation of the same under the title, "Judaism and Islam"
(Madras, 1898). See also the writings of Hirshfeld, Emmanuel Deutsch,
J. M. Arnold and others on this topic.

and fro between Safa and Marwa, in memory of her hurried steps in search of water. It was Abraham and Ishmael who built the temple, imbedded in it the Black Stone, and established for all Arabia the pilgrimage to Arafat. In imitation of him it was that stones were flung by the pilgrims, as if at Satan, and sacrifices offered at Mina, in remembrance of the vicarious sacrifice of Abraham. And so, altho the indigenous (Meccan) rites may have been little, if at all, altered by the adoption of Israelitish legends, they came to be received in a totally different light and to be connected in Arab imagination with something of the sanctity of Abraham, the Friend of God."[1]

For a detailed account of all the words, doctrines, ceremonies and stories that were borrowed from Judaism, adopted by Mohammed, and perpetuated in Islam, the reader is referred to Geiger or Tisdall; the accompanying table gives them in outline.[2] A careful study of the subject will show that most of the warp and woof of the new religion was taken from the old garment. *Islam is nothing more nor less than Judaism plus the apostleship of Mohammed.*

Christianity in Arabia before Islam.—The question how early and from what direction Christianity first entered Arabia is difficult to answer. Whatever is known on the subject can be found in Wright's essay.[3] Paul spent three years among the Arabs,[4] and Christianity was introduced in North Arabia very early. Bishops of Bosra, in Northwestern Arabia, are mentioned as having been

---

[1] Sir William Muir, "Life of Mahomet," third edition, introduction, xcii-xciii. See also "Reste Arabischen Heidentums," 232.
[2] Appendix B.
[3] Thomas Wright, "Early Christianity in Arabia." (London, 1855.)
[4] Gal. 1 17.

present at the Nicene Council (A. D. 325) with five other Arabian bishops. The Arabian historians speak of the tribe of Ghassan as attached to the Christian faith centuries before the Hegira.

There is no doubt that Christianity was widely diffused in other parts of Arabia at the time of Mohammed. According to Caussin de Perceval, who quotes from Arabic writers, Christianity existed among the Bni Taglib of Mesopotamia, the Bni Abd al Kais, the Bni Harith of Nejran, the Bni Ghassan of Syria, and other tribes between Medina and Kufa.[1] The picture of the Christian monk in his desert-cell, with his night-lamp and books, keeping vigil, is common in pre-Islamic poetry; and we have already seen that there were also Christian poets in the "Time of Ignorance." As the Arabs became more intimately connected with the Romans, the progress of Christianity increased. The name of Mavia, an Arabian queen, is mentioned by ecclesiastical writers as a convert to the faith, and it is stated that she invited a Christian bishop, named Moses, to live among her people. An unfortunate circumstance for the progress of Christianity in North Arabia, however, was its location between the rival powers of Rome and Persia. It was a sort of buffer-state, and suffered in consequence. The Persian monarchs persecuted the Christian Arabs, and one of their allies—a pagan Arab, called Naaman—forbade all intercourse with Christians, on the part of his subjects. This edict, we are told, was occasioned by the success of the preaching of Simon Stylites, the pillar saint, celebrated in Tennyson's poem.[2] The progress or even the toler-

[1] A. P. Caussin de Perceval, "Essai sur l'Histoire des Arabes avant l'Islamisme." (Paris, 1847 and 1902.) Three vols.

[2] Thomas Wright, "Early Christianity in Arabia," 77

Noldeke, "Sketches from Eastern History" (London, 1892). Chapter on Simon Stylites.

ance of Christianity in the kingdom of Hirah seems to have been always dependent on the favor of the Khosroes of Persia. Some became Christians as early as 380 A. D. And one of the early converts, Noman Abu Kamus, proved the sincerity of his faith by melting down a golden statue of the Arabian Venus worshipped by his tribe, and distributing the proceeds to the poor. Wright states that many of the tribe followed his example, broke their idols and were baptized. So early was idolatry doomed in North Arabia—long before the appearance of Mohammed.

It was in Southwestern Arabia, however, that the Christian faith exerted its greatest power and made largest conquest. We learn, from the monuments and inscriptions of Yemen, how, before the Christian preacher came, monotheism had already displaced polytheism in the cult of the Sabeans.[1] The names used for the Supreme Deity were, many of them, identical with those used later in the Koran. Add to this the large Jewish population, and it becomes evident that the soil was ready for the Christian faith to take root; altho it is also true that the Jews were often an obstacle to the early spread of Christianity, because of their bitter hostility. The legend that St. Bartholomew preached in Yemen, on his way to India, need not be considered; nor the more probable one of Frumentius and his success as first bishop to Himyar. But history relates that, in the reign of Constantius, Theophilus, the deacon of Nicomedia, a zealous Arian, being sent by the Emperor to attend a magnificent embassy to the court of Himyar, prevailed on the Arabian king to accept Christianity. He built three churches at Zaphar, Aden and Sanaa, as well as at Hormuz, in the

[1] Hubert Grimme, "Mohammed," 19-31, ff.

Persian Gulf. No less than four bishoprics were established. Ibn Khalikan, the Moslem historian, enumerates as Christian tribes the Bahrah, Tanoukh, and Taglab, while in Nejran, north of Yemen, and even in Medina there were Christians. In the year 560 A. D. there was a severe persecution of the Christians in Nejran, instigated by the Jews. "Large pits were dug, filled with fuel, and many thousands of monks and virgins were committed to the flames."[1] Yet, so firm a hold had the religion of Jesus Christ on the Arabs of Nejran that neither the fires of persecution nor the power of triumphant Islam in the later centuries could root it out speedily. Abbe Huc speaks of Christians in Nejran as late as the tenth century.[2]

In the year 567 A. D., Abraha, the Christian king of Yemen, built a new cathedral at Sanaa, with the intention of making it the rival of Mecca for the Arab pilgrimage. The church was defiled by pagan Arabs from the North, and then followed the famous expedition of Abraha against Mecca, and his defeat by the Koreish— forever after celebrated in the Koran chapter of "The Elephant."[3] Two months after this defeat was born the prophet whose character and career sealed the fate of Christianity in Arabia for many centuries.

From this short sketch of Christianity in early Arabia it is evident that Mohammed, like any other intelligent Arab of his day, could not have been wholly ignorant of the Christian faith. The picture of the Christian church of this period (323-692 A. D.) was dark indeed; yet it

---

[1] S. M. Zwemer, "Arabia; the Cradle of Islam," 307-308, following the account given by Wright.

[2] Abbe Huc, "Christianity in China, Tartary and Tibet," Vol. I, 88. (New York, edition 1857.)

[3] S. M. Zwemer, "Arabia; the Cradle of Islam," 308-313. See Moslem Commentators in loco.

COPIES OF THE KORAN WORN BY MOSLEMS WHEN
TRAVELING OR ON PILGRIMAGE

was not without true believers.[1] Arabia was full of heresies, and yet we have epigraphic evidence that the real doctrine of the Trinity obtained in Arabia, instead of that which Mohammed asserts the Christians hold. In 1888 Edward Glaser, the explorer, brought from Mareb, the Sabean capital, a copy of an inscription, telling of the suppression of a revolt against the Ethiopic rule then established in Yemen. This inscription, which dates from 542 A. D., opens with the words: *"In the Power of the All Merciful, and His Messiah and the Holy Ghost."*[2] Whatever may have been the condition or the teaching of Christianity in Arabia, Mohammed came in contact with it all through his life. One of the chief stories he heard in his boyhood was of the Christian invasion from the South, and the defeat of Abraha; later he went to Syria, met monks and passed through the territory of the Christian tribes of Northern Arabia; after he became a prophet he had as concubine a Christian Coptic woman, Miriam, the mother of his darling son, Ibrahim. For good or for ill, Mohammed could not remain wholly ignorant of Christianity, and therefore it is not surprising to find the evidence of this in Islam.[3] The Christian factor cannot be omitted in our study of the origin of Islam. Christian teaching, though often in corrupt form, was one of the sources of the new religion.

[1]Kurtz writes: "More and more the Church became assimilated and conformed to the world, church discipline grew lax, and moral decay made rapid progress. Passionate contentions, quarrels and schisms among bishops and clergy filled public life also with party strife, animosity and bitterness. . . . Hypocrisy and bigotry took the place of piety among those who strove after something higher, while the masses consoled themselves with the reflection that every man could not be a monk."—"Church History," Vol I, 386.

[2]Hilprecht, "Recent Explorations in Bible Lands," 149. (Article by Professor Fritz Hommel on "Arabia"); Zwemer, "The Moslem Doctrine of God," 27, 90

[3]See table of the Borrowed Elements, opposite page 86.

But Koelle goes much further than this, and shows negatively how, in Mohammed's own case, "not want of opportunity, but want of sympathy and compatibility kept him aloof from the religion of Christ. His first wife introduced him to her Christian cousin; one of his later wives had embraced Christianity in Abyssinia, and the most favored of his concubines was a Christian damsel from the Copts of Egypt. He was acquainted with ascetic monks, and had dealings with learned bishops of the orthodox church. In those days the reading of the Holy Scriptures in the public services was already authoritatively enjoined and universally practised; if he had wished thoroughly to acquaint himself with them, he could easily have done so. But, having no adequate conception of the nature of sin and man's fallen state, he also lacked the faculty of truly appreciating the remedy for it which was offered in the Gospel."[1] All these considerations have weight in determining the influence of Christianity on the origin of Islam.[2]

The Hanifs.—Besides the Jews and Christians, there were the Hanifs. The term was originally one of reproach (meaning to limp or walk unevenly, to pretend), and was applied to those who abandoned the worship of the popular deities.[3] With the decline of the old paganism, a number of men arose in Medina, Taif and Mecca

[1]S. W. Koelle, "Mohammed and Mohammedanism," 471.

A Moslem convert of El Azhar and a teacher of theology in Cairo holds that in his earliest years of manhood Mohammed was a nominal Christian and offers to prove it on Moslem authorities. See *Cairo Conference Reports,* Vol. II, 24.

[2]For a further consideration of the Moslem legends, stories and doctrines that were borrowed from Christianity, the reader is referred to Tisdall, "The Original Sources of the Qur'ân," Chap. IV.

[3]W. St. Clair Tisdall, "The Original Sources of the Qur'ân," 272; Pautz, "Mohammed's Lehre von der Offenbarung," 15; Hughes' "Dictionary of Islam" gives a different derivation.

who became convinced of the folly of the old religion, and were seekers after God, altho neither Jewish nor Christian proselytes. That they became numerous and honorable is evident from the Koran use of the term, and from the fact that Abraham the Patriarch is said to have been the first Hanif. Moslem history mentions twelve of Mohammed's companions who belonged to the Hanifs. And from Ibn Ishak, the earliest biographer of Mohammed, we learn what Zeid, Waraka and others of these reformers believed and taught. "They said, one to another: 'By God ye know that your nation is based upon nothing: truly, they have erred from the religion of their father, Abraham. What is a stone, that we should circle round it? It hears not, nor sees, nor injures, nor benefits. O people, seek for yourselves; for, verily by God, ye are based upon nothing.' Accordingly, they went into different lands, that they might seek *Hanifism*, the religion of Abraham. Waraka bin Naufal, therefore, became absorbed in Christianity, and he inquired after the Books among those who professed it until he acquired some knowledge from the People of the Book. But Ubaidullah bin Jahsh remained in the state of uncertainty in which he was until he became a Moslem. He migrated with the Moslems to Abyssinia . . . and when he arrived there became a Christian, and abandoned Islam, so that he perished there a Christian."[1] This testimony is remarkable. *So early was the first convert from Islam to Christianity.* And Ibn Ishak tells us he was not only a convert, but a witness. "When he became a Christian he used to dispute with the Companions of the Apostle, who were then in Abyssinia, and say: 'We see clearly, and you are yet blinking.' " Would that

[1] "Sirat-ur-Rasul," Vol. I, 76, 77. Quoted by W. St. Clair Tisdall.

Mohammed and his companions had accepted the testimony of Ubaidullah, and had come to the true light of the gospel!

The Hanifs expressed their piety in the words, "We have *surrendered* to God" (Islam) ; they prohibited the slaying of female infants; they acknowledged the unity of God; they rejected all idolatry; they promised a future garden of delight to the believer, and hell for the wicked; they used the words Merciful and Forgiving for Deity. Wellhausen states that these Hanifs were not found in Mecca and Medina alone, but that they were everywhere a symptom and an indication of the final dissolution of paganism and a proof that the soil was ripe for Islam.[1]

Islam a Composite Religion.—From the condition of Arabia at the time of Mohammed, and the whole religious environment of his day, it is natural that if there was to be a new religion for Arabia it must take account of the existing faiths. It is not at all surprising, therefore, that the result of a century of critical study by European and American scholars of every school of thought has established the fact that Islam is a composite religion. It is not an invention, but a concoction; there is nothing novel about it, except the genius of Mohammed in mixing old ingredients into a new panacea for human ills, and forcing it down by means of the sword. These heterogeneous elements of Islam were gathered in Arabia at a time when many religions had penetrated the Peninsula, and the Kaaba was a Pantheon. Unless one has a knowledge of these elements of the "Time of Ignorance," Islam is a problem. Knowing, however, these heathen, Christian, and Jewish factors, Islam is seen to be a per-

[1] J. Wellhausen, "Reste Arabischen Heidentums," 234.

fectly natural and comprehensible development. Its heathen, Christian and Jewish elements remain, to this day, perfectly recognizable, in spite of thirteen centuries of explanation by the Moslem authorities. And, logically, it was only a step from Hanifism to Islam, if one did not ·wish to embrace the old historic faiths of Moses or of Christ. The "Time of Ignorance" was a time of spiritual inquiry and seeking after God. But it was also a time of social and political chaos in Western Arabia. Everything was ready for a man of genius who could take in the whole situation—social, political, and religious—and form a cosmos. That man was Mohammed.

MOHAMMED, THE PROPHET OF ISLAM

"It has been truly said that Christianity is not a religious system, but a life; that it is *Christ*. With almost equal truth it may be affirmed that Islam is Mohammed. Certainly his spirit is infused into the religion which he founded, and still animates to an almost incredible extent the hearts of its professors in every Mohammedan land."—*W. St. Clair Tisdall.*

"The character of Mohammed is a historic problem, and many have been the conjectures as to his motives and designs. Was he an impostor, a fanatic, or an honest man—a very apostle of God?"—*T. P. Hughes*

"By a fortune absolutely unique in history Mohammed is a threefold founder—of a nation, of an empire and of a religion. . . . Scarcely able to read or write, he was yet the author of a book reverenced to this day by the sixth [seventh] of the whole human race as a miracle of purity of style, of wisdom and of truth."—*R. Bosworth Smith.*

II

MOHAMMED, THE PROPHET

Introductory.—About the year 570 A. D., Abdullah, the son of Abd ul Muttalib, a Mecca merchant, went on a trading trip from Mecca to Medina, and died there. A few months after his death his wife, Amina, gave birth to a boy, who was named Mohammed.[1] One hundred years later the name of this Arab, joined to that of the Almighty, was called out from ten thousand minarets five times daily from the Persian Gulf to the Atlantic, and his new religion was sweeping everything before it in three continents. What is the explanation of this marvel of history? Many theories have been given, and the true explanation of the spread of Islam is probably the sum of all these theories: The weaknesses of the Oriental churches; their corrupt state; the condition of the Roman and Persian empires; the easy-going moral character of the new religion; the power of the sword and of fanaticism; the great truths of Islam; the genius of Mohammed's successors; the hope of plunder, and the love of conquest—such are some of the causes given for the

---

[1] The name Mohammed was not unknown in pagan times. Ibn Khallikan states that three Arabs bore it in the Time of Ignorance, namely Mohammed bin Sufyan, Mohammed bin Uhaiyah, and Mohammed bin Humran He adds a story, however, to prove that each of these was so named in honor of the future prophet! (De Slane, "Translation of Ibn Khallikan's Biographical Dictionary," Vol. III, 620, ff.).

growth of the new religion from a minority of one to an immense army of believers. Yet none of these theories, nor all of them together, can omit, as the supreme cause of success, the genius of Mohammed. To the believing Moslem this is the *whole* explanation. And it is simple, because it is supernatural. All things are possible with God, and God sent Mohammed as the last and greatest apostle.

A Moslem Portrait of the Prophet.—Here is a description of Mohammed, the man and the prophet, by Kamal ud Din ad Damiri (A. D. 1349-1405), who was a theologian of the Shafi school, a prolific author and commentator, a scientist and a philosopher. The fact that this succinct pen-portrait of the prophet, which we quote, occurs incidentally in his "Dictionary of Zoology" as a digression does not detract from its value to a Moslem, and rather adds to it for us:[1] "Mohammed is the most favored of mankind, the most honored of all the apostles, the prophet of mercy, the head or imam of the faithful, the bearer of the banner of praise, the intercessor, the holder of high position, the possessor of the River of Paradise, under whose banner the sons of Adam will be on the day of judgment. He is the best of prophets, and his nation is the best of all nations; his companions are the most excellent of mankind, after the prophets, and his creed is the noblest of all creeds. He performed manifest miracles, and possessed great qualities. He was perfect in intellect, and was of noble origin. He had an absolutely graceful form, complete gen-

[1] The quotation is from Ad Damiri's Hayat ul Hayawan, a zoological lexicon with notes and digressions on the folk lore and history of the Arabs. Translation of Lt Colonel A. S G. Jayakar (London, 1906), Vol. I, 88, 89. The work is standard throughout the Arabic world and the passage given occurs at the beginning of his famous digression on the early caliphate under the article, Al Awizz, the Goose!

erosity, perfect bravery, excessive humility, useful
knowledge, power of performing high actions, perfect
fear of God and sublime piety. He was the most eloquent and the most perfect of mankind in every variety
of perfection, and the most distant of men from mean-
ness and vices. A poet says of him:

'The Merciful has not yet created one like Mohammed
And to the best of my knowledge never will do so.'

"Aisha stated that the prophet, when at home, used to
serve his household; he used to pick out the vermin from
his cloak, and patch it; mend his own shoes, and serve
himself. He used to give fodder to his camel, sweep the
house, tie the camel by the fore leg, eat with the female
slave, knead dough with her, and carry his own things
from the market. And he used to be constantly in a
state of grief and anxiety, and never had any peace of
mind. Ali stated that he asked the prophet, regarding
his mode of life, and that he replied: 'Knowledge is my
capital; love, my foundation; desire, my vehicle; the remembrance of God, my boon companion; grief, my
friend; knowledge, my arms; patience, my cloak; the
pleasure of God, my share of plunder; poverty, my distinction; renunciation of the world, my profession; faith,
my strength; truth, my interceder; obedience to God, my
sufficiency; religious war, my nature; and the refresher
of my eye is prayer.' As to his humility, liberality, bravery, bashfulness, fellowship, kindness, clemency, mercy,
piety, justice, modesty, patience, dignity, trustworthiness
and other praiseworthy qualities innumerable, they were
all very great. The learned have composed many books
regarding his life, his times, his mission, his wars, his
qualities, his miracles and his good and amiable actions;

to describe even a little of which would take several volumes. But that is not our purpose in this book. It is said that his death took place after God had perfected our religion, and completed this blessing for us, at noon on Monday, the 12th of Rabi'-al-Awal, 11 A. H., at the age of sixty-three years. His body was washed by Ali bin Abi Talib, and he was buried in the chamber which he had built for the mother of the faithful, Aisha."

Factors in Mohammed's Life.—Whether this naive and beautiful characterization of the prophet will stand the test of Moslem history, we shall see later on. Whatever we may deny Mohammed, we can never deny that he was a man of great talents. But he was not a self-made man. His environment accounts, in large measure, for his might and for his methods as a religious leader. What that environment was we have already seen in part in our study of the origin and sources of Islam. Four factors stand out clearly in the life of Mohammed:

There was, first of all, the political factor. The era known as the "year of the elephant" had seen the defeat of the Christian army from Yemen, which came, under Abraha, to attack Mecca and destroy the Kaaba. This victory was, to the young and ardent mind of Mohammed, prophetic of the political future of Mecca, and no doubt his ambition assigned himself the chief place in the coming conflict of Arabia against the Romans and the Persians.[1]

Next came the religious factor. The times were ripe for religious leadership, and Mecca was already the centre of a new movement. The Hanifs had rejected the

[1] Ignaz Goldziher, "Mohammedanische Studien," Vol I, 40-101; S W. Koelle, "Mohammed and Mohammedanism," first part, S. M. Zwemer, "Arabia; the Cradle of Islam," Chap. XVI.

old idolatry, and entertained the hope that a prophet would arise from among them.[1] There was material of all sorts at hand to furnish the platform of a new faith; it only required the builder's genius to call cosmos out of chaos. To succeed in doing this, it would be necessary to reject material also; to construct a comprehensive religion and a compromising religion, so as to suit Jew, and Christian, and idolater alike.[2]

In the third place, there was the family factor; or, in other words, the aristocratic standing of Mohammed. He was not a mere "camel driver." The Koreish were the ruling clan of Mecca; Mecca was the centre for all Arabia; and Mohammed's grandfather, Abd ul Muttalib, was the most influential and powerful man of that aristocratic city. The pet-child of Abd ul Muttalib was the orphan boy, Mohammed. Until his eighth year he was under the shelter and favor of this chief man of the Koreish. He learned what it was to be lordly and to exercise power, and he never forgot it. As in the case of so many other great men of history, his environment, his early training, and his wife were the determining *personal* influences in the character of Mohammed.

Finally, the ruling factor was the mind and genius of the man himself. Of attractive personal qualities, beautiful countenance, and accomplished in business, he first won the attention and then the heart of a very wealthy widow, Khadijah. Koelle tells us that she was "evidently an Arab lady of strong mind and mature experience, who maintained a decided ascendancy over her husband, and managed him with great wisdom and firmness. This appears from nothing more strikingly than from the very

[1] S. W. Koelle, "Mohammed and Mohammedanism," 27.
[2] J. Wellhausen, "Reste Arabischen Heidentums," (Berlin, 1897), 230-242.

remarkable fact that she succeeded in keeping him from marrying any other wife as long as she lived; though, at her death, when he had long ceased to be a young man, he indulged, without restraint, in the multiplication of wives. But, as Khadijah herself was favorably disposed toward Hanifism, it is highly probable that she exercised her commanding influence over her husband in such a manner as to promote and strengthen his own attachment to the reformatory sect of monotheists."

Mohammed married this woman when he had reached his twenty-fifth year. At the age of forty he began to have his revelations, and to preach his new religion. His first convert, and, perchance, the most ambitious one, was his wife: then Ali and Zeid, his two adopted children; then his friend, the prosperous merchant, Abu Bekr. Such was the nucleus for the new faith.

The First Period of His Life.[1]—The exact date of Mohammed's birth is unknown. Caussin de Perceval calculates that the date was August 20, A. D. 570.[2] According to Sprenger, it was April 13, A. D. 571.[3] Soon after his birth, according to Arab custom, he was sent to be nursed by Halimah, a woman of the tribe of Bni Saad, where he remained for a period of two years. In his sixth year Mohammed was taken by his mother to Medina, but on the return journey she fell sick and died. The orphan boy was then taken back to Mecca and put under the care of his grandfather, Abd ul Muttalib, and when the latter died, two years later, under that of his uncle, Abu Talib. The following beautiful verses

[1] For his genealogy, see the table opposite
[2] A. P. Caussin de Perceval, "Essai sur l'Histoire des Arabes avant l'Islamisme" (Paris, 1836), Vol. I, 282.
[3] Aloys Sprenger, "Das Leben und die Lehre des Mohammed," Vol. I, 138.

TABLE OF MOHAMMED'S GENEALOGY

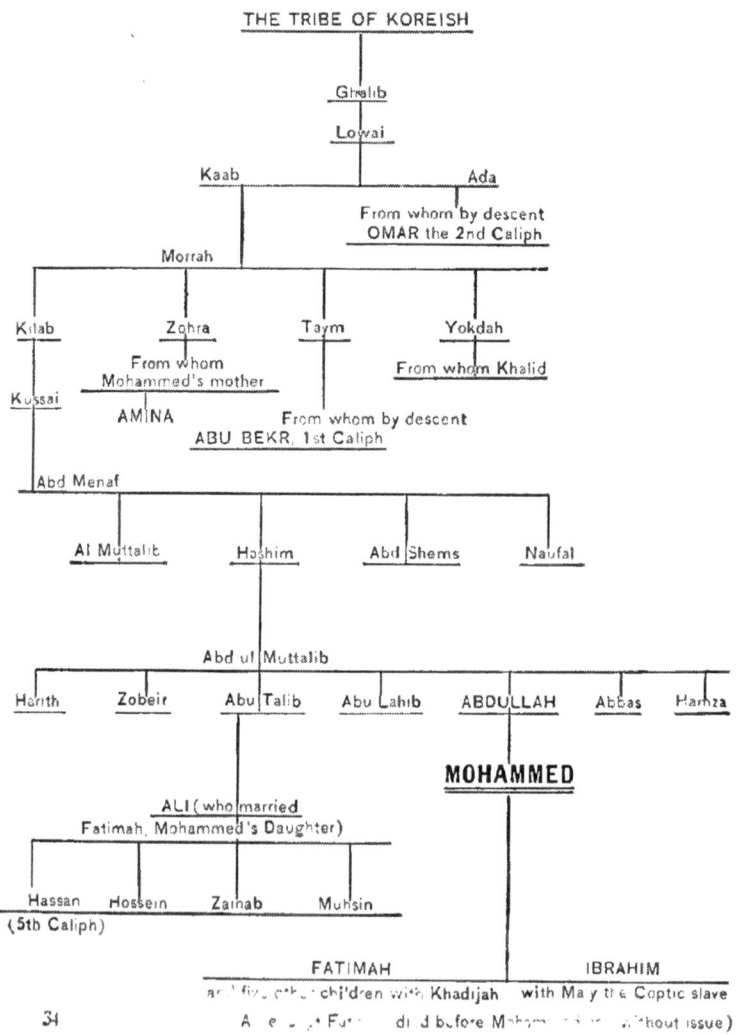

THE TRIBE OF KOREISH

Ghalib

Lowai

Kaab   Ada
                                    From whom by descent
                                    OMAR the 2nd Caliph

Morrah

Kilab   Zohra   Taym   Yokdah
          From whom   From whom Khalid
       Mohammed's mother
Kussai   AMINA   From whom by descent
                         ABU BEKR, 1st Caliph

Abd Menaf

     Al Muttalib   Hashim   Abd Shems   Naufal

Abd ul Muttalib

Harith   Zobeir   Abu Talib   Abu Lahib   ABDULLAH   Abbas   Hamza

                                          MOHAMMED

          ALI (who married
     Fatimah, Mohammed's Daughter)

Hassan   Hossein   Zainab   Muhsin
(5th Caliph)

          FATIMAH   IBRAHIM
and five other children with Khadijah   with Mary the Coptic slave
     A   Fati   died before Mohammed   without issue)

34

in the Koran are Mohammed's eloquent reference to this
period of his life:

"I swear by the splendor of light
And by the silence of night
That the Lord shall never forsake thee
Nor in His hatred take thee;
Truly for thee shall be winning
Better than all beginning.
Soon shall the Lord console thee, grief no longer control thee,
And fear no longer cajole thee
Thou wert an orphan-boy, yet the Lord found room for thy head.
When thy feet went astray, were they not to the right path led?
Did he not find thee poor, yet riches around thee spread?
Then on the orphan-boy, let thy proud foot never tread,
And never turn away the beggar who asks for bread,
But of the Lord's bounty ever let praise be sung and said."[1]

When twelve years old Mohammed was taken on a
mercantile journey as far as Syria. Here first he came
in contact with Christians and, according to tradition,
met the monk Buhaira. For the rest the youth of Mohammed was uneventful, and he was employed, as other
lads, in herding sheep and goats. To this he refers in
the traditional saying, "Verily there hath been no
prophet who hath not performed the work of a shep-
herd." At the age of twenty-five he entered the service
of Khadijah, a rich widow of Mecca, whose caravan of
merchandise he attended, and once more visited Busra
(near the Jordan), Aleppo and Damascus. As a reward
of faithful service he secured her hand in marriage, and
lived happily with her. His marriage gave him promi-
nence, and he took a leading part in renewing an old
federation at Mecca. In his thirty-fifth year he settled

[1]Surah 93 Translation printed in the *Edinburgh Review* for July, 1866.
Article "Mohammed" It has all the rhyme and beauty of the original.

a dispute regarding the placing of the Black Stone in reconstruction of the Kaaba. When he approached the age of forty he gave his mind to contemplation, and probably composed some of the earlier chapters of the Koran.[1] At last he received the call to become a prophet in the cave of Hira, and communicated his vision to his wife, Khadijah, who believed in its validity. After a period of mental depression other revelations followed, and he began to preach. The next two converts were Ali and Zeid, his adopted children; then Abu Bekr, Othman, Talha—until they numbered fifty souls. The hostility of the Meccans was aroused, persecution began, and some fled to Abyssinia. In the sixth year of his mission, Hamza and Omar joined Islam. In the tenth year Khadijah died, and the same year Mohammed negotiated two new marriages. Attempting to convert the people of Taif, he was driven out, but he won over a party of twelve from Medina, who came on pilgrimage and preached the faith on their return. At the next season seventy were ready to take the pledge of allegiance at Akaba. Shortly after Mohammed determined to flee from Mecca to Medina, and this flight dates the Moslem era (622 A. D.).

The Second Period.—The flight to Medina changed not only the scene, but the actor and drama. He who at Mecca was the preacher and warner, now becomes the legislator and warrior. This is evident from the Koran chapters revealed after the Hegira. The first year Mohammed built the great mosque and houses for his wives and his followers. The next year he began hostilities against the Koreish of Mecca, and the first pitched battle was fought at Bedr, where his force of

[1]Surahs 103, 100, 1, 101, 95, 104, 92, 91 and 106.

three hundred and five followers routed the enemy, three times as strong.[1]

The Koreish, aroused by the defeat at Bedr, advanced upon Medina, defeated the Moslem army at Ohod, and Mohammed himself was seriously wounded. The fourth year of the Hegira, war was waged against the tribe of Asad and the Jews of Bni Nazir; Mohammed also married a fifth and sixth wife. At the battle of the Ditch he defended Medina against a superior force, and broke up their siege. The next expedition was against the Jews of Bni Koraiza; seven hundred captives were slain, and the women and children sold into slavery.[2] Before the close of this year Mohammed married Zainab, the wife of his freed slave and adopted son.[3] In the sixth year of the Hegira there were other expeditions against the Jews and idolaters. The same year Mohammed wrote letters to foreign kings and princes, inviting them to embrace Islam.

In the seventh year of the Hegira Mohammed assembled a force of sixteen hundred warriors and marched against the Jewish strongholds at Khaibar; the Jews were subjugated or slain, and there was much booty, including a new wife—Safiyah—for the prophet. It was during the Khaibar expedition that Mohammed legalized

[1]The description of the battle by Muir is graphic in all its gruesome details. "Abu Jahl was yet breathing when Abdullah, Mohammed's servant, ran up and, cutting off his head, carried it to his master 'The head of the enemy of God,' cried Mohammed; 'God, there is no other god but He.' 'There is no other,' said Abdullah, as he cast the bloody head at the Prophet's feet. 'It is more acceptable to me,' cried Mohammed, 'than the choicest camel in all Arabia.'" After the battle Mohammed gave the law in regard to the division of the spoil, one-fifth for the prophet and for the rest share and share alike to all No quarter was given to the enemy, and even two days after the battle the chief prisoners, among them Okba and Nazir, were slain.

[2]This massacre is commended in Surah 33, verse 25.

[3]Surah 33:36-38.

"temporary marriages,"[1] altho it is said he afterward abolished the abominable custom. At Khaibar also a Jewess attempted to poison him, but the deed was discovered, and she was immediately put to death. Afterward Mohammed made the attempt to perform the sacred pilgrimage to the old Pantheon at Mecca, but was turned back. The next year, the eighth of the Hegira, in pursuance of the terms of the truce made at Hodaibiya, he entered Mecca and peacefully performed the ceremonies of the old pagan cult, thus forever perpetuating them in Islam. At Mecca he negotiated his last marriage, and through it won Khalid, "the Sword of God," and Omar, "the Valiant," as converts. The army sent under them to Southern Syria met with disaster, and there was also renewed hostility at Mecca. Therefore Mohammed resolved to attack his native city. He approached with ten thousand men, entered Mecca without a battle, destroyed the idols in the Kaaba, and administered the oath of allegiance to the people. When expeditions were sent to subdue the neighboring tribes, and Khalid was guilty of ordering a whole tribe to be slain, Mohammed rebuked him and sent money for the widows and orphans of the slain. The ninth year of the Hegira was the year of deputations, when the various Arabian tribes accepted Islam. Other warlike expeditions to Tabuk, Duma and Taif followed. In A. D. 631 Mohammed issued the famous command that, after four years, the Moslems would be absolved from every league or covenant with idolaters, and that thereafter no unbeliever would be allowed to make the pilgrimage. The same year he had a great sorrow in the death of his little son, Ibrahim. The next year, in great state, he made the

[1] See Chapter VI of this volume.

THE NORTHWESTERN PART OF MECCA AND THE SACRED MOSQUE

final pilgrimage, but the excitement and fatigue told on his health, for he was growing infirm. Three dangerous revolts by rival prophets—Musailimah, Iswad and Tulaiha—broke out in Arabia, which were all subdued, but not until after the death of Mohammed. The prophet's health grew worse; sixty-three years of checkered life had undermined his iron constitution, and perhaps the poison of Khaibar had left its trace in his system. From his sick-bed he sent out a last expedition, under Osama, against the Roman border; and, after a final address from the mosque pulpit, having given alms to the poor and counsel to his followers, he lay down to die on Aisha's lap.

Muir, following the oldest Moslem biographers, tells the rest of the story thus: "His strength now rapidly sank. He seemed to be aware that death was drawing near. He called for a pitcher of water and, wetting his face, prayed thus, 'O Lord, I beseech Thee to assist me in the agonies of death.' Then three times he ejaculated, most earnestly, 'Gabriel, come close to me!' . . . After a little he prayed in a whisper, 'Lord, grant me pardon, and join me to the companionship on high.' Then at intervals: 'Eternity in Paradise! Pardon! Yes, the blessed companionship on high.' He stretched himself gently. Then all was still. His head grew heavy on the breast of Aisha. The prophet of Arabia was dead."[1]

His Personal Appearance.—Mohammed is described in tradition as a man above middle height, of spare figure, as are nearly all the Arabs, commanding presence, massive head, noble brow, jet black hair, and a long bushy beard. His eyes were piercing. Decision marked his every movement, and he always walked rapidly. This

[1] Sir William Muir, "Life of Mahomet."

picture is doubtless reliable, and shows us something of
the man of whom the world has never seen contemporane-
ous portrait or sculpture.   All writers seem to agree that
he had the genius to command, and expected obedience
from equals as well as inferiors.   James Freeman Clarke[1]
says that to him, more than to any other of whom history
makes mention, was given

> "The monarch mind, the mystery of commanding,
>   The birth-hour gift, the art Napoleon
> Of wielding, moulding, gathering, welding, banding
>   The hearts of thousands till they moved as one."

His Character.—The character of Mohammed is one
of the great problems of history.   Altho the sources of
our information concerning his life and work are all
Mohammedan, and the Koran is his book, there is the
greatest diversity of opinion among students of history.
medanism in the twelfth century, concludes that Mohammed was in no sense of the word a *prophet;*[2] while
Bosworth Smith and Thomas Carlyle maintain that
he was "a very Prophet of God."[3]   Saiyad Ameer Ali suc-
ceeds, by clever argument, in eliminating every sensual,
harsh and ignorant trait from the character of Mohammed.[4]   In contrast to this, we may read what Hugh
Broughton quaintly wrote in 1662: "Now consider this
Moamed or Machumed, whom God gave up to a blind
mind, an Ishmaelite, being a poor man till he married

---

[1]James Freeman Clarke, "Ten Great Religions."
[2]"Zwei Bucher gegen den Mohammedanismus von Petrus Venerabilis, ins
Deutsche ubersetzt von John Thoma" (Leipsic, 1896, Akademische Buch-
handlung)
[3]R Bosworth Smith, "Mohammed and Mohammedanism," 340.
[4]"The Spirit of Islam; or, The Life and Teachings of Mohammed" (Calcutta, 1902), 78-85; 102-113, etc.

THE HERO AS PROPHET.

A LECTURE,

BY

THOMAS CARLYLE.

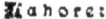

PUBLISHED BY

THE MOHAMMADAN TRACT AND BOOK DEPOT, PUNJAB.

Lahore:

PRINTED AT THE ISLAMIA PRESS.

1893.

M. V. PRESS. *(Price per copy two annas.)*

FACSIMILE TITLE PAGE OF A MOSLEM TRACT

A reprint of Carlyle's essay on Mohammed, published by the New Islam

a widow; wealthy then and of high countenance, having the falling sickness and being tormented by the devil, whereby the widow was sorry that she had matched with him. He persuaded her, by himself and others, that his fits were but a trance wherein he talked with the angel Gabriel. So, in time, the impostor was reputed a prophet of God and, from Judaism, Arius, Nestorius, and his own brain, he frameth a doctrine." Not altogether bad for a seventeenth-century synopsis!

In our day the critical labors of Arabic scholars, like Sprenger, Weil, Muir, Koelle, and others, have given us a more correct idea of Mohammed's life and character, but the pendulum is still swinging, and will come to rest probably between the two extremes. Sir William Muir, Marcus Dods, and others, claim that Mohammed was at first sincere and upright, himself believing in his so-called revelations, but that afterward, intoxicated by success, he used the dignity of his prophetship for personal ends, and was conscious of deceiving the people in some of his later revelations. Koelle finds the key to the first period of Mohammed's life in Khadijah, his first wife, who directed his ambitions and controlled his passions by her maturity and good management. After her death he revealed what he had always been, and gave vent to his hitherto restrained passions. Aloys Sprenger finds the solution of the problem in the epileptic fits to which Mohammed was subject, at least once in his youth, and often in later years: "The fit, after which he assumed his office, was undoubtedly brought on by long-continued and increasing mental excitement, and by his ascetic exercises. We know that he used frequently to fast, and that he sometimes devoted the greater part of the night to prayer. The bias of the Mohammedans is to gloss over the aberration of their prophet's mind and his intention to commit suicide. Most of his biographers pass over the transition period in silence. We may, therefore, be justified in stretching the scanty information which we can glean from them to the utmost extent, and in supposing that he was, for some time, a complete maniac, and that the fit after which he assumed his office was a paroxysm of cataleptic insanity. This disease is sometimes accompanied by such interesting psychical phenomena that, even in modern times, it gives rise to many superstitious opinions."[1]

Aside from the disputed question of Mohammed's sincerity, whether in his early career or throughout his life, no one can say that his moral character reached a high standard. It is possible to measure the prophet by three standards, of which two at least would seem to be a fair test: The law of the Pagan Arabs, the law he himself professed to reveal, and the law of the Old and New Testaments, *which he professed to approve and supersede.* By the New Testament law of Jesus Christ, who was the last Prophet before Mohammed and whom Mohammed acknowledged as the Word of God, the Arabian prophet stands self-condemned. The most cursory examination of his biography proves that he repeatedly broke every precept of the Sermon on the Mount, not only in his private life, *but in his prophetic office.* And the Koran itself proves that the spirit of Jesus was entirely absent from the mind of Mohammed.

The Arabs among whom Mohammed was born and grew to manhood also had a law, altho they were idolaters, slaveholders and polygamists. Even the robbers of the desert who, like Mohammed, lay in wait for cara-

[1]Aloys Sprenger, "Life of Mohammed," Vol. I, 949. (Allahabad, 1851.)

vans, had a code of honor. Three flagrant breaches of
this code stain the character of Mohammed.[1] It was
quite lawful to marry a captive woman, whose relatives
had been slain in battle, but not until three months after
their death. Mohammed only waited three days in the
case of the Jewess, Safiyah. It was lawful to rob merchants, but not pilgrims, on their way to Mecca. Mohammed broke this old law, and "revealed a verse" to
justify his conduct. In the "Time of Ignorance" it was
incest to marry the wife of an adopted son, even after
his decease. The prophet Mohammed fell in love with
the lawful wife of his adopted son, Zeid, prevailed on
him to divorce her, and then married her immediately;
for this also he had a "special revelation." The latest
biographer of Mohammed, Professor D. S. Margoliouth,
writes: "Of any moralizing or demoralizing effect which
Mohammed's teaching had upon his followers, we cannot speak with precision. When he was at the head of
a robber community (in Medina) it is probable that the
demoralizing influence began to be felt; it was then that
men who had never broken an oath learned that they
might evade their obligations, and that men to whom the
blood of the clansmen had been as their own began to
shed it with impunity in the cause of God; and that lying
and treachery, in the cause of Islam, received divine ap-
proval, hesitation to perjure oneself in that cause being
represented as a weakness. It was then, too, that Moslems became distinguished by the obscenity of their language. It was then, too, that the coveting of goods and
wives (possessed by unbelievers) was avowed without
discouragement from the prophet."[2]

[1] Sir William Muir, "Mahomet"; Sprenger, Koelle, etc
[2] D. S. Margoliouth, "Mohammed and the Rise of Islam" (New York
and London, 1905), 149. Every statement given is based on original Moslem

But Mohammed was not only guilty of breaking the
old Arab laws, and coming infinitely short of the law of
Christ; he never even kept the laws of which he claimed
to be the divinely appointed medium and custodian.
When Khadijah died he found his own law, lax as it
was, insufficient to restrain his lusts. His followers were
to be content with four lawful wives; according to tradition, he took to himself eleven lawful wives and two
concubines.[1] It is impossible to form a just estimate
of the character of Mohammed, unless we know somewhat of his relations with women. This subject, however, is, of necessity, shrouded from decent eyes, because of the brutality and coarseness of its charac-

sources, viz., for this paragraph· Bokhari IV, 90; Musnad IV, 256; Musnad IV, 79, Ishak 433, 744; Ibn Saad III, 116, 13, etc

[1]1 KHADIJAH.—A rich lady who had been twice married. She remained
Mohammed's only wife for twenty-five years. The mother of two sons and
four daughters.

2 SAUDAH.—Widow of Sakran. Married Mohammed two months after
death of Khadijah.

3. 'AISHA.—Daughter of Abu Bekr. Betrothed when seven years old;
married at ten His favorite wife.

4. JUWAIRIJAH —Widow of Al Harith. Ransomed for nine ounces of
gold by Mohammed.

5. HAFSAH —Daughter of Omar; widow of Khunais.

6 ZAINAB —Widow of Mohammed's cousin, Obaidah.

7. UM SALMAH.—Widow of Abu Salima, who died in battle.

8. ZAINAB —Wife of Mohammed's adopted son, Zaid, who divorced her
to please the prophet (Surah 33.36). By Arab law she was unlawful to him.

9. SAFIYAH.—Widow of a Khaibar chief, who was cruelly put to death.

10 UM HABIBAH —Widow of one of the four Moslems who emigrated to
Abyssinia, and there became Christians.

11. MAIMUNAH.—Daughter of El Harith.

12 MARY, THE COPTIC SLAVE (concubine) —A Christian slave-girl sent to
Mohammed by the Roman governor of Egypt.

13 RIHANAH —A Jewess, whose husband was slain in the massacre of the
Bni Koraiza. After the victory trenches were dug across the market-place
and, one by one, the male captives, by Mohammed's orders, were beheaded
on the brink of the trench and cast into it. The butchery lasted all day,
and it needed torchlight to finish it. After dark Rihanah was taken to Mohammed's tent.—*Majma'-ul-Bihar*, p. 528; Hughes, "Dictionary of Islam," p.
399.

ter.[1] A recent writer in a leading missionary magazine, touching on this subject, says: "We must pass the matter over, simply noting that there are depths of filth in the prophet's character which may assort well enough with the depraved sensuality of the bulk of his followers, . . . but which are simply loathsome in the eyes of all over whom Christianity, in any measure or degree, has influence." We have no inclination to lift the veil that, in most English biographies, covers the family-life of the prophet of Arabia. But it is only fair to remark that these love-adventures, and the disgusting details of his married life, form a large part of the "lives of the prophet of God," which are the fireside literature of educated Moslems in all lands where Mohammed is the ideal of character and the standard of morality. The list of Mohammed's wives will be a sufficient index to the subject for any student of Arabic literature.

Finally, we can only say, with Johnstone: "If it be thought that the judgment passed on the prophet of Arabia is harsh, let it be remembered that the evidence on which it rests comes all from the lips and the pens of his own devoted adherents. The voice of foes or detractors of his own time, or of time immediately following, has not yet reached the ears of later ages. Everything that could tend to his glory was eagerly sought out and treasured up by men jealous of his good name; and everything that might seem to detract therefrom was carefully suppressed. His lightest words were sacred to them, his most trifling actions were the example they strove to follow. To them he was the highest and

---

[1] See Insan el Ayun, Ibn Ishak, Bokhari, etc. Or Paul de Regla, quotations in "El Kitab des Lois Secrètes de l'Amour." (Paris, 1906.)

most excellent of the creatures of God's hand—last and
most perfect of the messengers who declared His will to
man. The vast body of tradition which was traced back
to the lips of those who had most closely companied
with him was jealously sifted and scrutinized, though not
tested by the canons of Western criticism; it is on this
that our knowledge is founded and our judgment passed.
*And the followers of the prophet can scarcely complain
if, even on such evidence, the verdict of history goes
against him.*"[1]

The Apotheosis of Mohammed.—The life and character of Mohammed, as portrayed by his earliest biographers—Ibn Ishak, Ibn Hisham, Wakidi, and others—is,
however, not the present-day conception of the prophet.
In the Koran and in these earliest sources Mohammed
is thoroughly human and liable to error. Later tradition
has changed all that, and made him sinless and almost
divine. The two hundred and one titles of honor given
him proclaim his apotheosis,[2] and orthodox tradition
establishes the claim. He is called Light of God, Peace
of the World, Glory of the Ages, First of all Creatures,
and names yet more lofty and blasphemous. He is at
once the sealer and abrogator of all former prophets
and revelations. They have not only been succeeded, but
also supplanted by Mohammed. No Moslem prays to
him, but every Moslem daily prays for him in endless
repetition. He is the only powerful intercessor on the
day of judgment. Every detail of his early life is attributed to divine permission or command, and so the
very faults of his character are his endless glory and his

[1]P. de Lacy Johnstone, "Muhammad and his Power."
[2]For the list of these lordly names, many of which are similar to those
given to God, see Sinajet et Tarb, Beirut edition, or any recent Moslem
biography. Zwemer, "Moslem Doctrine of God," 46.

sign of superiority.[1] God favored him above all creatures. He dwells in the highest heaven, and is several
degrees above Jesus in honor and station. His name is
never uttered or written without the addition of a prayer.
"Ya Mohammed" is the open sesame to every door of
difficulty—temporal or spiritual. One hears that name
in the bazaar and in the street, in the mosque and from
the minaret. Sailors sing it while hoisting their sails;
hammals groan it, to raise a burden; the beggar howls it,
to obtain alms; it is the Bedouin's cry in attacking a
caravan; it hushes babes to sleep, as a cradle-song; it
is the pillow of the sick, and the last word of the dying;
it is written on the door-posts and in their hearts as well
as, since eternity, on the throne of God; it is to the devout Moslem the name above every name; grammarians
can tell you how its four letters are representative of all
the sciences and mysteries by their wonderful combination. The name of Mohammed is the best to give a
child, and the best to swear by, for an end of all dispute, in a close bargain. In some biographies of Mohammed we are solemnly told that God created man in
the image of Mohammed's name, as written in Arabic
on His throne: مُحَمَّد viz., *M h m d*, and that
the four postures in prayer are indicative of the four
characters in his other name, احمد both of which
naïve theories seem very plausible to the devout Moslem of to-day.

The exceeding honor given to Mohammed's name
by his followers is only one indication of the place
their prophet occupies in their system and holds in
their hearts. From the fullness of the heart the mouth

[1] S. M. Zwemer, "Arabia; the Cradle of Islam," 185; Ameer Ali, "The Spirit of Islam," Arabic quotations, 1, 110, etc.

speaketh. Mohammed holds the keys of heaven and hell.
No Moslem, however bad his character, will perish finally; no unbeliever, however good his life, can be saved,
except through Mohammed.   One has only to question
the Moslem masses, whether in Morocco or Java, or to
read a single volume of "Traditions," for proof of this
statement.   Islam denies the need of a mediator or of
the incarnation, but it is evident that, in popular thought
and in Moslem writings, Mohammed *acts as a mediator,
without an incarnation, without an atonement, without
demand for change of character.*   For illustration, let
this story of the Jew suffice, altho it could be matched
with a hundred others equally absurd, yet equally
credited:

"In the days of the children of Israel there was a sinful and flagitious man who, for the space of two hundred years, wearied everyone by the enormity of his of-
fences. When he died they threw his corpse upon a
dunghill, but no sooner had this been done than Gabriel,
coming to Moses, said: 'Thus saith the Almighty God,
This day My friend has departed from this world, and
the people have cast his corpse upon a dunghill. Now
let that corpse be dressed and prepared for burial without delay: and ye shall speak unto the children of Israel,
that they forthwith recite the burial service over his bier
if they desire pardon.'   Then Moses marveled exceedingly, and inquired why forgiveness was required, and
God answered: 'The Lord well knoweth all the sins
which that sinner hath during these two hundred years
committed; and, verily, he never could have been par-
doned. But, one day, this wicked man was reading the
Torah and, seeing there the name of the blessed Mohammed, he wept and pressed the page to his eyes. This

honor and reverence shown to My beloved was pleasing
unto Me, and from the blessed effects of that single act
I have blotted out the sins of the whole two hundred
years.' Lovers of the blessed Mohammed! rejoice in
your hearts, and be assured that love for the holy prophet, the Lord of creation, is, in every possible condition,
the means of salvation."[1]

The "Coronation Hymn" of Islam.—Among all the
books and poems written in praise of Mohammed there
is none so popular, or so celebrated, as "the poem of the
mantle," "El Burda." It is the "Coronation Hymn" of
the Moslem world and, had Islam music in its public
worship, would hold the place among them that "All
Hail the Power of Jesus' Name" does among Christians.
It is read at public festivals, sung by travelling dervishes
and printed in books of devotion. It has been translated
into nearly all the languages of the Mohammedan world,
as well as into Latin, German, French and English. More
than thirty commentaries on the poem exist in Arabic,
and twenty-one Arabic poets have exercised their in-
genuity in poetical paraphrases of the text. One of
these books even sets forth the various medical benefits
to be derived from the poem when properly transcribed
for amulets and charms.[2]

The author of the poem was Sharif ud Din Moham-
mad el Busiri, of Berber origin, born in Egypt about
1212 A. D. His history is obscure, and even the date
and place of his death is uncertain. Although he wrote
other poetry, his fame is due solely to verses written in

---

[1] This story is given on page 3 of a life of Mohammed, published at
Agra, in 1852, and also in the book "Insan el Ayun," an authority in
Arabia and Egypt. There are many similar tales current, one relates that
even Satan has benefit from the coming of Mohammed

[2] See references in Brockelmann, "Geschichte der Arabischen Literatur"

praise of Mohammed. The occasion on which he wrote
"El Burda" is thus given in his own words: "It happened that I was struck with paralysis on my left side,
and besought Allah to cure me. Shortly after I was
composing my poem, in honor of the prophet, when he
appeared in a vision and passed his blessed hand over
my side. The result was a complete cure." Later traditions add that Mohammed also threw his mantle over
the poet, and thus the poem received its name. But this
part of the story happens to be borrowed from the "Life
of Kaab bin Zuhair," a contemporary of the prophet.
This man first mocked Mohammed's mission, and afterward, afraid of vengeance, appeased the prophet by
verses in his honor. On this occasion Mohammed for-
gave his enemy, and actually gave him a mantle. This
precious heirloom is still preserved in Constantinople,
according to Moslem authorities.

Not only the story of its composition, but the poem itself resembles the earlier one of Kaab bin Zuhair. The
original title of the later production was "The Glitter-
ing Galaxy of Stars in Praise of the Best of God's
Creatures." It consists of one hundred and seventy-two
rhymed couplets in ordinary Arabic metre, full of allite-
rations and the play upon words of which Orientals are
so fond. It gives a summary of the chief events in
Mohammed's life and an abridgment of Moslem beliefs.
From its form it can be easily memorized and, naturally,
its subject is one of which the pious Moslem never
grows weary. The poet wrote long after tradition and
orthodoxy had quenched the last spark of historical
criticism in the Mohammedan world. If the author had
read the Koran or Ibn Hisham with discrimination he
would hardly have written:

"Vainly would men strive to comprehend
The excellence of his mental endowments!
Just as when seen from far of day's bright orb
The enormous magnitude is not apparent,
But dazzles and confounds the vision
Of him who near beholds it."

The poem is really an attempt to put Mohammed on a par with Jesus Christ, by attributing to him Christian ideas and gospel miracles. There is no doubt that there were Christian influences moulding the form and furnishing the substance of later Mohammedan religious literature. Mohammed's biography, as given by later writers, is a palpable plagiarism and a parody on the life of our Saviour, as given in the gospels.[1] The poem of "The Mantle" calls the Mecca camel driver

"Prince of both of God's great worlds,
That of men and that of genii.
Sovereign likewise is he of the two races,
Arabians and Barbarians.
He is our prophet, who to us prescribeth
What we shall do and what we shall avoid.
Vast as the sea is his generosity,
His designs are as large and long as time."

Not only does Mohammed occupy so high a place in creation, but he is the sole hope of the dying, and the only intercessor on the last day; altho this teaching flatly contradicts the Koran. The poet voices the great need of the Moslem for a Saviour from sin when he bursts out with these words:

"O thou most excellent of all created beings!
To whom but thee can I flee for refuge
In that moment so terrible to every mortal?
O Apostle of God, thy glory will not be tarnished
By whatsoever aid thou mayest vouchsafe to me
In that tremendous day wherein the Mighty
Himself shall be manifest as the Avenger."

[1]See S. W. Koelle, "Mohammed and Mohammedanism."

It is natural that Mohammed's chief miracle, the matchless Arabic Koran, receives no small praise; in this portion of the poem there are lofty thoughts beautifully expressed, but the metaphors again seem borrowed from the Bible. The Moslem is told

> . . . "Therein to read to find a refuge sure
> Safe from Hell's scorching heat
> The refreshing waters of the Book divine
> Will cool the ardours of the infernal pit."
>
> .   .   .   .   .   .
>
> "As in some lofty mountain shines from far,
> Amid the darkness of a moonless night,
> A beacon lighted by some kindly hand
> To lead the traveller to some friendly hearth,
> So do these oracles irradiate with their beams
> The gloom and darkness of a sinful world."

Alas! that the only true commentary on these verses is the gloom and darkness that still rest on the sinful Moslem world, and which neither the Koran, with all its literary beauty, nor Mohammed has, in any way, removed, but rather increased. A stream cannot rise higher than its source, and this chapter has already shown one of the sources—the chief source—of Islam. The religion which Mohammed founded bears everywhere the imprint of his life and character. Mohammed was not only the prophet, but the *prophecy* of Islam.

THE SPREAD OF ISLAM

"Let there be no compulsion in religion."—*The Koran, Surah 2: 257.*

"When the holy months shall be past, then slay the polytheists wherever ye find them, and seize them, and besiege them, and lie in ambush for them in every ambuscade. But if they turn Moslems, and rise to prayer, and give the legal-alms, let them alone." —*The Koran, Surah 9:15.*

"Thus, from its very inception, Islam has been a missionary religion both in theory and practice, for the life of Mohammed exemplifies the same teaching, and the prophet himself stands at the head of a long series of Moslem missionaries who have won an entrance for their faith into the hearts of unbelievers. Moreover, it is not in the cruelties of the persecutor or the fury of the fanatic that we should look for the evidences of the missionary spirit of Islam any more than in the exploits of that mythical personage, the Moslem warrior with sword in one hand and the Koran in the other."—*T W. Arnold* in The Preaching of Islam.

III

THE SPREAD OF ISLAM

Islam a Missionary Religion.—The great religions of
the world may be divided into two classes—the non-
missionary and the missionary. Judaism, Zoroastrianism, Hinduism, for example, are non-missionary, while
Buddhism, Christianity and Islam *are* missionary.[1] Islam
was such from its very origin. Altho not in the Christian conception of the word "missionary," yet in zeal for
propagating their faith, in world-wide missionary enterprise and activity, whether by fire and sword or by word
of preaching, Islam affords a striking example of how
the rank and file in the Moslem army were missionaries
of the faith.

One hundred years after Mohammed's death his followers were masters of an empire greater than Rome at
the zenith of her power. They were building mosques
in China, in Spain, in Persia, and in Southern India!
The extent, the rapidity and the method of the early
Moslem conquest are a marvellous illustration of their
fanatic zeal.

Two hundred years after the Hegira Mohammed's
name was proclaimed on thousands of minarets from
the pillars of Hercules to the Pacific, and from Northern

[1] T. W. Arnold, "The Preaching of Islam," 1.

Turkestan to Ceylon. Only thirteen centuries have passed, and to-day there are over two hundred and thirty million Mohammedans—one-seventh of the population of the globe! Fifty-eight millions in Africa, sixty-two millions in India, thirty millions in China, thirty-five millions in the Malay Archipelago, and one-quarter of a million in the Philippines, not to speak of the lands that are almost wholly Mohammedan in Western Asia. It is easy enough to say that Mohammedanism was propagated by the sword. It largely was. But we may well ask, with Carlyle:[1] "Where did Mohammed get his sword?" What fires of faith and devotion must have burned in the hearts of the early champions of Islam, to make them gird the sword and fight and die for the new religion!

It swept across Syria, Egypt, Tunis, Tripoli, Algiers, Morocco, like the desert simoon—swift, fierce, impetuous irresistible, destructive—only to be curbed and cooled by the waves of the Atlantic. History tells of Akba, one of their leaders, that he rode his horse far out into the surf, and cried: "Great God! if I were not stopped by this raging sea, I would go on to the nations of the West, preaching the unity of Thy name and putting to the sword those who would not submit."[2] Tarik, finding no lands to the west, crossed over the straits into Spain, and named its promontory Jebel Tarik (the mountain of Tarik), Gibraltar—an everlasting monument to his missionary zeal.

Three Periods of Conquest.—The spread of Islam may be chronologically divided into three periods, and the dates when Islam entered the lands where it is now pre-

---

[1] Thomas Carlyle, in "Heroes and Hero Worship," The Hero as Prophet.
[2] Gibbon, "Decline and Fall of the Roman Empire."

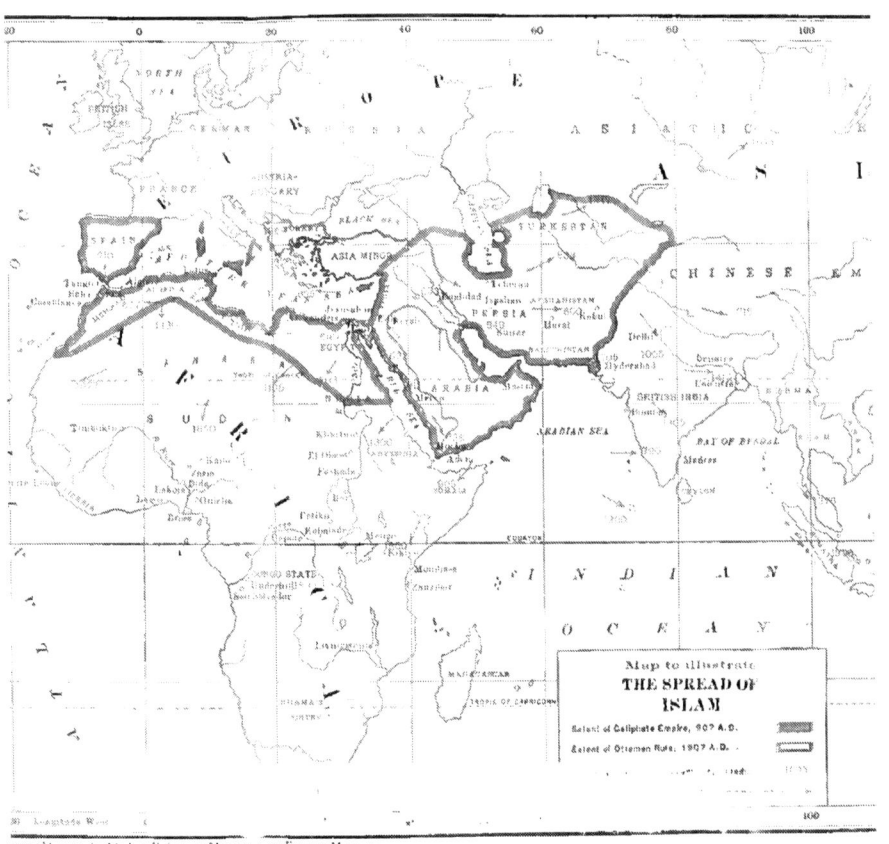

Map to illustrate
THE SPREAD OF
ISLAM

Extent of Caliphate Empire, 907 A.D.

Extent of Ottoman Rule, 1907 A.D.

dominant fall into three groups. Like Christianity, we may say Islam has had its apostolic, medieval and modern missions. The first period is from the death of Mohammed, 632 A. D. to 800 A. D.; a later period, under the Ottomans and Moguls, 1280 A. D. to 1480 A. D.; and lastly the modern spread of Islam, from 1780 A. D. and on, through the Wahabi revival and the Derwish movements in Africa.

During the first period, the days of the early caliphs, fire and sword carried Islam triumphant throughout all Arabia, Syria, Persia, Egypt, North Africa, and, by more peaceful means, as far as Canton and Western China. All these regions had received the faith, and it had become deeply rooted before the year 1000 A. D., while Christianity was put under tribute and oppression, as in Asia Minor and Egypt, or entirely swept away, as in Arabia itself, by the tornado power of the new religion in its political conquest.

That worldly motives played a considerable part in the early conversion of these lands cannot be doubted, and is admitted even by Moslem historians. When, for example, the Arabs of the pathless desert, who fed on "locusts and wild honey," once tasted the delicacies of civilization in Syria and reveled in the luxurious palaces of the Khosroes, they said: "By Allah, even if we cared not to fight for the cause of God, yet we could not but wish to contend for and enjoy *these,* leaving distress and hunger henceforth to others."[1]

The second chapter of Moslem conquest began with the rise of the Ottoman Turks and the Moguls of India. During this period Afghanistan, Turkestan, India, Java

[1]The Moslem historian, Et Tabari, attributes these words to Khalid. "Al Kindy," 85; C. R. Haines, "Islam as a Missionary Religion," 53.

and the Malay Archipelago, with Servia and Bosnia in
Europe, were more or less "converted" to Islam.

Lastly, we can chronicle the modern missionary efforts
of Islam by those apostles of fanaticism, the Derwish
orders in Africa, by the Oman Arabs in their slave-raids,
by the disciples of the Cairo University, or by returning
Meccan pilgrims. Their work has been chiefly in Africa,
but also in Russia, the Malay Archipelago, the Philippines, and even among the Finns of the Volga.[1]

Within the narrow limits of this chapter no attempt is
made to give the history of Moslem empires or dynasties, nor the rise, decline and fall of the early caliphate;
but the story of the spread of the Moslem faith is told
in brief outline, following the great geographical areas
now under its sway.

Arabia and Syria.—Whatever may have been the
method of propagating Islam in the later centuries, history leaves no doubt that its world-conquest began with
the sword. Mohammed, before his death, had announced,
as a prophecy, that "wars for the spread of Islam would
never cease until the anti-Christ appeared."[2]   And just
before he fell sick the prophet had given orders for an
expedition to the Syrian border. The great commission
of the apostle of Islam was "to slay the polytheists wherever ye find them"—and no sooner was Abu Bekr proclaimed Caliph than the faithful hastened to fulfil the
command. The army of invasion which was to carry the
Moslem standard into Syria was ordered to advance. El
Wakidi, the historian, leaves no doubt of the purpose of
their errand, and of how they executed it. He says:
"With the well-known cry of *Ya Mansur Umit!*—Strike,

[1] See the synchronological table in T. W. Arnold, "Preaching of Islam,"
389; also 204, 324, etc.

[2] Sir William Muir, "Life of Mahomet," Vol. IV, 204.

O ye conquerors!—they slew all who opposed them, and
carried off the remainder into captivity. They burned
the villages, the fields of standing corn, and the groves
of palm, and behind them there went up, as it were, a
whirlwind of fire and smoke."[1] Abu Bekr, in his address
to the people, emphasized the fact, as well he might, that
the very existence of the new religion now depended on
aggressive warfare. "When a people leaveth off to fight
in the ways of the Lord," said he, "the Lord also casteth
off that people." But Islam had so little real grip on the
Arabs themselves that, on Mohammed's death, the
Bedouin tribes, with one accord, fell away from Islam
and all the prophet's work in Arabia had to be done over
again. Medina and Mecca alone remained true to their
faith.[2]

Al Kindi, in his apology, states that the Arab tribes
started aside, like a broken bow, and were only brought
back gradually to hold fast to Islam by one inducement
or another, "by kindly treatment, persuasion and craft,
by fear and the terror of the sword, by the prospect of
power and wealth, and by the lusts and pleasures of this
life."[3]

When Osama had returned victorious from the Syrian
conquest eleven different expeditions were sent by Abu
Bekr against the apostate tribes throughout Arabia.
Muir observes that but for the simple faith and energy
of Abu Bekr himself "Islam would have melted away in
compromise with the Bedouin tribes, or, likelier still, have
perished in the throes if its birth."[4] It took over a year
of hard fighting against obstinate resistance to "convert"

[1]"Kitab el Wakidi," 139; Muir, IV, 298.
[2]C R. Haines, "Islam as a Missionary Religion," 52.
[3]"Al Kindy," 135, quoted in Haines, "Islam as a Missionary Religion," 52.
[4]Sir William Muir, "The Caliphate; Its Rise, Decline and Fall," 14

the Arabs of the Peninsula, altho they have ever since been true to Islam. Khalid, the Sword of Allah, was sent out against the rebel prophets, Toleiha and Mosei- lama. The first battle was with Toleiha, and the armies met at Bozakha. Victory came to the Moslems after a hard-fought field. The expedition against the Bni Te- mim, who occupied the plateau near the Persian Gulf, was also successful, and in the bloody battle of "the Garden of Death" Khalid overcame the forces of Mosei- lama. The Moslems lost twelve hundred men in the hand- to-hand slaughter, but Khalid, a true son of Islam, sig- nalized his victory by wedding a captive maid on the field of battle. When Abu Bekr heard of it, he wrote him a letter sprinkled with blood: "By my life! thou art a pretty fellow, living thus at thine ease. Thou weddest a damsel while the ground beneath the nuptial couch is yet moistened with the blood of twelve hundred."[1] Such were the early missionaries of Islam.

While Khalid was busy in Northern and Central Ara- bia, other similar campaigns were in progress in Bahrein and Oman. In the spring of 633 A. D., Yemen was sub- dued, and finally Hadramaut also submitted to the rule of the caliph and the religion of the prophet. In 634 the victorious Moslems, under Khalid, took Damascus. In 636 they utterly defeated the Persians at Kadesia, and the same year drove Heraclius out of Syria. Jerusalem fell the next year, and the conquest of Syria was then completed. Chaldea also was subdued by Khalid after the fashion of all these early and haughty champions of the faith.

To Hormuz, the satrap of the fertile delta region, Kha- lid wrote: "Accept the faith, and thou art safe; else pay

[1]Sir William Muir, "The Caliphate, Its Rise, Decline and Fall."

tribute, thou and thy people; which, if thou refusest, thou shalt have thyself to blame. A people is already on thee, loving death, even as thou lovest life." He refused to submit, and in the Battle of the Chains another province was added to the Arab dominions. Mohammed himself had so completely confused the functions of prophet and politician, warrior and preacher, that it is not surprising his successors knew no distinction between the word of Allah and the sword of Allah in the propagating of their faith. Yet the most remarkable fact in the spread of Islam is that political sway was *not* altogether synonymous with religious conversion. When Islam triumphed in Asia Minor, Christianity was dominant among the peoples speaking Greek, Armenian and Syriac, and these peoples, after twelve centuries of contact and conflict with Islam, are still Christian. The spread of Islam was not wholly a triumph. The victory more than once remained to the vanquished, and Islam often failed to win allegiance where it won subjection. Dr. William A. Shedd, in writing of this, says: "We are, perhaps, apt to forget this failure of Islam, the failure to attract and convert peoples who have lived for twelve and a half centuries under Moslem rule, accessible to the efforts of Mohammedan teachers, with material gain on the side of Islam; and yet to-day they are more averse to Islam than ever. It would be difficult to point out any similar failure of Christianity in its whole history."[1]

Africa.—The spread of Islam in Africa began in 638 A. D. and still continues. Bonet-Maury points out that there were three periods in the conflict for Africa. In the first, 638-1050 A. D., the Arabs, by rapid military conquest, overran the Mediterranean littoral from Egypt

[1] W. A. Shedd, "Islam and the Oriental Churches," 150.

to Morocco, where the stubborn resistance of the Berbers
and especially discord among the Moslem rulers prevented wider conquest until the tenth century. During
the second period, from 1050-1750, Morocco, the Sahara
region, and the Western Soudan became Moslem, and
the desire for conquest was, no doubt, provoked, in part,
as a reaction against the Christian crusades. The third
period, 1750-1900, was that of the revival of Islam and
its spread through the Mahdi movement and the Derwish
orders."[1]

While Khalid carried the Moslem banner to victory in
Syria and Western Persia, Amru-ibn-el-As, with equal
furor, invaded Egypt. Within two years (640 A. D.)
Alexandria was taken, and Egypt became a dependency,
like Syria and Chaldea. In 647 the armies moved westward, and within thirty years the victorious Moslems had
reached the Atlantic Ocean and were preparing to cross
over into Spain. It is impossible to give here, even in
summary, the story of these campaigns. The political victory was often an easy one, because the Christians were
divided. In Egypt one party, the Copts, welcomed the
Mohammedan invaders as a means of deliverance from
the orthodox Christian *Mukawkas*. However, they soon
had abundant reason to regret it,[2] and the religious victory of Islam was only partial, for there are still to-day
in Egypt 600,000 Copts.

Abdullah invaded Tripoli in 647 A. D.; Akba penetrated to Mauritania in 677 A. D.; yet their bloody vic-
tories were largely valueless to Islam, because Christian
civilization fought for its very life. It was not until

[1] G. Bonet-Maury, "L'Islamisme et Le Christianisme en Afrique" (Paris,
1906), 67, 68; 226-249
[2] Dr. A. Watson, in "The Mohammedan World of To-day," 23.

TUNIS—GENERAL VIEW AND MOSQUE ZEBONNA

754 A. D. that, by the conversion of the Christian "infidels," tribute was abolished.[1] Ibn Khaldun, the Moslem historian, states that those formerly Christians apostatized from Islam fourteen times.[2]

The Arabs, in their later efforts at "conversion," whether for trade, conquest or slave-raids, entered Africa from three different sides. These three streams of Moslem immigration and conquest were as follows: From Egypt they went westward as far as Lake Chad; from the northwest of Africa they came down to Lake Chad and the Niger region; and from Zanzibar the slave-dealers opened the way for Islam as far as the Great Lakes.

As early as the year 740 A. D. an Arab immigration brought Islam to Abyssinia, but the Swaheli tribes were not converted until 1700 by the Oman traders of Zanzibar. The period of the greatest Arab immigration was that following the Crusades and, therefore, the missionary expansion of Islam in North Central Africa falls between the years 1095 and 1300. Islam crossed the Sahara about the year 1200.[3] Its progress was slow, but irresistible.

In 1775 Othman, a Fulah of Gober, made a pilgrimage to Mecca, became imbued with the Wahabi desire for reform and conquest, returned and, transforming herdsmen into warriors, built up a strong Moslem empire at Sokoto. His power extended from the Atlantic to Lake Chad, and from the Binwe river to the Sahara.[4] From 1835 to 1853 Mohammed Othman of Mecca was a zealous propagandist of Islam in Kordo and Senaar, where many tribes were still pagan, and the order of

[1] T. W. Arnold, "Preaching of Islam," 103-111; F. P. Noble, "Redemption of Africa," Vol. I, 47.   [2] Ibid, Vol. I, 49   [3] Ibid, Vol. I, 49.
[4] Ibid, Vol. I, 53. Arnold, "Preaching of Islam," 265-268.

Derwishes he founded still carries on his work. In West Africa the Kadiriya and Tijani orders have been active propagandists as traders and missionaries. From 1832 to 1847 Abd ul Kader, poet and statesman, and a devout Algerian Moslem, strove to recall the Arabs of North Africa to the duty of preaching Islam, and a little later the Mahdist movement in the Egyptian Soudan extended the faith with fire and sword against the "infidels" and lukewarm believers.

But the latest and strongest Moslem missionary force in Africa is that of the Senusi brotherhood, the Jesuits of Islam. Of their rise, power and progress there are many and often conflicting accounts.[1] Noble gives the following summary:

"In 1843 Senusi, an Algerian sheikh, driven from Mecca on account of his pure life and principles, took refuge temporarily at Benghazi, on the Barkan coast. After founding military monasteries here, his order having arisen in 1837, he withdrew (1855) to Jarabub. . . . Altho within the western boundary of Egypt, and only one hundred and fifty miles from the Mediterranean, it lies on a borderland of the Libyan plateau, where no Egyptian khedive, no Turkish sultan exercises authority. Here is the true head of modern Islam's hostile movement against the giaour or infidel. It became such partly through its almost central position for African propaganda and through remoteness from European interference, but chiefly from Wahabi fanaticism and reaction. Senusi and, since 1859, his son developed their projects

[1]Compare, for example, the account of G Bonet-Maury in his "L'Islamisme et Le Christianisme en Afrique" with the interesting story of Arthur Silva White, "From Sphinx to Oracle; Through the Libyan Desert to the Oasis of Jupiter Ammon" (London, 1899). The book gives an account of his visit to the Senusi centre Siwa, near Jarabub, their capital. Other writers on the subject are Duveyrier and Rinn.

in secrecy. The sheikh is the undisputed head of the sect, blindly obeyed by the monastic orders of the Moslem world. The brethren are all in his hands as the corpse in those of the undertaker. The Senusi brotherhood is the Jesuit order of Islam. The monks regard the Senusi sheikh as the well-guided one, the true Mahdi to restore the Moslem power. Outwardly the Senusiya profess to aspire to no political aim. Their ideal goal consists in the federation of the orthodox religious orders into one theocratic body, independent of secular authority. They discountenance violence. To Mohammedans in districts under Christian sway they recommend not revolt, but withdrawal to Senusi convents. None the less, despite this ostensible condemnation of political agitation, the Senusiya aim at absolute independence. Their houses, at once church and school, arsenal and hospital, are found in the Libyan oases, Fezzan, Tripoli and Algeria, in Senegambia, the Soudan and Somalia."[1]

Europe.—Islam entered Europe very early. In 648 the Arabs crossed into Spain; in 711 they established their rule, and they and their descendants remained there for eight centuries until, in 1502, an edict of Ferdinand and Isabella forbade the exercise of the Mohammedan religion. Cyprus fell into the hands of the Saracens in 648, Rhodes five years later, while Constantinople itself was fruitlessly besieged in 668 and again in 716. Sixteen years later the battle of Tours set a limit to the Saracen conquests in Western Europe. However, in 823, Crete became Moslem, and Sicily in 878, while in 846 Rome was partially sacked by the Arabs and only saved by the bravery of Leo the Fourth.[2] In spite of their failure

[1] F P. Noble, "Redemption of Africa," Vol I, 54, 55. Compare also Bonet-Maury, "L'Islamisme," 245-263.
[2] C. R Haines, "Islam as a Missionary Religion," 58

to take Rome, the Moslems gained a foothold in Southern Italy, and were not driven out until 1058.

At the end of the thirteenth century Islam again attempted the conquest of Europe under the Ottoman Turks. "By the middle of the fourteenth century they had made good their footing in Europe. Thrace, Bulgaria, Wallachia, Servia were rapidly and thoroughly conquered, and by the end of the century Greece had become a Turkish province, and in 1453 the fall of Constantinople sealed the doom of the Eastern Empire. Seventy-six years later the unsuccessful siege of Vienna formed the high-water mark of Moslem conquest in that direction."[1] From that day until now Turkish rule and the Moslem faith have lost power in Europe. At present, while there are one hundred and sixty-nine million Moslems in Asia and nearly sixty millions in Africa, there are only five millions in Europe. Perhaps there is a physical reason for the limit of Moslem conquest toward the North. In the lands of ice and snow and shortened nights and days, the prayer-ritual is well-nigh impossible, and the fast becomes a crushing yoke [2] Gibbon tells us that the Tartars of Azoph and Astrakhan used to object to the prayer-ritual, because it was impossible in their latitude, and tried, therefore, to dissuade the Turks from attempting further conquest in that direction.[3]

[1]C. R. Haines, "Islam as a Missionary Religion," 126.
[2]Ibn Batuta, who went to Bulgar, a city in Siberia, to witness the short nights, says: "When I was saying the prayer of sunset in that place, which happened in the month of Ramadhan, I hasted, nevertheless, the time of evening prayer came on. This hastily repeated, I prayed the midnight prayer and the one termed *El Witr*, but was overtaken by the dawn!"—Haines, "Islam," 59
[3]Gibbon, "Decline and Fall of the Roman Empire," viii, 48. For a more detailed and interesting, although a one-sided account of the spread of Islam during the period of Ottoman supremacy among the Christian

Persia and Central Asia.—The entrance of Islam into Persia began with the Saracen invasion under Khalid, and was completed during the caliphate of Omar. At the bloody battle of Nehavend, 642 A. D., when thirty thousand Persian dead were left on the field, and eighty thousand refugees slain, the fate of Persia was decided.[1] Then, one after another, the various provinces were conquered—Fars, Kerman, Makran, Sejestan, Khorasan, Azerbijan—and converted to Islam. "But the people would, ever and anon, rise again in rebellion, and it was long before the invaders could subside into a settled life, or feel secure away from the protection of settled garrisons. But the privileges enjoyed by the professors of the faith were so great that the adherents of Zoroastrian worship were not long able to resist the attraction; by degrees the Persian race came over, in name at least, to the dominant creed and, in the end, opposition ceased. The notices of Zoroastrian families and of Fire temples destroyed in after reigns show indeed that in many quarters the conversion was slow and partial."[2] Yet it was sure and certain. The conquest of Persia was of the greatest significance for the future of Islam. Here for many centuries Mohammedan literature had its greatest impulse and glory, while the Aryan mind contributed to the Semitic faith poetry, philosophy and science. But Persia also became the mother of heresies and schisms, as we shall see later, and so was a source of weakness to Islam.

nations in Europe, the reader is referred to Arnold, "The Preaching of Islam," Chapter VI.

[1] Sir William Muir, "The Caliphate; Its Rise, Decline and Fall," 179.

[2] Ibid, 181. Contrast with the historical facts in Muir the account given by Arnold and his remark: "That this widespread conversion *was not due to force or violence* is evidenced by the toleration extended to those who still cling to their ancestral faith," 179. The italics are mine.

From Persia Islam spread to Central Asia. As early as 666 A. D. it had reached Balk, and in 672 the Saracens attacked Bokhara. The conquest was not an easy one, and the invaders were repulsed. In 704 Kuteiba, the Arab conqueror, appeared on the scene, and is said to have advanced even as far as Turfan, on the extreme border of Eastern Turkestan, imposing Islam as he went[1] We read that Bokhara was conquered and "converted" *three times,* only to revolt and relapse until the strongest measures were taken to establish the new religion. Every Bokharist, Vambery tells us, had to share his dwelling with a Moslem Arab, and those who prayed and fasted, like good Moslems, were rewarded with money.[2] Finally the city was wholly given over to the Arabs, and a little later Samarkand experienced the same fate. From Bokhara as a centre, Islam spread gradually by coercion or persuasion, by preaching or by the sword, in all directions throughout Afghanistan, Turkestan and Chinese Tartary for a period of two hundred years. When Marco Polo crossed these countries (1271-1294) he found Islam nearly everywhere dominant.[3]   But as late as the fifteenth century an Arab of Damascus was a preacher of Islam to the pagan tribes of Tunganis who lived between Ilia and Khamil. He was brought as a prisoner-of-war by Timur, and was so zealous for the faith that thousands were converted.[4]   Sometimes, also, Islam was spread by the influence or example of kings and princes who became Moslems and set the fashion for their court and their subjects. So Togoudar Ogoul, when he ascended the throne of Turkestan, renounced

[1]P D'Abry de Thiersant, "La Mahometisme en Chine," Vol. I, 257.
[2]A. Vambery, "Bokhara" (1873), 26.
[3]C. R. Haines, "Islam as a Missionary Religion," 86
[4]De Thiersant, Vol. I, 163   Haines, "Islam as a Missionary Religion," 86.

Christianity and became a Moslem, his subjects following his example.[1] Another example of this method in the spread of Islam is that of Taliclava, the ruler of Transoxiana, in the early years of the fourteenth century.[2] At present all of Persia and Central Asia, as well as a large part of Asiatic Russia, is Mohammedan. "In the Trans-Caucasus between the Black and Caspian seas are three million Tartars. In Turkestan, Bokhara, Khiva and Russian Turkestan together are about six millions. The capital city of Bokhara, which is a state vassal to Russia, is a stronghold at present for the spiritual power of Islam in Central Asia."[3]

China.—This land affords a striking example of a peaceful propaganda by Moslem preachers and merchants in distinction from the usual method of the military crusade. For centuries preceding Islam there had been commercial intercourse by sea between Arabia and China,[4] and when the Arab merchants, the Sinbads of history, became Moslems, it was only natural that they carried their religion with them on their long voyages for silk, spices, and gold. We read that Mohammed utilized these early trade-routes in the sixth year of the Hegira by sending his maternal uncle, Wahab bin Kabsha, with a letter and suitable presents to the Emperor of China, asking him to accept the new religion. Arriving at Canton the next year, he went to the capital and preached Islam for two years. His preaching, which is mentioned in an inscription on the mosque at Canton, produced considerable and permanent results, for there are over eight hundred Moslem families in Canton to-

[1]Dozy, "L'Islamisme," 400.
[2]A. Vambery, "Bokhara," 161.
[3]"The Mohammedan World of To-day," 243.
[4]Niemann, "Inleiding tot de Kennis van den Islam," 337.

day.[1] When Abu Kabsha returned, he found the prophet
had died, but, after Abu Bekr had published the Koran,
the venerable apostle of Islam returned to China with
a copy and remained there till his death. His tomb is
still held in honor by Chinese Moslems.[2]

The first body of Arab settlers in China was a contin-
gent of four thousand soldiers dispatched by the Caliph
Abu Jaafer, in 755 (or, according to others, by the Caliph Al Mansur in 758), to the assistance of the Emperor
Hsuan-Tsung, who was assailed by his commander, A
Lo Shan, a Tartar, appointed to lead an army against the
northwest frontier.[3] These soldiers, in reward for their
services and bravery, were allowed to settle in China,
where, by intermarriage and preaching, they won over
many to the faith. In the following century we read
that many thousands of Moslems were massacred in
China, while Marco Polo speaks of the large Moslem
population of Yunnan.

Following upon the great wars of Ghengis Khan a
vast number of Moslem traders and adventurers poured
into Western China. "Some came as merchants, artisans,
soldiers and colonists: others were brought in as prison-
ers-of-war. A great number of them settled in the country and developed into a populous and flourishing community, gradually losing their racial peculiarities by their
marriage with Chinese women."[4]

Regarding the present growth of Islam in China and
the total number of Moslems in the empire, there is the

---

[1]P. D'Abry de Thiersant, Vol. I, 31, ff. C. R. Haines, "Islam as a Missionary Religion," 82
[2]For further particulars see E M. Wherry, "Islam and Christianity in
India and the Far East," 74-84.
[3]T. W. Arnold, "Preaching of Islam," 251; "The Mohammedan World of
To-day," 252, 253.
[4]Ibid, 247.

INTERIOR OF A MOHAMMEDAN MOSQUE IN CHINA

The worshipper is kneeling toward Mecca, and the inscriptions are an
Arabic text giving verses from the Koran

greatest disagreement among writers. In 1889 Dr. Happer, of Canton, thought the numbers given by De Thiersant very excessive, and estimated the total Moslem population at not more than three millions. De Thiersant, who secured his data from Chinese officials, put it at twenty millions. A. H. Keane, in his geography of Asia, and in accordance with the "Statesmen's Year Book," one of the best authorities on statistics, says that China has thirty million Mohammedans, while an Indian writer, Surat Chandra Das, C.I.E., in the *Journal of the Asiatic Society*, estimates it at fifty millions; and Saiyad Sulayman, a prominent Moslem officer in Yunnan province, states that there are now seventy million Moslems in China! The total given by the Rev. W. Gilbert Walshe, in his paper for the Cairo Conference in 1906, was twenty millions.[1]

Some missionaries are not at all apprehensive of Islam in China, and look upon this faith as a negligible factor in the evangelization of the empire. But those who have studied its progress in the past may well ponder the following account of its methods, as given by Arnold in his interesting chapter: "In the towns, the Mohammedans tend, little by little, to form separate Mohammedan quarters, and finally do not allow any person to dwell among them who does not go to the mosque. Islam has also gained ground in China, because of the promptitude with which the Mohammedans have repeopled provinces devastated by the various scourges so familiar to China. In times of famine they purchase children from poor parents, bring them up in the faith of Islam and, when they are full-grown, provide them

[1] E. M Wherry, "Islam and Christianity in India and the Far East," 80 and 82; "The Mohammedan World of To-day," 258, 259.

T. W. Arnold, "Preaching of Islam," 257, 258.

with wives and houses, often forming whole villages of
these new converts.   In the famine that devastated the
province of Kwangtung, in 1790, as many as ten thousand children are said to have been purchased in this
way from parents who, too poor to support them, were
compelled by necessity to part with their starving little
ones.   Saiyad Sulayman says that the number of accessions to Islam gained in this way every year is beyond
counting.   Every effort is made to keep the faith alive
among the new converts, even the humblest being taught,
by means of metrical primers, the fundamental doctrines
of Islam.   To the influence of the religious books of the
Chinese Moslems, Saiyad Sulayman attributes many
of the conversions that are made at the present day.
They have no organized propaganda, yet the zealous
spirit of proselytism with which the Chinese Mussulmans are animated secures for them a constant suc-
cession of new converts, and they confidently look
forward to the day when Islam will be triumphant
throughout the length and breadth of the Chinese
Empire."[1]

India.—Here Islam has won a larger field and a
greater number of adherents than in any other part of
the world.   India to-day has a larger Moslem population than that of Persia, Arabia, the Turkish Empire and
Egypt combined.

The spread of Islam in India began with the sword,
and Haines declares: "The Arabs showed more clearly
in India than anywhere else that their object was not
so much the conversion of idolaters and polytheists as the plunder of temples and the enlargement
of the Moslem Empire.   We may search the record

[1]T. W. Arnold, "The Preaching of Islam," 257.

of bloodshed and spoliation in vain for any trace of a purely missionary effort to win over converts to Islam."[1]

While no less an authority than Lyall states that "the military adventurers who founded dynasties in North India and carved out kingdoms in the Deccan cared little for things spiritual; most of them had, indeed, no time for proselytizing, being continually engaged in conquest and civil war."[2]

The condition of the country was favorable to the Saracen invaders, as Dr. Wherry shows in his scholarly chapter on the Moslem conquest of India.[3] And the Arabs were not slow to learn the facts. As early as 712 the Caliph Walid sent an army to avenge an outrage on an Arab vessel.[4] Kasim, the Arab general, offered the Rajputs the alternative—Islam or tribute—and, having defeated them, he forcibly circumcised a number of Brahmans. This having failed to convert the people, he slew all males over seventeen years old and enslaved the rest.[5] Al Hajaj, the governor of Chaldea, sent an expedition to Daibul, the port of Sind, in 711. Two fierce battles were fought by the army on its way up the Indus, and Multan surrendered after a long siege. It was a victory of the sword. According to authorities, quoted by Dr. Wherry, three days of carnage followed the capture of Daibul. At Dahir "the Moslems were glutted with slaughter." So cruel were the conquerors that the Hindu king's sister called the women together and, "refusing to owe their lives to the vile 'cow-eaters,' at the

[1] C. R. Haines, "Islam as a Missionary Religion," 89
[2] "Asiatic Studies," Vol X, 289.
[3] E. M. Wherry, "Islam and Christianity in India and the Far East," 17-45.
[4] William Hunter, "Indian Empire," 213
[5] C. R Haines, "Islam as a Missionary Religion," 88, 89.

price of dishonor, they set their house ablaze and perished in the flames."

"This contempt for the lives of the rebellious or vanquished was exemplified over and over in the history of Islam in India. The slave emperor, Balban, once slew forty thousand Mongols, whom he suspected of disloyalty, notwithstanding that they had professed the Moslem religion. Timur (Tamerlane) felt encumbered by one hundred thousand Hindu prisoners taken at the capture of Delhi. He ordered them to be slain in cold blood. The Bahmanid Mohammed I, son of Hassan Gangu, once avenged the death of his Moslem garrison at Mudkal by the slaughter of seventy thousand men, women and children. Such were the deeds of the proselyting sword, which was unsheathed against the unbelieving world by the mandate of the prophet."[1]

The conquest of Sindh by the Arabs was only a beginning for the later conquest of India by the Moslems. In Sindh they gained a foothold and learned of the fabulous wealth in the hands of the unbelievers. Moreover, these converted Hindus were allies of the army of conquest in the tenth century, when Turks and Afghans poured into India from the northwest.

The Sultan of Ghazni, Mahmud, surnamed "the Idolbreaker," was the Napoleon of Islam who, after a score of invasions, established its power in the North, demolishing temples, slaughtering infidels and obtaining incredible quantities of loot. Delhi became the capital of the new kingdom, and was enlarged and strengthened by Mohammed Ghori and his successors in the latter part of the twelfth and the beginning of the thirteenth century.

[1] E. M. Wherry, "Islam and Christianity in India and the Far East," 49

A second Moslem kingdom was formed about this
time in Bengal and Behar by Mohammed Baktiyar, who
even attempted to carry Islam into Assam and Tibet.[1]
But it was during the period of 1525-1707, when the
Mogul Empire was dominant in India, that Islam made
its largest conquests, its most brilliant advances and the
greatest numerical increase. Wherry says: "The names
of Akbar, Jahangir, Jehan Shah, and Aurangzeb occupy
the chief places in the galaxy of Mogul emperors. They
most of all encouraged literature and the fine arts.
To them we owe those monuments in stone and
marble, of which Moslems may well be proud and
which still lend so much lustre to Mohammedan rule
in India."

Islam was introduced into Southern India by the conquest of Moslems from the north and by immigration
on the southeast coast. In the early part of the eighth
century some Arabs, driven from Irak by the persecution of Hajjaj bin Jusuf, settled near Cape Comorin and
their descendants and converts now number nearly half
a million. Other Moslems on the coast claim that they
are descended from Medina Arabs: and others again, the
Mapillas, were converted to Islam by one of their number who made the pilgrimage to Mecca and returned a
zealous propagandist.[2] The advance of Islam in India
during its twelve centuries of conquest has succeeded in
winning over nearly one-fourth of the entire population. According to the census of 1901 there are over
twenty-five million Moslems in Bengal, over ten millions
in the Punjaub, and in all North India about forty-five
millions. The remaining seventeen millions belong to

[1]C. R. Haines, "Islam as a Missionary Religion," 90.
[2]"The Mohammedan World of To-day," 175-178.

the Deccan, Central Western and Southern India, making a total of 62,458,077.

The Malay Archipelago.—A glance at the map opposite page 56, which illustrates the spread of Islam, will show that the nearest point in the Malay Archipelago to the Arab trader is the northern coast of Sumatra. Here Islam began its conquest, under Sheikh Abdullah Arif and Jehan Shah. In 1507 the King of Atjih, in Northern Sumatra, embraced the Moslem faith, while Ibn Batuta makes mention of a Moslem ruler in Sumatra as early as 1345. Next, Islam entered Java. A certain Arab, named Rahmat, who styled himself an apostle, began to preach and win converts. He built the first mosque in Java.[1] After the conversion of the chief, Raden Patah, proselytes became more numerous, force was used to extend the Moslem state, the capital fell into their hands and Islam was practically triumphant in 1478 A. D. Nine apostles or missionaries were sent out to convert the rest of the people.

Before the end of that century the King of Ternate, in the Moluccas, was converted, "and Islam was spread in the Spice Islands by Javanese traders who came there for the double purpose of procuring cloves and imparting Islam."[2] Arnold, quoting from a German writer, on the spread of Islam in the Philippines, tells us how these merchant missionaries carried on their propaganda, and the account is typical of how Islam won the whole Malay Archipelago: "The better to introduce their religion into the country, the Mohammedans adopted the language and many of the customs of the natives, married their women, purchased slaves, in order to increase their per-

[1] C. R. Haines, "Islam as a Missionary Religion," 98.
[2] Ibid, 99

sonal importance, and succeeded finally in incorporating themselves among the chiefs who held the foremost rank in the state."[1] In 1803 some Sumatra pilgrims, who had become followers of the Wahabi movement in Arabia, returned from Mecca to proclaim a holy war against all infidels, first the heathen Batta tribes and afterward the Dutch rulers. A seventeen-year war followed, and the Dutch government took the last stronghold of the zealots, but their propaganda did not cease with defeat on the field of battle. Even to-day the struggle is on between Christian missions and Islam for the conquest of the remaining heathen tribes in Java and Sumatra. The missionaries write (1906) that their chief task now is to bring into the church the mass of pagans as yet untouched by Islam and, *while there is yet time, to send workers to regions which are in danger of being brought over to Mohammedanism.*[2] So we see that the spread of Islam is not past history, but a present peril in the Malay Archipelago as well as in Western Africa. Among the four million inhabitants of Sumatra three and a half millions are Moslems, while in Java alone Islam has twenty-eight million adherents.

Had the Christian church entered upon the struggle for these island possessions earlier, who can tell what the result might have been for the kingdom of Christ? Haines writes: "The conversion of Macassar (Celebes) affords an interesting instance of the conflict between Christianity and Islam. The king apparently considered the question of the true religion to be an open one, and desired instruction in both religions from their respective professors before he decided which he should adopt. The

[1] T. W. Arnold, "Preaching of Islam," 295.
[2] "The Mohammedan World of To-day," 232.

missionaries from Mecca, however, arrived sooner than the Jesuits from Portugal, and the king became a Mohammedan."[1]   The spread of Islam in three continents for well-nigh twelve centuries was due to the power of the sword *and to the low moral standards of the new faith,*[2] but was doubtless greatly facilitated also by the lack of missionary zeal in the churches of Christendom. Beyond the boundaries of the Oriental churches Islam advanced in her world-conquest unchallenged.   There were no missions to Islam.

Islam Our Example.—The history of the spread of Islam is not without significance for us to-day.   In spite of cruelty, bloodshed, dissension and deceit, the story of the Moslem conquest is full of heroism.   If so much was done in the name and after the example of Mohammed, what should we not do in the name of Jesus Christ and in obedience to His marching orders?   A careful study of these early Moslem conquests impresses one with the fact that some measure of their success was due to their enthusiasm and fanatic faith, as well as to the character of their creed and the mere power of the sword.   The preaching of Islam was earnest, and demanded as unconditional a surrender as did their weapons.   The thunder of their cavalry was not more terrible to the enemy than the clamor of their short, sharp creed in the ears of an idolatrous and divided Christendom, or the ears of ignorant pagans: "La-ilaha illa Allah!   Allahu Akbar!" These men of the desert carried everything before them, because they had the backbone of conviction, knew no compromise, and were thirsting for world-conquest.   Not Khalid alone, but every Moslem warrior felt himself to be the "Sword of God."

---

[1]C. R. Haines, "Islam as a Missionary Religion," 100.   [2]See Chapter VI.

MOSLEM PILGRIMS FROM SOUTH BORNEO AT MECCA

Nor did they shrink from hardship, danger or death itself, in this holy war for their faith. Had not Mohammed said: "The fire of hell shall not touch the legs of him who is covered with the dust of battle in the road of God"? And was not Paradise itself under the shadow of the spears of the thickest fight?

To the modern Christian world, missions imply organization, societies, paid agents, subscriptions, reports, etc. All this is practically absent from the present Moslem idea of propagation, and yet the spread of Islam goes on. With loss of political power, the zeal of Islam seems to increase, for Egypt and India are more active in propagating the faith than are Turkey or Morocco.

In Burma (where Indian merchants are the Moslem missionaries) the Moslem population increased 33 per cent. in the past decade. In the Western Soudan and on the Niger whole districts once pagan are now Mohammedan, and this has been, to a large extent, the work of lay missionaries—merchants, travelers and artisans. It would be an exaggeration to say that every Moslem is a missionary, but it is true that, with the exception of the Derwish orders (who resemble monks), the missionaries of Islam are the laymen in every walk of life, rather than its priesthood. For example, a pearl merchant at Bahrein, East Arabia, recently, at his own expense and on his own initiative, printed an entire edition of a Koran commentary for free distribution. On the streets of Lahore and Calcutta you may see clerks, traders, bookbinders, and even coolies, who spend part of their leisure time preaching Islam or attacking Christianity by argument.

The merchants who go to Mecca as pilgrims from Java return to do missionary work among the hill-tribes.

In the Soudan the Hausa merchants carry the Koran and the catechism wherever they carry their merchandise. No sooner do they open a wayside shop in some pagan district than the wayside mosque is built by its side. And is it not a remarkable proof of the earnestness even of the Arab *slave-dealers,* that, in spite of the horrors of the traffic, the very slave-routes became highways for Islam, and the negroes adopted the religion of Mohammed, to escape the very curse which brought it to them?

The laity in Islam are, in one sense, all preachers. The shop-keeper and the camel-driver are ashamed neither of their proud creed nor of their prophet and his book. They proclaim the creed from the housetop, they never utter Mohammed's name without a prayer, and they carry the Koran everywhere, altho 80 per cent. of the Moslem world is illiterate. If they cannot read it they can, at least, kiss it or wear it as an amulet! All ranks of society are propagandists. By such incessant, spontaneous and almost fanatic parading, preaching, pushing of their faith by the mass of believers, and not solely by the power of the sword, Islam grew to its gigantic proportions. And if they used the sword, so also can we. "The Word of God is sharper than any two-edged sword, piercing even to the dividing of soul and spirit to the joints and marrow, and is a discerner of the thoughts and intents of the heart." *That* blade we can all wield. It is a better sword than theirs, and slays to give Life Eternal.

If they did so much with theirs, surely we can do more with ours. We can do it, if we will. We have a better message, a more glorious faith, a higher motive, a richer reward, a more certain victory, a nobler inspiration, a better comradeship, and a Leader before Whose

great white throne and great white life the mock majesty
and the whitewashed immorality of Mohammed shrink
in abject terror. *They* did it for Mohammed. Shall we
not do it for our Saviour in the spread of Christianity?

THE FAITH OF ISLAM

"A prophet without miracles; a faith without mysteries; and a morality without love; which has encouraged a thirst for blood, and which began and ended in the most unbounded sensuality."—*Schlegel's Philosophy of History.*

"As we conceive God we conceive the universe; a Being incapable of loving is incapable of being loved."—*Principal Fairbairn.*

IV

THE FAITH OF ISLAM

Scope of This Chapter.—All Moslems describe the character and content of their religion under two heads, or divisions, called *Iman* and *Dîn*. The first concerns their articles of faith, or what an orthodox follower of the prophet must believe. The second refers to the outward practice of religion, including the ritual and other requirements of Moslem piety. This resembles the division of the Christian system into faith and practice, as given in the "Westminster Shorter Catechism."

This chapter treats only of *Iman,* and tells what a Moslem must believe; the relation of creed to character is, however, not merely a formal one, but vital and organic in all religion. Because Moslems believe as they do, therefore their religious duties, privileges and practices are what they are. The accompanying table (Appendix) sets forth in outline an analysis of Islam as a system developed from its creed. The original material for that system is found in the Koran text, but the logical development of it took place after the death of Mohammed, by the interpretation of the Koran and the collection (sometimes the invention[1]) of a mass of so-called

---

[1] Out of 40,000 persons who have been instrumental in handing down tradition, Buchari (died 256 A. H.) only acknowledges two thousand as reliable authorities! Sir William Muir says "there are abundant indications of actual fabrication throughout Mohammedan tradition." Muir, "Mahomet," Intro. Vol. I, xxviii.

"Traditions" of what Mohammed did and taught, as an example to true believers.

It is incumbent on all orthodox believers to have a firm faith in six articles: God, His Angels, His Books, His Prophets, the Day of Judgment, and Predestination of Good and Evil. The sources of Moslem teaching on these topics are apparent from what we have learned in previous chapters. Islam was not an invention, but a concoction. The genius of Mohammed mixed old ingredients into a new panacea for humanity, sugar-coated it with an easy-going morality, and forced it down by means of the sword. At a time when many religions existed in Arabia, and the Kaaba was a Pantheon, the heterogeneous elements of Islam were molded into one system. These elements, as we have seen, were partly heathen (Arabian), partly Christian (Abyssinian); but, for the most part, they were borrowed from Talmudic Judaism. In the following summary of Islam's creed and practice, one may read between the lines the sources of Mohammed's teaching.[1]

1. The Moslem Idea of God.—Moslems believe in God's unity, omnipotence and mercy. "There is no god but Allah" is the first clause in the Moslem creed. Gibbon calls it an eternal truth, but Palgrave, Noble, Osborn, Hauri, and other students of Islam have questioned whether the monotheism of Islam is worthy to be compared with that of Judaism, or of Christianity. Islam reduces God to the category of the will. The Koran shows that Mohammed had a measurably correct idea of the physical attributes of God, but an absolutely false conception of His moral attributes. The conception of God is negative. Absolute sovereignty and ruthless om-

[1] Compare also the table opposite page 86.

I From HEATHENISM
(As existing in Mecca or prevalent
in other parts of Arabia.)

a Saheanism
- Astrological superstitions, e g , that met⟨
- Oaths by the stars and planets (Sural⟨

b Arabian Idolatry
- Circumambulation of Kaaba—and the ⟨
- Allah (as name of supreme deity), used
  and others
- Mecca—Centre of religious pilgrimage—
- Pilgrimage—in every detail hair, dress
- Polygamy, slavery, easy divorce and soc
- Ceremonial cleanliness, forbidden foods

c Zoroastrianism
- Cosmogony—The different stories of th⟨
- Paradise—Its character—the houris=pe⟨
- Doctrine of Jinn and their various kind⟨

d Buddhism.
- The use of the rosary (See Hughes' "⟨

II From JUDAISM
(As found in the old Testament, but
more especially the Talmud, the
source of Jewish ideas prevalent in Arabia just be-
fore Mohammed.)

A Ideas and Doctrines
(According to the division of
Rabbi Geiger.)

1 Words that represent Jewish ideas, and are not Arabic but Hebrew
- Taboot ⟨
- Rabbi, Ar
- gboot—(u⟨
- Furkan, e⟨

2 Doctrinal Views
- Unity of God
- Resurrection
- Sevens hells an⟨
- Final judgmen⟨
- Gog and Mago⟨

3 Moral and Ceremonial laws
- Prayer · its time, pos⟨
- Laws regarding imp⟨
- "   "   purific⟨

4 Views of Life Use of "inshallah"

B Stories and Legends
(According to Rabbi Geiger.)
- Adam, Cain, Enoch, the fabulous thing⟨
- Noah—the flood—Eber (Hud)—Isaac,
- Abraham—his idolatry—Nimrod's oven
- Moses—The fables related of him and A⟨
- Jethro (Shuaib), Saul (Taloot), Goliath (⟨

III From CHRISTIANITY
(In its corrupt form, as found in the apo-
cryphal gospels, especially the "Gospel of Barnabas.")

1. Reference for New Testament—Injil—(Zacharias, John, Gabriel)
2. Respect for religious teachers, the Koran references to priests and
3. Jesus Christ—His names—Word of God, Spirit of God, etc—Pne⟨
    —Denial of crucifixion (Basilidians, etc)
4. The Virgin—Her sinlessness—and the apostles—"hawari," an Aby⟨
5. Wrong ideas of the Trinity As held by Arabian heretical sects
6. Christian legends, as of "Seven Sleepers," "Alexander of the horns⟨
7. A fast month Ramadhan to imitate lent.
    ⟨...⟩ ship.

nipotence are His chief attributes, while His character is impersonal—that of a Monad. The Christian truth, that "God is love," is to the learned Moslem blasphemy and to the ignorant an enigma. "Islam," says Palgrave, "is the Pantheism of Force." Johannes Hauri, in his classical study of Islam, says:[1] "What Mohammed tells of God's omnipotence, omniscience, justice, goodness and mercy sounds, for the most part, very well indeed and might easily awaken the idea that there is no real difference between his God and the God of Christianity. But Mohammed's monotheism was just as much a departure from true monotheism as the polytheistic ideas prevalent in the corrupt Oriental churches. Mohammed's idea of God is out and out deistic. God and the world are in exclusive, external and eternal opposition." And James Freeman Clarke calls it the "worst form of monotheism," and sums up the distinction thus: "Islam saw God, but not man; saw the claims of deity, but not the rights of humanity; saw authority, but failed to see freedom—therefore hardened into despotism, stiffened into formalism, and sank into death. . . . Mohammed teaches a God above us; Moses teaches a God above us, and yet *with us;* Jesus Christ teaches God above us, God with us, and God in us."[2]

2. The Doctrine of Angels.—The Moslems assert their belief in three species of spiritual beings, viz., angels, jinn, and devils. This belief is not theoretical, but is intensely practical, and touches everyday life at many points.

(a) Angels are very numerous, were created out of light, and are endowed with life, speech, and reason. Of

[1]"Der Islam in seinem Einfluss auf das Leben seiner Bekenner," 44, 45. (Leyden.)

[2]James Freeman Clarke, "Ten Great Religions," Vol II, 68.

the four archangels, Gabriel reveals truth, Michael is patron of the Jews, Israfil will sound the last trump, and Israil is the angel of death. Angels are inferior to the prophets.[1] There are two recording angels for each person, who write down his good and his ill. Therefore Mohammed enjoined his people not to spit in front, or on the right, but on the left, as on that side stands the recording angel of evil.[2] Munkar and Nakir are two black angels, with blue eyes, who interrogate men after burial in the grave, and mete out terrible blows to those whose replies prove them not Moslems. Therefore, at a funeral, parting instructions are given the deceased in the grave. The Koran seems to teach that angels intercede for men.[3] The names of guardian angels are used in exorcism; eight special angels support Allah's throne; and nineteen have charge of hell-fires.

(b) Jinn, or genii, are either good or evil. They were created from fire, are of diverse shapes, marry and propagate, and are mortal. The Koran and orthodox Moslem theology are full of teaching about their origin, office, power, and destiny. One needs only to read the "Arabian Nights" to get an idea of the effect of this belief on life and morals. No pious Moslem to-day doubts that they exist, nor that Solomon sealed some of them up in brass bottles! In Arabia, Persia, and Morocco they tell stories of everyday Moslem life and encounters with jinn that rival the tales of Sheherzade to the King. The chief abode of jinn is in the mountains of Kaf, which encompass the world; they also frequent baths, wells, ruined houses, etc. For fear of jinn millions of the ignorant in Moslem lands are, all their lifetime, subject to bondage. This article of their creed is the mother

[1]Surah 2:32.   [2]Mishkat, Book 4, Chapter 8   [3]Surah 42:3.

of a thousand foolish and degrading superstitions, yet it can never be abandoned without doing violence to the Koran. Read, for example, Surahs 46 and 72, which tell how the jinn listened to Mohammed's preaching and were converted to Islam.

(c) The devil (Sheitan, or Iblis) has a proper name— Azazil. He was expelled from Eden for refusal to prostrate before Adam when God commanded it.[1] His demonic host is numerous and terrible. Noteworthy among them are Harut and Marut, two evil spirits which teach men sorcery at Babylon.

3. The Books of God.—Islam is decidedly a bookish religion, for Moslems believe that God "sent down" one hundred and four sacred books. Their doctrine of inspiration is mechanical. Adam received ten books; Seth, fifty; Enoch, thirty; and Abraham, ten; all of these are utterly lost. The four books that remain are the Torah (Law), which came to Moses; the Zabur (Psalms), which David received; the Injil (Gospel) of Jesus, and the Koran. The Koran is uncreated and eternal; to deny this is rank heresy. And while the three other books are highly spoken of in the Koran, they now exist, Moslems say, only in a corrupted form, and their precepts have been abrogated by the final book to the last prophet, Mohammed. This is the belief of all *orthodox* Moslems. Thousands of Mohammedans now, however, say the Bible is not corrupted, and read it willingly and gladly.

The Koran.—This book is considered by Moslems the great standing miracle of their prophet, and it is a remarkable production. It is a little smaller than the New Testament in bulk, and has one hundred and fourteen chapters, bearing fanciful titles borrowed from some

[1]Surah 7:10-17.

word or phrase in the chapter, e. g., the Cow, the Bee, Women, Spoils, the Ant, the Spider, Smoke, the Pen, etc. The book has no chronological order, logical sequence, or rhetorical climax. Its jumbled verses throw together, piecemeal, fact and fancy, laws and legends, prayers and imprecations. It is unintelligible without a commentary, even for a Moslem. Moslems regard it as supreme in beauty of style and language, and miraculous in its origin, contents, and authority. From the Arab's literary standpoint it is, indeed, a remarkable book. Its musical jingle and cadence are charming, and, at times, highly poetical ideas are clothed in sublime language. The first chapter and the so-called verse of the "Throne" are striking examples:

THE OPENING CHAPTER

"In the name of God, the Compassionate, the Merciful.
Praise be to God, Lord of the worlds!
The Compassionate, the Merciful!
King of the Day of Judgment!
Thee do we worship, and to Thee do we cry for help!
Guide Thou us on the right path!
The path of those to whom Thou art gracious!
Not of those with whom Thou art angered, nor of those who go
     astray."

THE VERSE OF THE THRONE.

"God! there is no God but He; the living, the Eternal.
Slumber doth not overtake Him, neither sleep.
To Him belongeth whatsoever is in heaven and on the earth.
Who shall intercede with Him except by His permission? He
     knows what is between their hands and behind them;
And they can not encompass aught of His knowledge except as
     He please. His throne is as wide as the heavens and the
     earth.
The preservation of both is no weariness unto Him.
He is the high, the mighty."

THE COURT OF THE UNIVERSITY MOSQUE EL AZHAR, CAIRO

The great bulk of the Koran is either legislative or legendary; the book consists of laws and stories. The former relate entirely to subjects which engrossed the Arabs of Mohammed's day—the laws of inheritance, the relation of the sexes, the law of retaliation, etc.—and this part of the book has a local character. The stories, on the other hand, go back to Adam and the patriarchs, take in several unknown Arabian prophets or leaders, tell of Jesus Christ, Moses and Solomon, and do not venture beyond Jewish territory, except to mention Alexander the Great and Lokman (Æsop).

The defects of its teaching are many: (a) It is full of historical errors; (b) it contains monstrous fables; (c) it teaches a false cosmogony; (d) it is full of superstitions; (e) it perpetuates slavery, polygamy, divorce, religious intolerance, the seclusion and degradation of women, and it petrifies social life. All this, however, is of minor importance compared with the fact that the Koran ever keeps the supreme question of salvation from sin in the background, and offers no doctrine of redemption or atonement by sacrifice. In this respect the Koran is inferior to the sacred books of ancient Egypt, India, an China, though, unlike them, it is monotheistic. It cannot be compared with the Old or the New Testament.

4. *The Major and Minor Prophets.*—According to Moslem writers, a prophet is one who is directly inspired by God, while an apostle is one entrusted with a special mission. Mohammed is related to have said that there were 124,000 prophets (anbiya) and 315 apostles (rusul). Six of the latter are designated by special titles, and are the major prophets of Islam. They are as follows: Adam is the chosen of God; Noah, the

preacher of God; Abraham, the friend of God; Moses, the spokesman of God; Jesus, the word of God; and Mohammed, the apostle of God. In addition to this common title, Mohammed has two hundred and one other names and titles of honor by which he is known among the faithful. Their devotion to him is intense and sincere.

Only twenty-two others—minor prophets—are mentioned in the Koran besides these six, altho the host of prophets is so large. They are: Idris (Enoch), Hud (Heber), Salih (Methusaleh), Ishmael, Isaac, Jacob, Joseph, Lot, Aaron, Shuaib (Jethro), Zacharias, John the Baptist, David, Solomon, Elias, Elijah, Job, Jonah, Ezra, Lokman (Æsop, Balaam?), Zu'l-Kifl (Isaiah or Obadiah?), and Zu'l Karnain (Alexander the Great). The account of these prophets is confused, yet we must give credit to some Moslem commentators for doubting whether Lokman and Alexander were really prophets! Moslems say that they make no distinction between the prophets, but love and reverence them all. Mohammed, however, supersedes all, supplants all in the hearts and lives of his followers.

The Mohammed of history and the Mohammed of Moslem tradition are two different persons. In the Koran Mohammed is thoroughly human and liable to error. He is now, because of the traditional halo which surrounds him, considered to have had a pre-existence before creation, to have been perfectly sinless, and he is the only powerful intercessor on the Day of Judgment. He is the standard of character and the model of conduct. Every detail of his early life is surrounded with fantastical miracles which prove his divine commission. Even the evil in his life is attributed to God's permission or command, so that his very faults of character become his endless glory and the signs of his superiority, e. g., his polygamy and cruel wars are interpreted as special privileges. He dwells in the highest heaven and is several degrees above Jesus, our Saviour, in honor and station. His name is never uttered or written without the addition of a prayer. Yet, a calm and critical study of his life proves him to have been an ambitious and sensual enthusiast, who did not scruple to break nearly every precept of the moral law to further his own ends.[1]

What Moslems Believe Concerning Jesus Christ.—A Christian studying the faith of Islam soon learns not only that Christ has no place in the Moslem idea of God, as they deny the Trinity, but that the portrait of our Saviour, as given in the Koran and in tradition, is a sad caricature. According to Moslem teaching, Jesus was miraculously born of the Virgin Mary; He spoke while still a babe in the cradle; performed many puerile miracles in His youth; healed the sick and raised the dead when He reached manhood. He was specially commissioned to confirm the Law and reveal the Gospel. He was strengthened by the Holy Spirit (Gabriel). He foretold another prophet, whose name should be Ahmed (Mohammed). They believe that Jesus was, by deception and substitution, saved from crucifixion and taken to heaven, and that He is now in one of the inferior stages of celestial bliss; that He will come again at the last day, slay anti-Christ, kill all the swine, break the Cross, and remove the poll-tax from infidels. He will reign as a just King for forty-five years, marry and

[1]See Muir, Koelle, Sprenger and Weil, the earliest Moslem biography by Ibn Hisham and also Chapter II in this volume

leave children, then die and be buried near Mohammed
at Medina. The place of His future grave is already
marked out between the graves of Omar and Fa-
timah.[1]

5. *The Day of Judgment.*—This occupies a large place
in the creed and the Koran. It is called the Day of
Resurrection, of Separation, of Reckoning, or simply the
Hour. Most graphic and terrible descriptions portray
the terrors of that day. Moslems believe in a literal
resurrection of the body from a living principle which
resides in the *os sacrum.* This bone will be impregnated
by a forty-days' rain before the resurrection takes place.
The souls of martyrs for the faith, however, remain,
after death, in the crops of green birds which eat of the
fruits and drink of the rivers of Paradise.[2]

Moslems believe also in an everlasting life of physical
joys, or physical tortures. The Moslem paradise, in the
words of the Koran, is "a garden of delight, . . .
with couches and ewers, and a cup of flowing wine;
their brows ache not from it, nor fails the sense; theirs
shall be the Houris, . . . ever virgins." What commentators say on these texts is often unfit for translation. The orthodox interpretation is literal, and so was
that of Mohammed, because the traditions give minute
particulars of the sanitary laws of heaven, as well as of
its sexual delights.

According to Al Ghazzali[3] (A. H. 450), Mohammed
said: "The believer in Paradise will marry five hundred
houris, four thousand virgins and eight thousand divorced women." Al Ghazzali is one of the greatest theolo-
gians of Islam, and no orthodox Moslem would dispute

---

[1]S M Zwemer, "Arabia; the Cradle of Islam," 49   [2]Surah 3:163.
[3]IV, 337.

his statement. In this very connection Ghazzali quotes the words, "things which eye saw not and which did not enter into the heart of man!"[1]

The Moslem hell is sevenfold, and "each portal has its party." All the wealth of Arabic vocabulary is exhausted in describing the terrors of the lost, and Dante's "Inferno" is a summer-garden compared with the Jehennom of Islam. It is terribly hot, its fuel are men and stones, its drink liquid pus, the clothes of the inhabitants burning pitch, while serpents and scorpions sting their victims. Connected with the Day of Judgment are the signs of its approach, viz., the coming of the anti-Christ (Dajjal), the return of Jesus as a Moslem prince, the rising of the sun in the West, the war of Gog and Magog, etc.

6. Predestination.—This last article is the keystone in the arch of Moslem faith. It is the only philosophy of Islam, and the most fertile article of the creed in its effects on everyday life. As in the Christian church, this doctrine has been fiercely discussed, but what might be called ultra-Calvinism has carried the day. The terminology of their teaching is Calvinistic, but its practical effect is pure fatalism. Most Moslem sects "deny all free-agency in man, and say that man is necessarily constrained by the force of God's eternal and immutable decree to act as he does." God wills both good and evil; there is no escaping from the caprice of His decree. Religion is Islam, i. e., resignation. Fatalism has paralyzed progress. Hope perishes under the weight of this iron bondage; injustice and social decay are stoically accepted; no man bears the burden of another. Hauri and Osborn show, in their study of this subject, how its blasting and deadening influence is felt in every Moslem

[1] Ghazzali, IV, 338.

land. Omar Khayyam voices the sentiment of millions when he writes:

> " 'Tis all a chequer-board of nights and days
> Where Destiny with men for pieces plays.
> Hither and thither moves and mates and slays,
> And one by one back in the closet lays."

To the Moslem, God's will is certain, arbitrary, irresistible, and inevitable before any event transpires. To the Christian, God's will is secret until He reveals it; when He does we feel the imperative of duty. Were a Moslem to pray to Allah "Thy will be done on earth as it is in heaven," he would be guilty of folly, if not of blasphemy. An archangel and a murderer, a devil and a gnat equally execute the will and purpose of Allah every moment of their existence. As He wills, and because He wills, they are what they are, and continue what they are.

No wonder that this article of the Moslem faith has left no place for progress in the lands under Mohammedan rule. For, as Canon Sell says: "It is this dark fatalism which, whatever the Koran may teach on the subject, is the ruling principle in all Moslem countries. It is this which makes all Mohammedan nations decay."

THE RITUAL OF ISLAM

"The five pillars of the Mohammedan faith are all broken reeds by the solemn test of age-long experience, because their creed is only a half-truth, and its 'pure monotheism' does not satisfy the soul's need of a mediator and an atonement for sin. Their prayers are formal and vain repetitions, without demanding or producing holiness in the one that uses them. Their fasting is productive of two distinct evils wherever observed; it manufactures an unlimited number of hypocrites who profess to keep the fast and do not do so and, in the second place, the reaction which occurs at sunset of every night of Ramazan tends to produce revelling and dissipation of the lowest and most degrading type. Their almsgiving stimulates indolence, and has produced that acme of social parasites—the derwish or fakir. Finally their pilgrimages to Mecca, Medina, and Kerbela are a public scandal even to Moslem morality, so that the holy cities are hotbeds of vice and plague-spots in the body politic."—*Missionary Review of the World,* October, 1898.

V

THE RITUAL OF ISLAM

The Religion of Good Works.—While everyone who confesses the faith of Islam is a Moslem or true believer, yet it is incumbent on all who believe to show their faith by outward observance of the religious duties of Islam. The preceding chapter dealt with the theoretical part of Islam, called *Iman*. This treats of its practical requirements, called *Din*. That told of faith, this of works. In Moslem phraseology, the former is also called *'Ilm-ul-Usool*, or science of the roots of religion; the latter *'Ilm-ul-Feroo'a,* or science of the branches of religion. While, generally speaking, Islam means resignation to the will of God, Mohammed stated that it was, especially, to be submissive to His will in the observance of *five duties*. These five duties merit reward and are called "the pillars," or foundation, of religion. Their pious observance is the mark of a true Moslem; to break loose from any one of them is to be in peril of damnation. Mohammed said: "A Moslem is one who is resigned and obedient to God's will, and (1) *bears witness* that there is no god but God, and that Mohammed is His Apostle; and (2) is steadfast in *prayer,* and (3) gives *zakat* (legal alms); and (4) *fasts* in the month of Ramazan; and (5) makes a *pilgrimage* to Mecca, if he have the means."[1] Before we give a

[1] T. P. Hughes, "Dictionary of Islam," 220.

99

summary of these five duties, it is necessary to understand something of what Moslems mean by Tradition, because all the *details* of these duties are in accord with the example and precept of the Prophet, altho in substance they are mentioned in the Koran.

The Traditions.—The Traditions of Islam are called *Hadith,* or *Sunnat-en-nebi.* The former term means "that-which-is-related"; the latter signifies the custom, habit or usage of the Prophet. They supplement and interpret the Koran, and have therefore exercised tremendous power on Moslem thought and life from the early days of Islam with ever-growing force. There are one thousand four hundred and sixty-five collections of Traditions in existence, but only six of them are counted classical or standard by the orthodox school. The six authors of the classical collections were "higher critics" in a measure and attempted to sift the chaff from the wheat according to their way of thinking. Abu Daood, one of their number, states in his massive work that he received as trustworthy only four thousand and eight hundred traditions out of five hundred thousand. And yet after this careful selection he says he has given "those which seem to be authentic and those which are nearly so."

For many of the details of their daily religious practice, and for nearly all of their jurisprudence, Moslems depend on Tradition. Here is a specimen of the traditions which will indicate the way in which all of them are recorded by a chain of witnesses:

A Specimen Tradition.—"Abu Kuraib said to us that Ibrahim ibn Jusef ibn Abi Ishak said to us, from his father, from Abu Ishak, from Tulata ibn Musarif, that he said, I have heard from Abd-ur-Rahman ibn Ausajah that he said, I have heard from Bara ibn Azib that he said, I have heard that the Prophet said, whoever shall give in charity a milch-cow, or a piece of silver, or a leathern bottle of water, it shall be equal to the freeing of a slave."

From this sample it is evident that in Islam the genuineness of a Tradition depends on the chain of narrators and their trustworthy character. Nearly all tradition was orally handed down and its authority necessarily depends on the memory of those who handed it down. Yet there is no doubt that these "collections of recollections" recorded two centuries after Mohammed's death contain much that is reliable concerning the life and practice of the Prophet and his companions. "That the collectors of Tradition," says Muir, "rendered an important service to Islam and even to history cannot be doubted." The table opposite page 86 gives the list of the six orthodox authorities on Tradition.

The Traditions have high authority in Islam. "An orthodox Moslem places the Gospels in the same rank as the Hadith; that is, he looks upon them as a record of what Jesus said and did, handed down to us by His companions."[1] There is not a single Moslem sect that looks to the Koran as the only rule of faith and practice. It is well to remember this when superficial students of comparative religion tell us that the Mohammedan religion is all contained in the Koran. Who seeks to understand what Islam is from the Koran alone will succeed about as well as one who should draw his ideas of Roman Catholicism in Mexico from the New Testament.

The five chief duties of a pious Moslem are carefully described in these collections of tradition and leave no

[1] E. Sell, "The Faith of Islam."

doubt as to the importance of each duty if the believer would be assured of eternal salvation. The first of the five pillars of religion, according to the Koran and Tradition, is Confession.

1. *The Confession of the Creed.*—It is the shortest creed in the world, has been oftener repeated, and has perhaps had more power over those that uttered it than any other. The creed is so brief that it has needed no revision for thirteen centuries. It is taught to infants and whispered in the ears of the dying. Five times a day it rings out in the call to prayer in the whole Moslem world: *"La-ilaha-illa-'llahu; Muhammadu-Rasulu-'allah."* "There is no god but God; Mohammed is the apostle of God." It is related in Tradition that the Prophet said, "Whosoever recites this creed shall receive rewards equal to the emancipating of ten slaves and shall have one hundred good deeds put to his account and one hundred of his sins shall be blotted out, and the words shall be a protection from the devil." On every occasion this creed is repeated by the believer. It is the key to every door of difficulty. *It is the watchword of Islam.* These words they inscribe on their banners and on their door-posts. They appear on all the early coins of the caliphs. This creed of seven Arabic words rings out in every Moslem village from the Philippines to Morocco. One hears it in the bazaar and the street and the mosque; it is a battle-cry and a cradle-song, an exclamation of delight and a funeral dirge. There is no doubt that this continual, public repetition of a creed has been a source of strength to Islam for ages, as well as a stimulus to fanaticism; witness the use of this creed by the Derwish orders in their nightly meetings.

When anyone is converted to Islam he or she is re-

THE DOCTRINE OF GOD "Pantheism of Force"

1, Negative (*Nafi*) "There is no god"—
His names . { of t / of t

2 Positive (*Athbat*) ' but Allah '
His attributes { Th / De

His nature . { Ex

THE DOCTRINE OF REVELATION

(Mohammed the Apostle of God is the sole channel of revelation and abrogates former revelations)

Orthodox Moslems acknowledge two kinds of revelation and one authority beside them

1 By the KORAN

(*Wahi el Matlu*)

Verbal revelation which teaches the two fold demands of Islam —

(The Book)

A FAITH

(what to believe)

"Iman"

[The six articles of faith]

1 In God

Moslems believe that 104 "books" were heaven in the following order

2 Angels { angels / jinn / devils

To Adam — ten books
beth—fifty "
" Enoch—thirty "
Abraham—ten
" Moses—the TORAH
" David—the ZABOOR
" Jesus—the INJIL
Mohammed—the KORAN

these are utte

3 Books—

{ These are hig / in corrupted / the final book / eternal i / character

5 Last Day (Judgment)

6 Predestination

A The Greater,

Adam—"Chosen of Go
Noah— Preacher of Go
Abraham— Friend of (
Moses—'Spokesman of (
Jesus—called "Word (
' Spirit of God
MOHAMMED, (*who has J / titles*)

4 Prophets,—

B The Of these there have been thousa
Less Twenty-two are mentioned in the

B PRACTICE

(what to do)

"Din"

[the five pillars]

1 Repetition of Creed

2 *Prayer* (five times daily) including

3 Fasting (month of Ramadhan)

4 Alms-giving (about 1-40 of income)

5 Pilgrimage

1 Purification

{ washing various par / three times a cordin / rules

2 Posture(prostrations) { facing the K / prostrations

3 Petition

Declarat'n {genuflections
the Fatihah or first Sura
Praise and Confession—

{ Mecca (incumbent)
Medina (meritorious but volun
Kerbela (Meshed Ali etc (Sh

II By TRADITION

(*Wahi gheir el Matlu*)

Revelation by example of the perfect prophet

(The Man)

1 Records of what Mohammed *did* (Sunnat-el-fa il) (example)

2 Records of what Mohammed *enjoined* (Sunnat-el-kaul) (precept)

3 Records of what Mohammed *allowed* (Sunnat-et-takrir) (license)

Verbally handed down from mouth to mouth and finally sifted and recorded by both sects

A The Sunnite
(collected and i
following six

B The Shiah T
(five auth

III Other Authority

a Among the *Sunnites*

IJMA'A or unanimous consent of the leading compan
cerning source I i e, the Koran
KIYAS or the deductions of orthodox teachers from

e IJTAMA (beginning with

[1] By Abu Jaafer

quired to repeat this formula; and a thorough conversion requires:

1. That it be repeated aloud at least once in a lifetime, and the oftener the better.
2. That the meaning of it be fully understood.
3. That it shall be believed in by the heart.
4. That it shall be professed until death.
5 That it shall be recited correctly.
6. That it shall be always professed and declared without hesitation.[1]

Surely this diligent, constant, almost fanatic use of their short creed as a public confession has been not only a strength to Islam, but one of the chief factors in its rapid spread. The very impetuosity and frequency of its repetition has often persuaded ignorant men of its truth by the impetus of its proclamation.

2. *Prayer.*—The fact that Moslems pray often, early and earnestly has elicited the admiration of many travelers, who, ignorant of the real character and content of Moslem prayer, judge it from a Christian standpoint. What the Bible calls prayer and what the Moslem calls by the same name are, however, to a degree, distinct conceptions. One who was for many years a missionary in India, and who is an authority on Islam, says: "Prayer is by them reduced to a mechanical act; and, in judging of the spiritual character of Mohammedanism, we must take into careful consideration the precise character of these devotional services five times daily."[2] The devotions of Islam are essentially vain repetitions, for they must be said in the Arabic language by all Moslems, whether in China or Calcutta, in the Soudan or Singapore.

[1] T P. Hughes, "Dictionary of Islam," 63.
[2] Ibid, 471; and Dean Stanley, "Eastern Church," 279

Three-fourths of the Mohammedan world pray five times daily in an unknown tongue. Yet their prayers are persistent and often sincere. Mohammed used to call prayer "the pillar of religion" and "the key of Paradise."

The first requirement of correct prayer is that it be in the right direction, i.e., toward the Kaaba at Mecca. Because of this, private houses, as well as mosques, all over the Mohammedan world, are built accordingly, and not on meridian lines. It is often pathetic to hear a wayfarer or a Moslem who travels on an ocean steamer ask which is the proper direction to turn at the hour of prayer. To pray with one's back to Mecca would be unpardonable. Many Moslems carry a pocket-compass on their journeys to avoid all possible errors of this character.

Purification.—Another necessary preliminary to every Moslem prayer is legal purification. Whole books have been written on this subject, describing the occasions, method, variety and effect of ablution by water, or, in its absence, by sand. The ritual of purification is one of the chief shibboleths of the many Moslem sects. In Mohammedan works of theology there are chapters on the proper way of washing, on the use of the toothbrush,[1] on the different kinds of water allowed for ablution, and on all the varieties of uncleanness. As a sample of the puerile details of their ritual, here is a verbatim transcript of the correct religious use of the toothbrush, as given in orthodox tradition: "Abŭ Huraira said that Mohammed (on him be prayers and peace) said, Had I not doubted con-

[1] All Moslems use a vegetable toothbrush made of a root or twig and called *miswak.* 'Brushes for the head and teeth have not yet been introduced into Moslem families, nor is it ever likely they will, unless some other material than pigs' bristles can be used in their manufacture. The swine is abominable to Moslems."—Mrs. Meer Hassan Ali, "Observations on the Mussulmans of India," 105. T. P. Hughes, "Dictionary of Islam," 353.

FOUNTAIN IN A MOSQUE, ALGIERS

The inscription over the door is from the Koran, and reads "And wash

cerning my people I would have commanded them to burn incense at night and to use the toothbrush before every prayer. This is a sure tradition.—Shuraib said, I asked Ayesha what the Prophet (on him be prayers and peace) first did on entering a house, and she said, He used a toothbrush. Huthaifa relates that the Prophet (on him be prayers and peace) when he got up for night prayers would brush his teeth with a *miswak*. . . . Ayub said, The Prophet (on him be prayers and peace) said, On four things all the prophets of former times agreed: Salutation, circumcision, perfumes and the use of the toothbrush. . . . Ayesha said, The Prophet would not lie down at night nor in the day and rise again without using the toothbrush before washing for prayers. She said, The Prophet would take the toothbrush and then give it to me to wash and then use it. Then I would use it and wash it and return it to him. . . . Abu Imam say that the Prophet (on him be prayers and peace) said, Gabriel never came to me except he commanded me to use the toothbrush. Ayesha said, The Prophet (on him be prayers and peace) said, The prayer after using a toothbrush is better than the prayer without, seventy-fold . . . "[1] The book from which this is quoted is accepted by all orthodox Mohammedans of North Africa, the Levant and India as one of the highest authorities on piety. All Moslem books on Practical Theology (*Fiqh*) contain page after page, which cannot be given here, of most minute and often obscene and disgusting explanations on what constitutes impurity and defilement. Altho in theory it is mentioned, in practice *moral purity* as a preparation for prayer is never alluded to, nor does the Koran allude to it. After proper purification and lustration according

[1]Mishkat, Book III, On Purification, Part 3.

to the degree of ceremonial uncleanness or the particular practice of his sect, the Moslem is ready for prayer. Ordinary purification always includes washing various parts of the body three times, according to fourteen rules.

The Five Proper Times for Prayer are at dawn, just after high noon, two hours before sunset, at sunset, and again two hours after. It is forbidden to say morning prayers after the sun is risen.

Posture is of prime importance, and includes facing the Kibla, i.e., Mecca, as well as a series of prostrations and genuflections more easily imitated than described.

The words repeated during this exercise consist of Koran phrases and short chapters, which include praise, confession and a prayer for guidance. Often the chapters chosen have no connection with the topic of prayer. Personal private petitions are allowed after the liturgical prayers, but they are not common. The least departure from the rule in purification, posture or method of prayer nullifies its effect, and the worshipper must begin over again. Special prayer is obligatory at an eclipse of the sun or moon and on the two Moslem festivals. It has been calculated that a pious Moslem repeats the same form of prayer at least seventy-five times a day!

The Call to Prayer heard from minarets five times daily in all Moslem lands is as follows. The muezzin cries it in a loud voice and always in the Arabic language: "God is most great! God is most great! God is most great! I testify that there is no god but God! I testify that there is no god but God! I testify that Mohammed is the Apostle of God! I testify that Mohammed is the Apostle of God! Come to prayer! Come to prayer! Come to prosperity! Come to prosperity! God is most great! God is most great! There is no god but God!"

In the call to early morning prayer the words "prayer is better than sleep" are added twice after the call to prosperity.[1]

3. *The Month of Fasting.*—This was probably borrowed by Mohammed from the Christian Lent. There are many traditions that tell how important fasting is. Let one suffice: "Every good act that a man does shall receive from ten to seven hundred rewards, but the rewards of fasting are beyond bounds, for fasting is for God alone and He will give its rewards." The chief Moslem fast is that of the month of Ramazan. This is the ninth month of the Moslem year, but because they have a lunar calendar it can occur at any season. At present Ramazan corresponds to December, and the days are short. On the other hand, the fast is extremely hard upon the laboring classes when, by the changes of the lunar calendar, it falls in the heat of summer, when the days are long. Even then it is forbidden to drink a drop of water or take a morsel of food. Yet it is a fact that Mohammedans, rich and poor, spend more on food in that month than in any other month of the year; and it is also true that physicians have a run of patients with troubles from indigestion at the close of this religious fast! The explanation is simple. Although the fast extends over one lunar month, it only begins at dawn and ends at sunset each day. During the whole night it is usual to indulge in pleasure, feasting and dinner parties. This makes clear what Mohammed meant when he said that "God would make the fast an ease and not a difficulty."

The hours during which fasting is prescribed are to be

[1]For further details of the prayer-ritual, see F. A Klein, "The Religion of Islam," 120-156.

sacredly observed. Not only is there total abstinence from food and drink, but bathing, smoking, taking snuff, smelling a flower and the use of medicine are prohibited. I have even heard Moslem jurists discuss whether hypodermic medication was allowed during the fast period. In Eastern Arabia the use of an eye-lotion even is considered as equivalent to breaking the fast. The law provides, however, that infants, idiots, the sick, and the aged are exempted from observing this fast.

Voluntary fasting on certain other days is also very common in imitation of the Prophet's example. It is customary for the pious to spend the hours of Ramazan in reading the Koran or the Traditions. Mohammed said: "He who forsakes the fast of Ramazan becomes an infidel, whom to deprive of his wealth and his life is lawful."[1]

4. *Zakat, or Legal Alms.*—This pillar of religion, like all the others, rests rather upon the authority of tradition than upon the precepts of the Koran, since every detail in its observance is borrowed from the example of the Prophet himself. In its primitive sense the word *zakat* means purification, and it was applied to legal alms, or the poor-rate, since the gift of a portion of one's gain or property would purify, or sanctify, the remainder. These compulsory alms were in the early days of Islam collected by the religious tax-gatherer, as they are still in some Mohammedan countries. Where Moslems are under Christian rule, however, the rate is paid out by each Mohammedan according to his own conscience. The rate varies greatly, and the different sects disagree as to what was the practice of the Prophet. Moreover, it is difficult to find a precedent in

[1] F. A. Klein, "The Religion of Islam," 164.

the customs of pastoral Arabia for the present methods of acquiring and holding property in lands touched by civilization. The greatest details are given, e.g , regarding *zakat* on camels, but there is no precedent for *zakat* on city lots or on railway bonds! One-fortieth of the total income is about the usual rate. The tithe of the Old Testament was a much larger portion and was supplemented by many free-will offerings. Charitable offerings are also common in Islam, but, generally speaking, the Moslem who gives his *zakat* is satisfied that he has fulfilled all righteousness. There are seven classes to whom this legal alms may be given, viz., the poor, the homeless, the tax-collector, slaves, debtors, those engaged in fighting for Islam, and wayfaring travellers. The wonderful and cheerful hospitality of so many Moslem peoples finds here, in part, its religious ground and explanation. It is a religious duty to be hospitable. Mohammed excelled in this Semitic virtue himself, and left a noble example to his followers. Arabia is a land without hotels, but with lavish hospitality nearly everywhere.

5. *The Pilgrimage.*—The pilgrimage (*Hajj*) to Mecca is not only one of the pillars of the religion of Islam, but it has proved one of the strongest bonds of union and has always exercised a tremendous influence as a missionary agency. Even to-day the pilgrims who return from Mecca to their native villages in Java, India and West Africa are fanatical ambassadors of the greatness and glory of Islam. From an ethical standpoint, the Mecca pilgrimage, with its superstitious and childish ritual, is a blot upon Mohammedan monotheism. But as a great magnet to draw the Moslem world together with an annual and ever-widening *esprit de corps,* the Mecca pilgrimage is without a rival. The number of pilgrims that come to Mecca varies from

year to year; although Tradition says that it is always 72,-
000, the angels completing any deficiency in the number
of earthly pilgrims! The vast majority arrive by sea
from Egypt, India and the Malay archipelago. The pilgrim caravan from Syria and Arabia by land is growing
smaller every year, for the roads are very unsafe. It will
probably increase again on the completion of the Hejaz
railway from Damascus to Mecca. All told, from sixty
to ninety thousand pilgrims reach Mecca at the time of
the *Hajj*.

For the details of the pilgrimage one must read Burckhardt, Burton, or other of the dozen travellers who have
risked their lives in visiting the forbidden cities of Islam.
In brief, the ceremonies are as follows: After donning
the garb of a pilgrim and performing the legal ablutions,
the *Hajji* visits the sacred mosque and kisses the Black
Stone. He then runs around the Kaaba seven times—
thrice very rapidly and four times slowly—in imitation
of the motions of the planets. Next he offers a prayer:
"O Allah, Lord of the Ancient House, free my neck from
hell-fire and preserve me from every evil deed; make me
contented with the daily food Thou givest me, and bless
me in all Thou hast granted." At "the place of Abraham" he also prays; he drinks water from the sacred
well of Zemzem and again kisses the Black Stone. Then
the pilgrim runs between the hills of Safa and Marwa.
He visits Mina and Arafat, a few miles from Mecca, and
at the latter place listens to a sermon. On his return he
stops at Mina and stones three pillars of masonry known
as the "Great Devil," "the middle pillar," and the "first
one" with seven small pebbles. Finally there is the sacrifice of a sheep or other animal as the climax of the pilgrim's task. Snouck Hurgronje and Dozy have given

us the philosophical origin of these strange ceremonies in their monographs.[1] The whole pilgrimage is, in the words of Kuenen, "a fragment of incomprehensible heathenism taken up undigested into Islam." And as regards the veneration for the Black Stone, there is a tradition that the Caliph Omar remarked: "By God. I know that thou art only a stone and canst grant no benefit or do no harm. And had I not known that the Prophet kissed thee I would not have done it."

The Kaaba and Its Black Stone.—These merit at least a paragraph, since they are the centre toward which, as toward the shrine of their religion, the prayers and pilgrim-journeys of millions have gravitated for thirteen centuries. The story goes that when Adam and Eve fell from Paradise, Adam landed on a mountain in Ceylon and Eve fell at Jiddah, on the western coast of Arabia. (Jiddah signifies "grandmother.") After a hundred years of wandering they met near Mecca and here Allah constructed for them a tabernacle on the site of the present Kaaba. He put in its foundation the famous stone, once whiter than snow, but since turned black by the kisses of pilgrims.

The name Kaaba means a cube; but the building is not built true to line and is in fact an unequal trapezium.[2] Because of its location in a hollow and its black-cloth covering, these inequalities are not apparent to the eye.

The Kaaba proper stands in an oblong space 250 paces

---

[1] Snouck Hurgronje, "Het Mekkaansche Feest" (Leyden, 1880) Dozy, "De Israelieten te Mekka van David's tijd enz" (Haarlem, 1864). These are in the Dutch language, and contain matter nowhere else accessible, as far as the author is aware

[2] Its measurements, according to Ali Bey, are 37 ft. 2 in., 31 ft. 7 in., 38 ft. 4 in., 29 ft. and its height is 34 ft. 4 in. The student could construct a model from these measurements, Burton's full description, and Hurgronje's photographs.

long by 200 broad.   This open space is surrounded by
colonnades used for schools and as the general rendez-
vous of pilgrims.   It is in turn surrounded by the outer
temple wall, with its nineteen gates and six minarets.
The Mosque is of much more recent date than the Kaaba,
which was well known as an idolatrous Arabian shrine
long before the time of Mohammed.   The Sacred Mosque
and its Kaaba contain the following treasures: the Black
Stone, the well of Zemzem, the great pulpit, the staircase
and the Kubattein, or two small mosques of Saab and
Abbas.   The remainder of the space is occupied by pave-
ments and gravel arranged to accommodate and distinguish the four orthodox sects in their devotions.   (See
Plan of the Mosque, opposite.)

The Black Stone is undoubtedly the oldest treasure of
Mecca.   Stone-worship was an Arabian form of idolatry
in very ancient times, and relics of it remain in many
parts of the Peninsula.   Maximus Tyrius wrote in the
second century, "The Arabians pay homage to I know not
what god, which they represent by a quadrangular stone."
The Guebars, or ancient Persians, assert that the Black
Stone was an emblem of Saturn and was left in the Kaaba
by Mahabad.   It is probably an aerolite and owes its rep-
utation to its fall from the sky.   Moslem historians do
not deny that it was an object of worship before Islam,
but they escape the moral difficulty and justify their
Prophet by further traditions about its origin and miraculous character.

The Mecca pilgrimage is incumbent on every free Moslem, male or female, who is of age and has sufficient
means for the journey.   Many of them, unwilling to un-
dergo the hardship of the journey, engage a substitute,
and thus purchase the merit for themselves.   Most Mos-

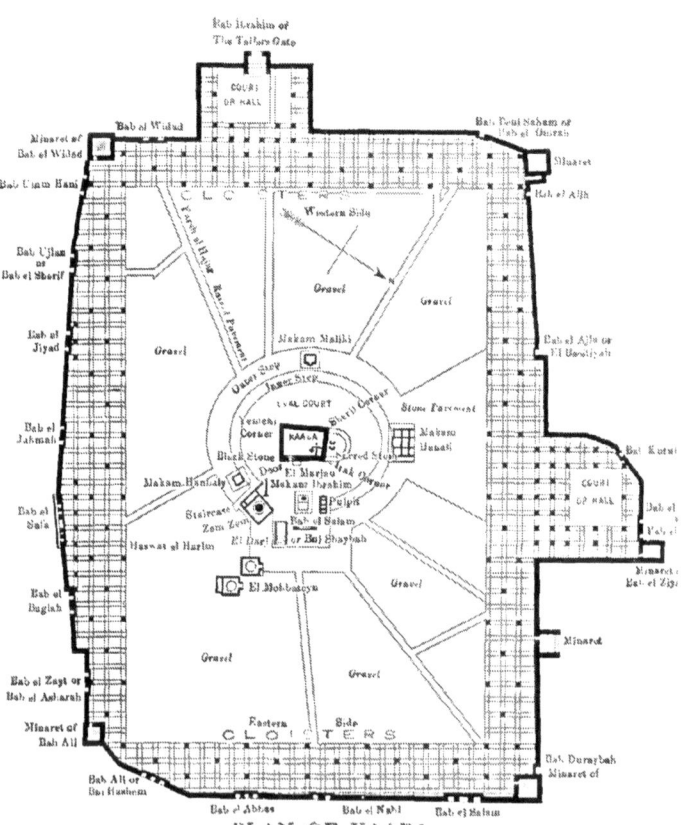

PLAN OF KAABA

lems also visit the tomb of Mohammed at Medina and claim the Prophet's authority for this added merit. The Shiah Moslems visit Kerbela and Meshad Ali, where their martyr-saints are buried. Pilgrimages to tombs of local saints and ancient prophets, to "foot-prints" of the Apostle, or to graves of his companions are exceedingly common. But none of these pilgrimages equal in merit that to the House of God in Mecca. In conclusion, it is necessary to state that the two sacred cities of Islam, Mecca and Medina, are hotbeds of every form of immorality, and, by the witness of Moslems themselves, sink-holes of iniquity and dens of robbers.[1]

Other Religious Practices.—In addition to what is said about these "five pillars" of the faith, a word is necessary regarding certain other Moslem practices. if we are to complete the sketch of every-day religion.

(a) *Circumcision*, although not once alluded to in the Koran, is the initiative rite among all Moslems everywhere, and in that respect it corresponds somewhat to baptism. Its performance is attended with religious festivities, and its omission is equivalent to a denial of the faith. Its observance is founded upon tradition, i.e., the custom of Mohammed. The abominable practice of female circumcision (mutilation) is common in many Moslem lands, and is also founded on the precept of Mohammed.[2]

(b) *Feasts and Festivals.*—The two great feast days of Islam are the '*Idu-l-Fitr*, or the first day after Ramazan, when the long fast is broken, and the '*Id-ul-Azha*, or *Bairam*, the great feast, which is the Feast of Sacrifice.

The first of these feasts is especially a time for rejoic-

[1] S. M. Zwemer, "Arabia; the Cradle of Islam," 30-52.
[2] F. A. Klein "The Religion of Islam," 131.

ing and alms-giving.   Special public prayer is held and
a sermon delivered to the vast assemblies in the open air.
All wear their best dress, generally new clothing, and
even the women don all their jewels while they celebrate
the feast in the Zenana or the Harem with amusements
and indulgences.

The Feast of Sacrifice is observed by animal sacrifices
in addition, and these are really a part of the rite of the
Meccan pilgrimage, but the feast is simultaneously celebrated everywhere.   It is held in commemoration of
Abraham's willingness to sacrifice Isaac, or, as the Moslems believe, Ishmael.

It is a notable fact and an enigma that while Mohammed professed to abrogate the Jewish ritual and
ignored the doctrine of an atonement, even denying the
fact of our Saviour's crucifixion, he yet made the Day
of Sacrifice the great central festival of his religion.

(c) *Jihad.*—It is unaccountable why this greatest force
in Islam, religious warfare, or Jihad, is not mentioned
as a pillar of religion.   A religious war against infidels
is a duty plainly taught by the Koran and by tradition,
e.g.: "Kill those who join other gods with God, wherever
ye shall find them."[1]   And a dozen other passages command believers to make war, to kill, and to fight in the
path of God.   Some apologists for Islam—T. W. Arnold,
Saiyad Ameer Ali, and others—attempt to avoid the fact
of an appeal to use the sword by interpreting these passages in a semi-spiritual way, and they even try to make
Jihad mean a sort of Christian Endeavor Society for
propagating Islam!   To this Marcus Dods replies: "The
man must shut his eyes to the broadest and most con-
spicuous facts of the history of Islam who denies that

[1] Surah 9:5.

the sword has been the great means of propagating this religion. Until Mohammed appealed to the sword his faith made very little way." The history of the Wahabis in the nineteenth century, the Armenian massacres, the Mahdis of the Soudan and of Somali-land, and the almost universal hope among Moslems to use the power of the sword again—all these are proofs that Jihad is one of the religious forces of Mohammedanism which Christendom cannot afford to ignore. The sword is in its sheath, but the giant still wears it at his side, and it has never been rusty.

Only last year the Arabic paper, *Ez-Zahir,* published in Egypt, said: "Has the time not come yet when uniting the suppressed wailings of India with our own groans and sighs in Egypt, we should say to each other, Come, let us be one, following the Divine words, 'Victory belongs to the united forces'? Certainly the time has come when we, India and Egypt, should cut and tear asunder the ties of the yoke imposed on us by the English." On the other hand, Mohammed Husain, the editor of a paper at Lahore, wrote a Treatise on Jihad (1893), stating: "The present treatise on the question of Jihad has been compiled for two reasons. My first object is that the Mohammedans, ignorant of the texts bearing on Jihad and the conditions of Islam, may become acquainted with them, and that they may not labor under the misapprehension that it is their religious duty to wage war against another people solely because that people is opposed to Islam. Thus they, by ascertaining the fixed conditions and texts, may be saved forever from rebellion, and may not sacrifice their lives and property fruitlessly nor unjustly shed the blood of others. My second object is that non-Mohammedans and the government under whose protection the Mohammedans live, may not suspect Mohammedans of thinking that it is lawful for us to fight against non-Mohammedans, or that it is our duty to interfere with the life and property of others, or that we are bound to convert others forcibly to Mohammedanism, or to spread Islam by means of the sword."

So the question of "religion and the sword" is still an open one among Moslems. It must needs be so long as they obey the Koran and Tradition, for Mohammed said: "He who dies and has not fought for the religion of Islam, nor has even said in his heart, 'Would to God I were a champion that could die in the road of God,' is even as a hypocrite." And again, still more forcibly: "The fire of hell shall not touch the legs of him who is covered with the dust of battle in the road of God." In spite of cruelty, bloodshed, dissension and deceit, the story of the Moslem conquest with the sword of Jihad is full of heroism and inspiration.

If so much was done in the name of Mohammed, what should we not dare do in the name of Jesus Christ, without carnal weapons, to carry His gospel and the practical precepts of His religion to every Moslem people, who are groaning under the intolerable burden of the "five pillars" of practice, a yoke which neither they nor their fathers were able to bear.

THE ETHICS OF ISLAM

"Mohammedanism is held, by many who have to live under its shadow, to be the most degraded religion, morally, in the world We speak of it as superior to the other religions, because of its monotheistic faith, but I would rather believe in ten pure gods than in one God who would have for His supreme prophet and representative a man with Mohammed's moral character. Missionaries from India will tell you that the actual moral conditions to be found among Mohammedans there are more terrible than those to be found among the pantheistic Hindus themselves, and the late Dr. Cochran, of Persia, a man who had unsurpassed opportunities for seeing the inner life of Mohammedan men, told me, toward the close of his life, that he could not say, out of his long and intimate acquaintance as a doctor with the men of Persia, that he had ever met one pure-hearted or pure-lived adult man among the Mohammedans of Persia. Can a religion of immorality, or moral inferiority, meet the needs of struggling men?"—*Robert E. Speer.*

VI

THE ETHICS OF ISLAM

Basis of Moslem Ethics.—Martensen defines Christian ethics as "the science of morals conditioned by Christianity." If we use the same definition for Mohammedan ethics, we already know from the two previous chapters what articles of faith and religious conceptions of duty are behind the moral-teaching of Islam and fundamental to it.

The three fundamental concepts of Christian ethics are all of them challenged by the teaching of Islam. The Mohammedan idea of the Highest Good, of Virtue and of the Moral Law are not in accord with those of Christianity. "The highest good is the very outwardly and very sensuously conceived happiness of the individual." Ideal virtue is to be found through imitation of Mohammed. And the moral law is practically abrogated because of loose views as to its real character, its teaching and finality.

Its Real Character.—"Islam," says Adolph Wuttke, in his system of ethics, "finds its place in the history of the religious and moral spirit not as a vital organic member, but as violently interrupting the course of this history, and which is to be regarded as an attempt of *heathenism* to maintain itself erect under an outward monotheistic form against Christianity.

"The ethics of Islam bear the character of an outwardly and crudely conceived doctrine of righteousness;
conscientiousness in the sphere of the social relations,
faithfulness to conviction and to one's word, and the
bringing of an action into relation to God, are its bright
points; but there is a lack of heart-depth, of a basing of
the moral in love. The highest good is the very outwardly and very sensuously conceived happiness of the
individual. The potency of sin is not recognized; evil
is only an individual, not an historical power; hence
there is no need of redemption, but only of personal
works on the basis of prophetic instruction; Mohammed
is only a teacher, not an atoner. God and man remain
strictly external to, and separate from, each other; God
—no less individually conceived of than man—comes into
no real communion with man; and man, as moral, acts
not as influenced by such a communion, but only as an
isolated individual. . . . Man has nothing to receive
from God but the Word, and nothing to do for God
but good works; of inner sanctification there is no
thought; the essential point is simply to let the *per se*
good nature of man manifest itself in works; there is no
inner struggle in order to attain to the true life, no peni-
tence-struggle against inner sinfulness; and instead of
true humility we find only proud work-righteousness.
To the natural propensities of man there is consequently
but little refused—nothing but the enjoyment of wine, of
swine-flesh, of blood, of strangled animals, and of games
of chance, and this, too, for insufficient (assigned) reasons. The merely individual character of the morality
manifests itself especially in the low conception that is
formed of marriage, in which polygamy is expressly con-
ceded, woman degraded to a very low position, and the

dissolution of the marriage bond placed in the unlimited discretion of the man; there hence results a very superficial view of the family in general; the moral community-life is conceived of throughout in a very crude manner. Unquestionably this form of ethics is not an advancing on the part of humanity, but a guilty retrograding from that which had already been attained."[1]

After this philosophical summary of the real character of Mohammedan Ethics, an account of its practical teaching and effect will make the picture more vivid, altho still darker.

The Moslem Idea of Sin.—Moslem doctors define sin as "a conscious act of a responsible being against known law." Wherefore sins of ignorance and of childhood are not reckoned as real sin. They divide sin into "great" and "little" sins. Some say there are seven great sins. idolatry, murder, false charge of adultery, wasting the substance of orphans, taking interest on money, desertion from Jihad and disobedience to parents! Others say there are seventeen, and include wine-drinking, witchcraft and perjury among them. Mohammed himself said: "The greatest of sins before God is that you call another like unto the God who created you, or that you murder your child from an idea that it will eat your victuals, or that you commit adultery with your neighbor's wife."[2] All sins except "great" ones are easily forgiven, as God is merciful and clement. The words permitted (*hallal*) and forbidden (*haram*) have superseded the terms for guilt and transgression. Nothing is right or wrong by nature, but becomes such by the fiat of the Almighty. What Allah or his Prophet forbids is sin, even should he forbid

[1]Adolf Wuttke, "Christian Ethics," Vol. I, 172.
[2]Mishkat, Book I, Chap. 2.

what seems right to the conscience. What Allah allows is not sin and cannot be sin *at the time He allows it*, though it may have been before or after. One has only to argue the matter of polygamy with any intelligent Moslem to have the above statement confirmed. There is no clear distinction between the ceremonial and the moral law implied in the Koran. It is as great an offence to pray with unwashed hands as to tell a lie, and "pious" Moslems, who nightly break the seventh commandment (even according to their own lax interpretation of it) will shrink from a tin of English meat, for fear they be defiled eating swine's flesh. The lack of all distinction between the ceremonial and the moral law is very evident in the traditional sayings of Mohammed, which are, of course, at the basis of ethics. Take one example: "The Prophet, upon whom be prayers and peace, said, One *dirhem* of usury which a man takes knowing it to be so is more grievous than thirty-six fornications, and whosoever has done so is worthy of hell-fire."[1]

One cannot read the Koran without coming to the conclusion that according to its teaching *Allah himself does not appear bound by any standard of justice.* For example, the worship of the creature is heinous to the Moslem mind, yet Allah punished Satan for not being willing to worship Adam.[2] Allah is merciful in winking at the sins of His favorites (the prophets and those who fight His battles), but is the quick avenger of all infidels and idolaters. The moral law changes according to times and circumstances. God can do what He pleases. The Koran often asserts this. Not only physically but morally He is *almighty*, in the Moslem sense of the word. Allah, the

[1] S. M. Zwemer, "Moslem Doctrine of God," 52.
[2] Surah 2:28-31.

Koran says, is the best plotter. Allah mocks and deceives. Allah "makes it easy" for those who follow Mohammed.[1]

The Low Ideal of Character in Islam.—A stream cannot rise higher than its source; a tower cannot be broader than its foundation. The measure of the moral stature of Mohammed is the source and foundation of all moral ideals in Islam. His conduct is the standard of character. We need not be surprised, therefore, that the ethical standard is so low. Raymund Lull, the first missionary to Moslems, used to show in his bold preaching that Mohammed had none of the seven cardinal virtues and was guilty of the seven deadly sins; he doubtless went too far. But it would not be difficult to show that pride, lust, envy and anger were prominent traits in the Prophet's character. To read the pages of Muir or Koelle or Sprenger is convincing.[2]

[1]Surahs 8:29; 3 53: 27 51; 86 15; 16·4; 14:15; 9:51.

[2]The following instances, taken from Koelle, "Mohammed and Mohammedanism," are sufficient proof:

"The first to fall as victims of Mohammed's vengeance were some individuals of the Jewish persuasion who had made themselves obnoxious above others by attacking him in verse. He managed to produce an impression amongst the people that he would like to be rid of them. The hint was readily taken up by persons anxious to ingratiate themselves in the prophet's favor The gifted woman, Asma, and the hoary poet, Abu Afak, were both murdered in their sleep: the former while slumbering on her bed, with an infant in her arms; the latter whilst lying, for coolness' sake, in an open verandah No one dared to molest the assassin of either of these victims; for it was no secret that the foul deeds had been approved by the prophet, and that he had treated the perpetrators with marked favor." (P. 169)

Another instance is as follows: "One of their more influential Rabbis was Kab Ibn Ashraf, who had looked favorably upon Mohammed, till he changed the Kibla from Jerusalem to Mecca. Then he became his decided opponent, attacking him and his religion in verse, and working against him in various ways He was first to fall as a victim to Mohammed's vindictiveness. The prophet despatched four men, amongst them Kab's own foster-brother, to assassinate him, and sanctioned beforehand any lie or stratagem which they might see fit to employ, so as to lure him aside It was dark when they arrived at his house, and he was already in bed; but they cunningly prevailed upon him to come out to them, and when they had him alone in the dark they foully murdered him.

And to take another example, what did Mohammed teach regarding truthfulness? There are two authenticated sayings of his given in the traditions on the subject of lying: "When a servant of God tells a lie, his guardian angels move away to the distance of a mile because of the badness of its smell." That seems a characteristic denunciation; but the other saying contradicts it: "Verily a lie is allowable in three cases—to women, to reconcile friends, and in war."[1] The dastardly assassination," says Muir, "of his political and religious opponents, countenanced and frequently directed as they were in all their cruel and *perfidious* details by Mohammed himself, leaves a dark and indelible blot upon his character." With

Mohammed remained up, to await their return, and when they showed him Kab's head, he commended their deed, and praised Allah But on the following morning, when the assassination had become generally known, the Jews, as Ibn Ishak informs us, were struck with terror, and none of them regarded his life safe any longer" (P 172)

Further on we read: "But, some time before it was actually carried out, the inhabitants of Khaibar were horrified by one of the dastardly assassinations to which Mohammed did not scruple to stoop, for the purposes of revenge. The victim selected this time was Sallam, a leading man of the Beni Nadhir who, after the expulsion of the tribe from Medina, had settled in Khaibar and enjoyed great influence there. He was accused of having had a hand in stirring up the Meccans to the war in which they laid siege to Medina. Mohammed never had any difficulty in finding, amongst his followers, willing tools for executing such secret missions Ibn Ishak mentions it as one of the Divine favors to Mohammed, that 'the two tribes of the Awsites and Khazrajites were as jealous about his head as two male camels.' Accordingly, as the former had assassinated Kab bin Ashraf, the latter aspired after an equal distinction, and asked the prophet's permission, which was gladly given, to do away with Sallam. Five Khazrajites, one of whom Mohammed had appointed chief for the occasion, reached Khaibar after dark and, professing to have come for the purpose of buying corn, were admitted to Sallam's upper apartment, where he was already lying on his bed But, as soon as they had him thus in their power, they fell upon him with their daggers and massacred the defenceless man, without the slightest shame or compunction. By the time the startled Jews came to see what had happened, the assassins had decamped and were on their way to their master, to receive his thanks" (P. 179.)

[1]S. M. Zwemer, "Moslem Doctrines of God," 41. El Hidayah, Vol. IV, 81.

such a prophet it is no wonder that among his followers
and imitators "truth-telling is one of the lost arts," and
that perjury is too common to be noticed. Since Mohammed gathered ideas and stories from the Jews of
Medina and palmed them off as a new revelation from
God, it is no wonder that Arabian literature teems with
all sorts of plagiarisms,[1] or that one of the early authorities of Islam laid down the canon that it is justifiable to
lie in praise of the Prophet. In regard to the Mohammedans of Persia, Dr. St. Clair Tisdall says: "Lying has
been elevated to the dignity of a fine art, owing to the
doctrine of *Kitman-ud-din,* which is held by the Shiah
religious community."[2]

Islam and the Decalogue.—According to a remarkable
tradition,[3] Mohammed was confused as to the number
and character of the commandments given Moses. "A
Jew came to the Prophet and asked him about the *nine*
(*sic*) wonders which appeared by the hand of Moses.
The Prophet said: "Do not associate anything with God,
do not steal, do not commit adultery, do not kill, do not
take an innocent before the king to be killed, do not practice magic, do not take interest, do not accuse an innocent
woman of adultery, do not run away in battle, and especially for you, O Jews, not to work on the Sabbath."

The lax and immoral interpretation by Moslem theolo-
gians of the Third, Sixth, Seventh, Eighth and Ninth
commandments of the decalogue are very evident. But
that interpretation is based on the Koran itself, which is
full of the vain use of God's name and needless oaths,
which permits murder in Jihad, which allows polygamy,
divorce and the capture of slaves. How Mohammed re-

[1]See Brockelmann, "Geschichte der Arabischen Literatur," Introduction
[2]"The Mohammedan World of To-day," 117.
[3]Mishkat, Book I, Chap. II, Part II.

garded the Tenth commandment is plain from the story of Zainab.[1]

There are certain things which the ethics of Islam allow of which it is also necessary to write. They exist not in spite of Islam, but because of Islam and because of the teaching of its Sacred Book.

Polygamy, Divorce and Slavery.—These three evils are so closely intertwined with the Mohammedan religion— its book and its Prophet—that they can never be wholly abandoned without doing violence to the teaching of the Koran and the example of Mohammed. In Moslem books of theology, jurisprudence and ethics there are long chapters on each of these subjects. Nor can there be the least doubt that polygamy and slavery have had a tremendous power in the spread and grasp of Islam. It is the testimony of history that the slave-traders of Zanzibar were also the missionaries of Islam, in darkest Africa; and the last census report of Bengal states that the increase of the Mohammedan population there is due, not to conversions from Hinduism, but to polygamy and concubinage as open doors into a higher caste for submerged Hindu womanhood. We must also consider that the loose moral code of Islam is ever an attraction to the unregenerate.

It is impossible to give here, even in outline, the true character, extent and effect of these three "religious institutions" of Islam. A Moslem who lives up to his privileges and who follows the example of "the saints" in his calendar can have four wives and any number of slave-concubines; can divorce at his pleasure; he can remarry his divorced wives by a special though abominable arrangement; and, in addition to all this, if he belong to

[1] See Surah 33:37.

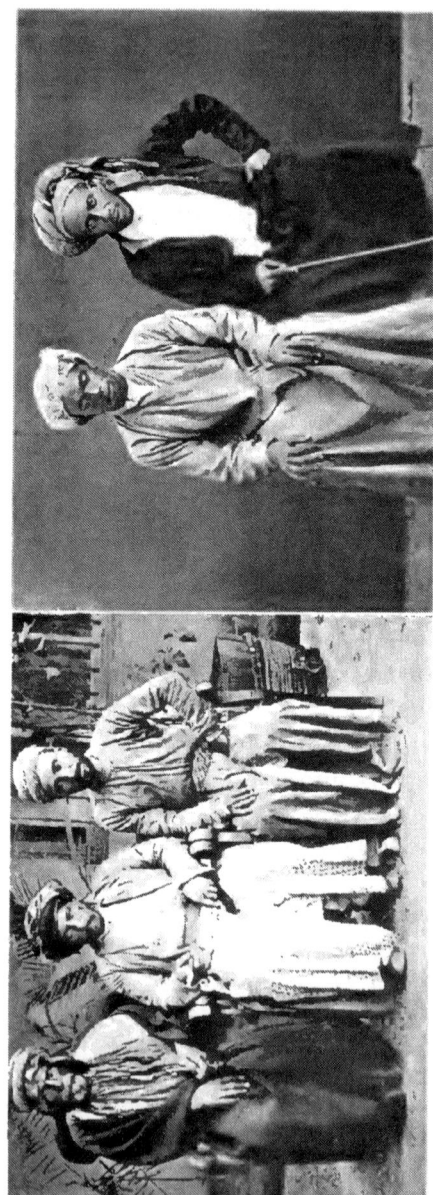

Busrah

Zanzibar

TYPES OF MOSLEM PILGRIMS AT MECCA

the Shiah sect he can contract marriages for fun (*Metaa'*), which are temporary.

As Robert E. Speer said at the Student Volunteer convention at Nashville, 1906: "The very chapter in the Mohammedan Bible which deals with the legal status of woman, and which provides that every Mohammedan may have four legal wives, and as many concubines or slave girls as his right hand can hold, goes by the title in the Koran itself of 'The Cow'."[1] Altho, of course, the title of the chapter was not given it for that reason.

The degrading views held as regards the whole marriage relation are summed up by Ghazzali when he says: "*Marriage is a kind of slavery,* for the wife becomes the slave (*rakeek*) of her husband, and it is her duty absolutely to obey him in everything he requires of her except in what is contrary to the laws of Islam." Wife-beating is allowed by the Koran, and the method and limitations are explained by the laws of religion.[2]

The Slave-Trade.—Arabia, the cradle of Islam, is still a centre of the slave-trade, and, according to the Koran, slavery and the slave-trade are divine institutions. Some Moslem apologists of the present day contend that Mohammed looked upon the custom as temporary in its nature; but slavery is so interwoven with the laws of marriage, of sale, of inheritance, and with the whole social fabric, that its abolition strikes at the foundations of their legal code. Whenever and wherever Moslem rulers have agreed to the abolition or suppression of the slave-trade they have acted contrary to the privileges of their religion in consenting to obey the laws of humanity. From

[1] In Turkey the word "cow" is actually applied to women by the Moslems. "Our Moslem Sisters," 198.
[2] See F. A. Klein, "The Religion of Islam," 190; and Moslem Commentaries on Surah 4:38.

the Koran we learn[1] that all male and female slaves taken as plunder in war are the lawful property of the master, that the master has power to take to himself any female slave, either married or single, as his chattel; that the position of a slave is as helpless as that of the stone idols of old Arabia; and that, while a man can do as he pleases with his property, slaves should be treated kindly and granted freedom when able to purchase it. Slave-traffic is not only allowed, but legislated for by Mohammedan law and made sacred by the example of the Prophet.[2] In Moslem books of law the same rules apply to the sale of animals and slaves.

In 1898 the late J. Theodore Bent wrote respecting the slave-trade in the Red Sea: "The west coast of the Red Sea is in portions still much given to slave-trading. From Suez down to Ras Benas the coast is pretty well protected by government boats, which cruise about and seize dhows suspected of traffic in human flesh, but south of this, until the area of Suakin is reached, slave-trading is still actively carried on. The transport is done in dhows from the Arabian coast, which come over to the coral reefs of the western side ostensibly for pearl fishing. At certain seasons of the year slave-traders in caravans come down from the derwish territory in the Nile valley, and the petty Bedouin sheiks on the Red Sea littoral connive at and assist them in the work."

Dr. C. Snouck Hurgronje describes the public slave-market at Mecca in full swing every day during his visit. It is located near Bab Derebah and the holy mosque, and open to everybody. Altho he himself apologizes for the traffic, and calls the anti-slavery crusade a swindle, he yet

---

[1]Surahs 4 3, 28 40; 23·49; 16 77; 30 27, 24·33, etc.
[2]Mishkat, Book XIII, Chap. 20.

confesses to all the horrible details in the sale of female slaves, and the mutilation of male slaves for the markets. Eunuchs are plentiful, and are specially imported to act as guards for mosques; they can be bought for $120 apiece.[1]

The explorer, Charles M. Doughty, who spent years in the interior of Arabia, wrote: "Jiddah is the staple town of African slavery for the Turkish empire; Jiddah, where are Frankish Consuls. But you shall find these worthies, in the pallid solitude of their palaces, affecting (great Heaven!) the simplicity of new-born babes; they will tell you they are not aware of it! . . . But I say again in your ingenuous ears, Jiddah is the staple town of the Turkish slavery, or all the Moslems are liars. . . . I told them we had a treaty with the Sultan to suppress slavery. "Dog," cries the fellow, "thou liar—are there not thousands of slaves at Jiddah that every day are bought and sold? Wherefore, thou dog, be they not all made free if thou sayest sooth?"[2]

The Social Bankruptcy of Islam.—A system forever handicapped in any effort toward social progress by the incubus of such gigantic evils, sanctioned in their Prophet's life and in his book, could not escape social bankruptcy. Islam has been on trial for thirteen centuries. "By their fruits ye shall know them."

It has often been asserted that Islam is the proper religion for Arabia The miserable, half-starved, ignorant but canny Bedouins now say: "Mohammed's religion can never have been intended for us; it demands ablution, but we have no water; fasting, but we always fast; almsgiving, but we have no money; pilgrimage, but Allah is everywhere." Islam has had fair trial in other than des-

[1]"Mekka." Vol II, 15-24.   [2]"Arabia Deserta," Vol. II, last chapter.

ert lands. For five hundred years it has been supreme in Turkey, the fairest and richest portion of the Old World. And what is the result? The Mohammedan population has decreased; the treasury is bankrupt; progress is blocked; "instead of wealth, universal poverty; instead of comeliness, rags; instead of commerce, beggary—a failure greater and more absolute than history can elsewhere present."[1] In regard to what Islam has done and can do in Africa, the recent testimony of Canon Robinson is conclusive. Writing of Mohammedanism in the central Soudan, he says:

"Moreover, if it be true, as it probably is to some extent, that Mohammedanism has helped forward the Hausas in the path of civilization, the assistance rendered here, as in every other country subject to Mohammedan rule, is by no means an unmixed good. *Mohammedan progress is progress up an impasse;* it enables converts to advance a certain distance, only to check their further progress by an impassable wall of blind prejudice and ignorance. We cannot have a better proof of this statement than the progress, or rather, want of progress, in Arabia, the home of Mohammedanism, during the last thousand years. Palgrave, who spent the greater part of his life among Mohammedans, and who was so far in sympathy with them that on more than one occasion he conducted service for them in their mosques, speaking of Arabia, says: 'When the Koran and Mecca shall have disappeared from Arabia, then, and only then, can we expect to see the Arab assume that place in the ranks of civilization from which Mohammed and his book have, more than any other cause, long held him back.' "

---

[1] Cyrus Hamlin, "Five Hundred Years of Islam in Turkey." American Board of Commissioners for Foreign Missions, 1888.

And Professor A. Vambery, speaking of the impossibility of political independence for Egypt, says: "I am the last to wish to blacken the leaders of Mohammedan society, but I beg leave to ask: Does there exist a Mohammedan government where the deep-seated evil of tyranny, anarchy, misrule and utter collapse does not offer the most appalling picture of human caducity?"[1]

Moslem Ethics a Plea for Missions.—When Canon Taylor and Dr. Blyden, some years ago, published their extravagant glorifications of Islam, Mr. R. Bosworth Smith accused them of plagiarism from *his* life of Mohammed, and subsequently, in an address before the fellows of Zion's College, on February 21, 1888, he said: "The resemblances between the two creeds are indeed many and striking, as I have implied throughout; but if I may once more quote a few words which I have used elsewhere in dealing with this question, the contrasts are even more striking than the resemblances. *The religion of Christ contains whole fields of morality* and whole realms of thought which are all but outside the religion of Mohammed. It opens humility,[2] purity of heart, for-

---

[1] *The Nineteenth Century* for October, 1906.

[2] The following account of Moslems at prayer is typical: "Personal pride, which, like blood in the body, runs through all the veins of the mind of Mohammedanism, which sets the soul of a Sultan in the twisted frame of a beggar at a street corner, is not cast off in the act of adoration These Arabs humbled themselves in the body. Their foreheads touched the stones. By their attitudes they seemed as if they wished to make themselves even with the ground, to shrink into the space occupied by a grain of sand Yet they were proud in the presence of Allah, as if the firmness of their belief in him and his right dealing, the fury of their contempt and hatred for those who looked not toward Mecca nor regarded Ramazan, gave them a patent of nobility Despite their genuflections they were all as men who knew, and never forgot, that on them was conferred the right to keep on their head-covering in the presence of their King. With unclosed eyes they looked God full in the face. Their dull and growling murmur had the majesty of thunder rolling through the sky."—"The Garden of Allah," 153.

giveness of injuries, sacrifice of self, to man's moral nature; it gives scope for toleration, development, boundless progress to his mind; its motive power is stronger, even as a friend is better than a king, and love higher than obedience. *Its realized ideals in the various paths of human greatness have been more commanding, more many-sided, more holy, as Averroes is below Newton, Harun below Alfred, and Ali below St. Paul.* Finally, the ideal life of all, is far more elevating, far more majestic, far more inspiring, even as the life of the founder of Mohammedanism is below the life of the Founder of Christianity. If, then, we believe Christianity to be truer and purer in itself than Islam and than any other religion, we must needs wish others to be partakers of it; and the efforts to propagate it is thrice blessed—it blesses him that offers no less than him who accepts it; nay, it often blesses him who accepts it not "[1]

And so the most famous apologist for Islam himself pleads for missions to the Mohammedan world on the ground of its ethical needs.

[1] Quoted by F. F. Ellinwood in "Oriental Religions and Christianity," 218.
For further statements concerning the social results of the ethics of Islam consult Dennis, "Christian Missions and Social Progress," Vol. I, 389-391 and 446-448.

DIVISION, DISINTEGRATION AND REFORM

"We stand in the midst of a great world of wrecked religions. Heresy after heresy has shot schism upon schism through what we used to look upon as a solid mass of Mohammedanism, and all the other non-Christian religions are attempting, in greater or less degree, to transform themselves beneath our eyes They are confessing, every one of them, their inadequacy to meet the needs of men."—*Robert E. Speer,* in the "Non-Christian Religions Inadequate to Meet the Needs of Men," an address at the Student Volunteer Convention, Nashville, 1906.

"Verily, it will happen to my people even as it did to the Children of Israel The Children of Israel were divided into seventy-two sects, and my people will be divided into seventy-three. Every one of these sects will go to hell, except one sect." —*Mohammed* (Mishkat, Book I, chap. 6, part 2).

VII

DIVISION, DISINTEGRATION AND REFORM

Why Islam Became Divided.—In the Koran there was given to Moslems a religion, but no religious system. It was all accepted by the first believers without asking questions of the how and why. But when once Islam left the deserts of Arabia and conquered Syria and Persia and the regions beyond, the conquerors were faced by a fully formed Christian belief and by Zoroastrian and Brahmanic thought.

It is true that the Arabs assumed everywhere the leading position. They were a military aristocracy, and the proof of it is the fact that conquered nations with an old and superior civilization accepted *the language* of their conquerors. But when the new converts in Persia and Syria interpreted the new religion and began to write its dogmatics, the rise of dispute and the multiplication of divisions was inevitable. The new wine of Aryan thought and philosophy burst the leathern bottles of the Semitic creed. As Sir Lewis Pelly remarks: "Though the personal history of Ali and his sons was the exciting cause of the Shiah schism, its predisposing cause lies far deeper in the impassable ethnological gulf which separates the Aryan and Semitic races."[1]

[1]"The Miracle Play of Hassan and Husain," Introduction, xvi. (London, 1879.)

It is evident from the saying of Mohammed, quoted on the page facing this chapter, that he himself anticipated division among his followers, for in his own family jealousies and rivalries were already preparing the way for the first great schism. The story of Ayesha, Mohammed's daughter, as given by Muir, is a striking example. She died fifty-eight years after the Hegira.

Number of Moslem Sects.—The number of Moslem sects has far exceeded the prediction of Mohammed, for they are more in number and variety than those of the Christian religion. Several of the sects, especially the orthodox Sunnis, arrogate to themselves the title of *Najiyah*, or "those who are being saved." Most of them agree with the dictum of the Prophet that there is no salvation for heretics; while for rancor, bitterness, hatred and bloodshed the sad divisions of Christendom are far outmatched by the history of sects in Islam. Sheikh Abd ul Kader says there are no less than one hundred and fifty sects in Islam;[1] others, like the author of *Ghiyas-ul-Lughat*, have been very careful to so prepare a list of all the Moslem sects as to tally exactly with Mohammed's prophecy that they would number seventy-three! By this artificial classification there are six divisions, of twelve sects each, from which one can choose a way of destruction, and the seventy-third (that of the author) is the path of *Najiyah*, or salvation. The table on page 138 gives the chief Moslem sects and their relation one to another.

The Sunnis—This sect far outnumbers all others today, and was also the most influential in the history of Islam. The Sunnis, as their name imports, are the fol-

[1] T. P. Hughes, "Dictionary of Islam," 569.

From Morocco

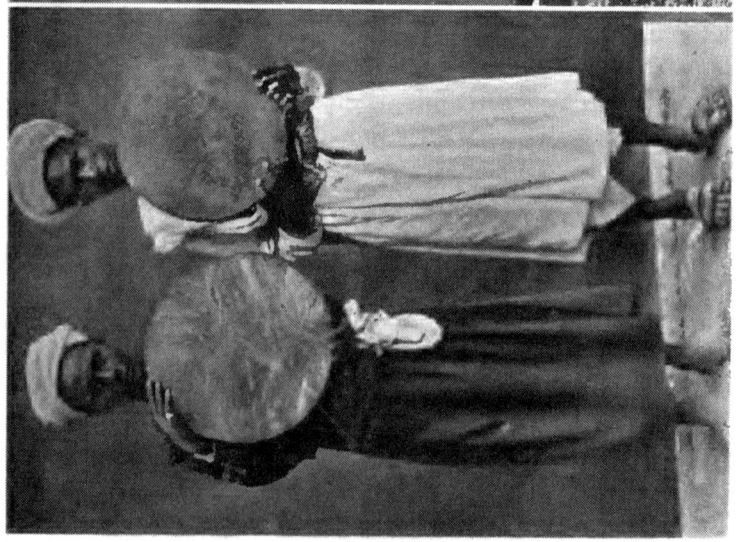

Mendicants from Yemen

lowers of *tradition* and the foes of all innovation. To them the Koran was the Procrustean bed for the human intellect. Everything was measured by it and by orthodox tradition. Especially on the doctrine of predestination they were opposed to all compromise. When we consider the deadening influence of their doctrine of fatalism, it is not surprising that they are opposed to all new philosophy. The attainments of the Arabs in philosophy have been greatly overrated; they were translators and transmitters of the Greek philosophy, and whatever was added to Plato and Aristotle came not from the side of orthodoxy, but was entirely the work of heretics such as Averroes, Alfarabi and Avicenna.[1]

The philosopher of the Sunnis is Al Ghazzali, and the result of his work was the complete triumph of unphilosophical orthodoxy. So utterly barren of ideas and opposed to all reason did this orthodoxy become that Sprenger sarcastically remarks concerning it: "The Moslem student marveled neither at the acuteness nor yet at the audacity of his master; he marveled rather at the wisdom of God, which could draw forth such mysterious interpretations. Theology, in fact, had now made such happy progress that *men looked on common sense as a mere human attribute—the reverse being that which was expected from Deity!*"

The Sunni sect has four orthodox schools of theology and jurisprudence, founded by the four great doctors, Abu Hanifa, Ibn Malik, As Shafi and Ibn Hanbal. These agree in essentials, but differ in their interpretation of ceremonial laws and are more or less rigid. Generally speaking, central Asia, northern India and the Turks everywhere are *Hanifite;* lower Egypt, southern India

---

[1]Ueberweg, "History of Philosophy," Vol. I, 405.

and the Malay archipelago are *Shafite;* upper Egypt and north Africa are *Malikite;* while the sect of *Hanbalites* exists only in central and eastern Arabia.   All of them agree on the Faith and Practice set forth in Chapters IV and V.

But the four schools have disputes over unimportant trivialities, such as whether one should first wash the wrist or the elbow before prayer, whether a cat can be allowed to enter a mosque, etc.   Each of these four orthodox sects has its special place of prayer around the Kaaba at Mecca.   A very mountain of voluminous literature on jurisprudence and tradition proves the literary activity of the disciples of these four orthodox fathers.   *Scribendum est* seems to have been their motto!

The Shiahs.—These are the partisans of the house of Ali and they assert that he should have been the first of the caliphs after Mohammed's death.   So great is their hatred toward the earlier caliphs that on one of their festivals three images of dough filled with honey are made to represent Abu Bekr, Omar and Othman, which are then stuck with knives and the honey is sipped as typical of the blood of the usurping caliphs!   The festival is named *Ghadir,* from the place in Arabia where their traditions say Mohammed declared Ali his rightful successor.

There are thirty-two subdivisions of the Shiah sect, and the most important are given in the table.[1]   The chief

¹TABLE OF CHIEF MOSLEM SECTS

1. THE SUNNIS, or Orthodox Sect, divided into four schools of jurisprudence, with date of the death of their founders:
    1. Hanafis, 767 A. D
    2. Shafis, 820 A. D.
    3. Malakis, 795 A D
    4. Hanbalis, 855 A. D.   From this school arose the Puritan Reformation under the Wahabis. (1787 A. D.)

point of difference between the Shiahs and Sunnis is the
doctrine of the Imamate.   This consists in the belief that
the "light of Mohammed" descended to Ali and from him
passed to the true Imams or religious leaders   The Imam
is the successor of the Prophet, he is free from all sin and
his authority is infallible.   The Imam is the Vicar of God
on earth.   There have been twelve regular Imams according to Shiah belief.   The last of the twelve Imams,
Abu el Kasim, is supposed to be still alive, though hidden
from view.   He is the *Mahdi,* or expected Guide, "who
will fill the earth with justice, even though it be covered
with tyranny."   This expected *Mahdi* has always been
the life and the hope of Moslem fanaticism and faith.
"The whole of the Shiah doctrine of the Imamate," says
Canon Sell, "seems to show that there is in the human
heart a natural desire for some Mediator—some Word of
the Father who shall reveal Him to His children.   At
first sight it would seem as if this dogma might to some
extent reconcile the thoughtful Shiah to the Christian
doctrine of the incarnation and mediation of Jesus Christ,
to His office as the perfect revealer of God's will and as
our Guide in life; but it is not so.   The mystic lore connected with Shiah doctrine has sapped the foundation of
moral life and vigor.   A system of religious reservation,
too, is a fundamental part of the system.   It thus becomes

2 THE MU'TAZILIS, the followers of Wasil-ibn'Ata (110 A H), the first
   teacher of scholastic divinity among Moslems   His method of interpretation is partly adopted by the "New Islam" of India and Egypt.
3 THE SIFATIS, who held the contrary opinions of the Mu'tazilis.
4 THE KHARIJIS, or Aliens, who revolted from Ali.
5. THE SHIAHS, or the followers of Ali, divided into:
        1. Imamis, who believe in the twelve Imams
        2 Zaidis, the followers of *Zaid* as one of the Imams.
        3. Ismailis, the followers of *Ismail.*
            "The Veiled Prophet of Khorasan" (Lalla Rookh), Babek,
            "the Old Man of the Mountains," the Assassins, and the Car-
            mathians all came from this branch.

impossible to place dependence on what a Shiah may profess, as pious frauds are legalized by his system of religion.   If he becomes a mystic, he looks upon the ceremonial and moral law as restrictions imposed by an Almighty Power.   The advent of the *Mahdi* is the good
time when all such restrictions shall be removed, when
the utmost freedom shall be allowed.   Thus the moral
'sense in many cases becomes deadened to an extent such
as those who are not in daily contact with these people can
hardly credit."[1]

The Shiahs also differ from the Sunnis in the following
points: They still possess *Mujtahids*, or enlightened doctors of the law, whose interpretation is final; they observe
the Moharram ceremonies and then have a sort of miracle-play to commemorate the death of Hassan and Husain,
the sons of Ali; they also allow *Muta'a,* or temporary
marriages, and differ in liturgical practice and in civil
law from the orthodox on many points.

"With the Shiahs extremes meet," says Mr. Wilfred
S. Blunt.   "No Moslems more readily adapt themselves
to the superficial atheisms of Europe than do the Persians,
and none are more ardently devout, as all who have wit-
nessed the miracle-play of the two Imams will be obliged
to admit.   Extremes, too, of morality are seen, fierce
asceticisms and gross licentiousness.   By no sect of Islam
is the duty of a pilgrimage more religiously observed or
the prayers and ablutions required by their rule performed with a stricter ritual.   But the very pilgrims who
go on foot to Mecca scruple not to drink wine there, and
Persian morality is everywhere a by-word."[2]

The Shiah sect does not number much over twelve mil-

<hr/>

[1] E Sell, "The Faith of Islam."
[2] "Future of Islam," quoted in Hughes' "Dictionary of Islam," 579.

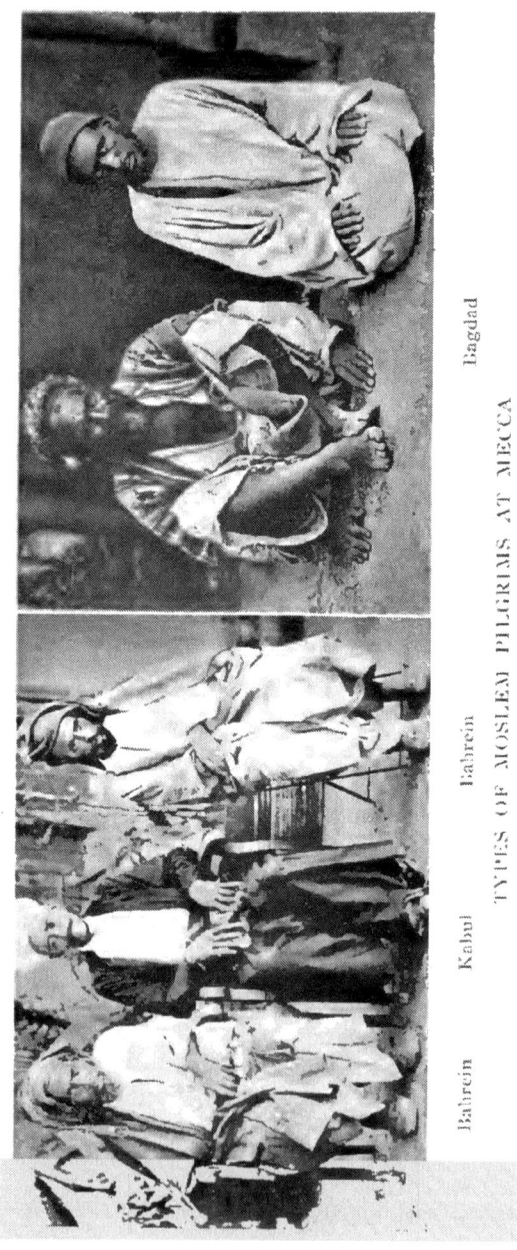

Bahrein   Kabul   Bahrein   Bagdad

TYPES OF MOSLEM PILGRIMS AT MECCA

Those from Bahrein and Bagdad belong to the Shiah sect

lion. Outside of Persia they are found chiefly in Mesopotamia and India, with a few in Syria and Afghanistan.

Other Sects.—The Ghalia sect of Shiahs exceeded all bounds in their veneration for their Imams, and raised them to deity.   The Abadiyah hold Ali alone to have been divine, and practically worship him as such.

Among the subdivisions of the Khawariji sect there are those "who believe that God is indifferent to the actions of men as if He were in a state of sleep."   Others who require a complete bath five times a day before prayer is considered legal!   Another sect holds that there is no punishment for sin, and still another holds the transmigration of souls!

The Jabariyah sect, with its twelve minor divisions, deny free-will.   Some of them say "that inasmuch as God doeth everything and everything is of God, man cannot be made responsible for either good or evil."   The many sects of Kadariyahs, on the contrary, assert free-will and some go so far as to teach "that the actions of men are of no consequence, whether they be good or evil."

All sorts of heretical sects sprang up because of speculation on the being and attributes of Allah.   Orthodox Moslems were greatly averse to the doctrine of the Incarnation, yet there was much absurd teaching about the form of Allah.   "Some went so far as to ascribe to Him all the bodily members together, with the exception of the beard and other privileges of oriental manhood."[1]   What a contrast to the wild speculations or ignorant groping for light on such topics by Moslem authors are the words of St. John: "No man hath seen God at any time; the only begotten Son, which is in the bosom of the Father, he hath declared Him."[2]   Or of Jesus Christ

[1] T. J De Boer, "Philosophy of Islam," 44.   [2] John 1 18

Himself : "The hour cometh and now is when the true worshippers shall worship the Father in spirit and in truth, for the Father seeketh such to worship Him. God is a spirit and they that worship Him must worship Him in spirit and in truth.[1]

Disintegration.—In addition to all these divisions on doctrinal and party lines Islam has suffered disintegration for centuries through pantheism, rationalism, and asceticism, which at various times and in various ways swept through all the sects alike, and exerted a powerful influence everywhere, without producing permanent reform or progress.

"Christian heresies, Greek philosophy, oriental, and Aryan mysticism made short work with the Shiah division ; and altho the Persians have furnished Islam with only ten million votaries at its most flourishing period (hardly more than one-twentieth in all), yet it has had from the earliest times more antagonizing and heretical sects than all the rest of the world of Islam put together. Mohammedan rationalism has always found its home in Persia."[2] And so also Mohammedan mysticism found its cradle in Persia, altho according to learned orientalists its ideas are mainly borrowed from Indian philosophy of the Vedanta school.

Sufism.—From the earliest days of Islam there has existed among Moslems a kind of mysticism in protest against the barren formalism of its ritual and the dead orthodoxy of its dogma. Those who followed this system were called Sufis.[3]

---

[1] John 4·23, 24

[2] H. W. Hulbert, "The Philosophical Disintegration of Islam," in *Bibliotheca Sacra,* January, 1899

[3] The word is severally derived· From *suf* (wool), because they wore a woolen garment ; or from σοφια (wisdom) ; or from *safa'* (purity).

Sufiism in the early days of Islam consisted in spending one's time in worship and fleeing the pleasures of the world. Its later development was pantheistic and speculative rather than ascetic in character.

The leading doctrines of the Sufis can be stated as follows:

1. God alone exists, and is all in all.

2. Religions are matters of indifference, altho Islam is the most advantageous for the present life.

3. There is no distinction between good and evil, as God is the real author of both.

4. Man has no real free-will.

5. The soul dwells in the body like a bird in a cage, and the sooner it is released the better.

6. Spiritual union with God is the highest good.

7. Without God's grace we cannot attain to this union, but we receive it by asking fervently.

8. The chief duty while in the body is to meditate (*Zikr*) on God's unity and His attributes (names), and so progress in the journey of life (*tarika*).[1]

Their definition of the Perfect Man (*Insan-ul-Kamil*) is very remarkable: "He should have four things in perfection: good words, good deeds, good principles, and knowledge. He should have four additional characteristics, viz., renunciation, retirement, contentment, and leisure. He who has the first four is virtuous but not free; he who has the whole eight is perfect, liberal, virtuous and free." Among the names they give to this ideal man are: Guide, Beacon, Mirror of the World, Mighty Elixir, Isa (Jesus), the Raiser of the Dead, Khizar (the Discoverer of the Water of Life), and Solo-

---

[1] Particulars of their belief in "the journey" and its various mystical stages can be found in Hughes, "Dictionary of Islam."

mon, who knew the language of the Birds! It is strange
that Mohammed's name is not mentioned.

The very essence of Sufiism is poetry, and the celebrated Masnavi, the poems of Sa'adi and the odes of
Hafiz afford Scriptures to the Moslem mystic. Yet each
of these authors contains passages unfit for publication in
English and at times advocates morals that are corrupt.
Here are some specimens of their teaching on the Divine
love and unity:

> "One knocked at the door of the Beloved, and a voice from
> within inquired, 'Who is there?' Then he answered, 'It is I.'
> And the voice said, 'This house will not hold me and thee.'
> So the door remained shut Then the Lover sped away into the
> wilderness, and fasted and prayed in solitude. And after a year
> he returned, and knocked again at the door, and the voice again
> demanded, 'Who is there?' And the Lover said, 'It is Thou.'
> Then the door was opened."

>> "Are we fools? We are God's captivity.
>> Are we wise? We are His promenade
>> Are we sleeping? We are drunk with God
>> Are we waking? Then we are His heralds.
>> Are we weeping? Then His clouds of wrath.
>> Are we laughing? Flashes of His love."

The story of the Indian convert from Islam, Dr. Imad
ud Din, as told in his autobiography, will make clear the
hopelessness of Sufi-teaching: "I sought for union with
God from travellers and fakirs, and even from the insane
people of the city, according to the tenets of the Sufi
mystics. The thought of utterly renouncing the world
then came into my mind with so much power that I left
everybody, and went out into the jungles and became a

fakir, putting on clothes covered with red ochre, and wandered here and there, from city to city, and from village to village, step by step, alone, for about 2,000 *cos* (2,500 miles), without plan or baggage.   Faith in the Mohammedan religion will never, indeed, allow true sincerity to be produced in the nature of man; yet I was then, although with many worldly motives, in search only of God. In this state I entered the city of Karuli, where a stream called Cholida flows beneath a mountain, and there I stayed to perform the *Hisb ul bahar*.   I had a book with me on the doctrines of mysticism and the practice of devotion, which I had received from my religious guide, and held more dear even than the Koran.   In my journeys I slept with it at my side at nights, and took comfort in clasping it to my heart whenever my mind was perplexed.   My religious guide had forbidden me to show this book, or to speak of its secrets to any one, for it contained the sum of everlasting happiness; and so this priceless book is even now lying useless on a shelf in my house. I took up the book, and sat down on the bank of the stream, to perform the ceremonies as they were enjoined, according to the following rules: The celebrant must first perform his ablutions on the banks of the flowing stream, and, wearing an unsewn dress, must sit in a particular manner on one knee for twelve days, and repeat the prayer called *Jugopar* thirty times every day with a loud voice.   He must not eat any food with salt, or anything at all, except some barley bread of flour, lawfully earned, which he has made with his own hands, and baked ' with wood that he has brought himself from the jungles. During the day he must fast entirely, after performing his ablutions in the river before daylight; and he must remain barefooted, wearing no shoes; nor must he touch

any man, nor, except at an appointed time, even speak to
any one.   The object of it all is that he may meet with
God, and from the longing desire to attain to this I under-
went all this pain.   In addition to the above, I wrote the
name of God on paper during this time 125,000 times,
performing a certain portion every day; and I cut out
each word separately with scissors and wrapped them up
each in a little ball of flour, and fed the fishes of the river
with them, in the way the book prescribed.   My days
were spent in this manner, and during half the night I
slept, and the remaining half I sat up, and wrote the name
of God mentally on my heart, and saw Him with the eye
of thought.   When all this toil was over, and I went
thence, I had no strength left in my body; my face was
wan and pale, and I could not even hold myself against
the wind."[1]

The Derwish Orders.—The Derwish Orders are the
direct result of Sufiism.   They are one of the most powerful factors in present-day Islam, and altho they are in
disfavor among the orthodox they have spread everywhere, and in Constantinople alone they have two hundred monasteries.   All of them are absolutely obedient to
their spiritual leaders or Sheikhs and the various orders
are bound together by secret oaths and symbolism after
the fashion of Free Masonry.   Hypnotism is used in their
initiation ceremonies, and after their initiation they are
told to be "in the hands of their superior, as the body of a
deceased person is in the hands of those that wash the
dead."

The derwish, or *fakir* (for that is his name in Arabic)
generally obtains his living by begging from door to door,

---

[1]"A Mohammedan Brought to Christ   The Autobiography of the Late
Rev. Imad-ud-Din, D D." (Church Missionary Society, London, 1900)

but this does not signify that he is poor. I remember one who came to me in Arabia in tattered garments and asked me to keep a bag of silver money for him! He had made large sums writing talismans and amulets for women and children. They wander from country to country, and it is not at all uncommon to meet derwishes from Tunis, Calcutta or Java on the streets of Bagdad and Constantinople.

There are two classes of derwishes—those who govern their conduct according to the law of Islam and those who profess to be free from the yoke of any creed, altho calling themselves Moslems.

There are thirty-two orders of derwishes founded by various leaders between A. D. 766 and A. D. 1750.[1] Their influence is widespread and everywhere opposed to Christianity and Christian governments. *The derwish orders are the tentacles of the Pan-Islamic movement,* and the Sultan of Turkey uses their leaders as spies and to work out his own ambitions.[2]

The Babis and the Beha'is.—Altho these are not Moslem sects, but arose rather in protest against some of the teaching of Islam, they yet sprang up on Moslem soil, and their opinions are closely connected with the Shiah doctrine of the Imamate. They share their mystical mode of thought and thousands of Shiahs in Persia were the first to hail the Bab as the great Deliverer.

When Abd ul Kasim, the last of the twelve Imams, disappeared in 329 A. H. he is supposed to have held intercourse through a successive number of men who were called *"Doors"* (singular=Bab). Abu el Hassan, the last of these "Doors," refused to appoint a successor.

[1] For a full account of their worship, shrines, doctrines and aim, the student is referred to the bibliography on this chapter.
[2] See R. P. Louis Petit, "Les Confréries Musulmanes."

Many centuries passed by and then, in 1826-1843, the Shaiki sect revived this belief and sought for a new Bab. He was found in the person of Mirza Ali Mohammed, who was born at Shiraz in 1820. After having studied, meditated and led an austere life until he was about twenty-four years of age, he announced himself as a duly authorized teacher and guide, and assumed the title of the Bab, declaring that whosoever wished to approach God must do it through him. Notwithstanding the opposition of a number of Mullas (priests), crowds of people, among whom there were learned men also, followed him and became his disciples. In 1848 the Shah of Persia severely persecuted the Babis and put the Bab himself to death. In 1852 an attempt was made to assassinate the Shah and a new persecution of the sect followed. But they continued to increase and spread their teachings.

After the death of the Bab, Mirza Yahya and his half-brother, Beha Ullah, became the leaders of two rival sects of Babis, viz , the Ezelis and the Beha'is. Both leaders were deported, Beha and his followers to Akka and Mirza to Famgusta, in Cyprus.

Babism and its derived sects are all a protest and a revolt against orthodox Islam, whether the "orthodoxy" of the Shiahs or the Sunnis. The whole movement in its origin, extent and present decline is indicative of the disintegration of Moslem philosophy and religion. It is the beginning of the end. Islam as an intellectual system can no longer appeal to the thoughtful. They are groping elsewhere for a Deliverer, and seeking an ideal of character higher than Mohammed. The Babis forbid the traffic in slaves, and deprecate violence in religion; they do not observe Ramazan and do not pray toward Mecca.

Concerning the Beha'is an American missionary in Persia writes: "They are not more open to the gospel than the Moslems. In fact, many consider them less so, for although they profess to accept the whole Bible, yet by their allegorical interpretation and denial of all miracles they effectually change its meaning. Having incorporated into their books some of the moral precepts of Christ and having adopted a semi-Christian vocabulary, they delight to discourse at length on love, on a tree being known by its fruits, and on kindred themes; but having left out Christ, the centre, they have missed the essential thing, and now in Persia are notorious as being religious in word rather than in deed. In fact, many of them are simply irreligious rationalists. By neither Moslem, Jew nor Christian are they considered morally superior to the Moslems, while in some respects they are rightly judged less so. They have grossly exaggerated the number of their converts, so that Moslems now say of them that the Bahai claims for a convert every man who speaks to him on the street. The outside figure for all Persia is 200,-000, with all probability that half that number is nearer the truth The one promising aspect of the movement is that it is an opening wedge making for religious liberty."[1]

The Wahabis.—The rise of this remarkable movement in Islam cannot be called the birth of a new sect. They themselves do not consider it so. It was an honest attempt to reform or renew Islam on radical lines; an endeavor to return to the golden days by setting back the hands of the clock. But, like every other attempt to reform Islam, it failed signally and piteously.

Mohammed bin Abd ul Wahab was born at Ayinah, in

[1] S. M. Jordan, in "The Mohammedan World of To-day," 129.

Nejd, in 1691. Carefully instructed by his father in the tenets of Islam according to the school of Hanbali, the strictest of the four great sects, Abd ul Wahab visited the schools of Mecca, Busrah and Bagdad, to increase his learning. At Medina, too, he absorbed the learning of the Moslem divines and soaked himself in the "six correct books" of Traditions. In his travels he had observed the laxity of faith and practice which had crept in, especially among the Turks and the Arabs of the large cities. He tried to distinguish between the essential elements of Islam and its later additions, some of which seemed to him to savor of gross idolatry and worldliness. What most offended the rigid monotheism of his philosophy was the almost universal visitation of shrines, invocation of saints, and the honor paid at the tomb of Mohammed. The use of the rosary, of jewels, silk, gold, silver, wine and tobacco, were all abominations to be eschewed. These were indications of the great need for reform. The earlier teaching of the companions of the Prophet had been set aside or overlaid by later teaching. Even the four orthodox schools had departed from the pure faith by allowing pilgrimage to Medina, by multiplying festivals and philosophizing about the nature of Allah. Therefore it was that Abd ul Wahab not only preached reform, but proclaimed himself the leader of a new *jihad*. His teaching was based on the Koran and the early traditions; his sword was found in the desert of Arabia and his followers fought, as did the companions of the Prophet, to destroy all infidels.

The movement is chiefly distinguished from the orthodox system in the following particulars:

1. The Wahabis reject *Ijma*, or the agreement of later interpreters.

2. They offer no prayer to prophet, wali, or saint, nor visit their tombs for that purpose.

3. They say Mohammed is *not yet* an intercessor; although at the last day he will be.

4. They forbid women to visit the graves of the dead.

5. They allow only four festivals.

6. They do not celebrate Mohammed's birthday.

7. They use their knuckles for prayer-counting, and not rosaries.

8. They strictly forbid the use of silk, gold, silver ornaments, tobacco, music, opium, and every luxury of the Orient, except perfume and women.

9. They have anthropomorphic ideas of God by strictly literal interpretation of the Koran texts about "His hand," "sitting," etc.

10. They believe *jihad,* or religious war, is not out of date, but incumbent on believers everywhere.

11. They condemn minarets, tombstones and everything that was not in use during the first years of Islam.

There is no doubt that Abd ul Wahab honestly tried to bring about a reform, and that in many of the points enumerated his reform was strictly a return to primitive Islam. But it was too radical to last. It took no count of modern civilization and the ten centuries that had modified the character of the city Arabs, not to speak of those outside of Arabia. It is impossible here to give even the outline of the rise of the Wahabi state, its bloody conflicts with the Arabs, the Turks and the English, and the final collapse of Wahabi empire in Arabia. The story can be read elsewhere.

The Wahabi reformation resembled the Reformation in Europe (with which it has been often compared) in only three respects. It was iconoclastic and waged war against every form of saint-worship. It acknowledged the right of private judgment and demanded a return to primitive beliefs. It was fruitful in results beyond its own horizon.

But it is very doubtful whether Blunt does not go too far when he says: "Wahabiism has produced a real desire for reform, if not reform itself, among Moslems Islam is no longer asleep, and were another and a wiser Abd ul Wahab to appear, not as a heretic, but in the body of the orthodox sect, he might play the part of a Loyola or Borromeo with success."[1]

The present intellectual, social and moral condition of the old Wahabi empire, Central Arabia, is sufficient commentary on the fact that even a Reformed Islam cannot save or elevate a people. There is no hope, for Arabia at least, in Islam. It has been tried for thirteen hundred years and signally failed. The Wahabis and their history only emphasize the fact. Nor has there been a permanent moral or social reformation of Islam in any land since the day of its origin. It is a hopeless system.

[1] In the "Future of Islam," quoted in Hughes, "Dictionary of Islam," 662.

THE PRESENT CONDITION OF THE MOSLEM WORLD

"The number of the followers of Mohammed is, I believe, still larger than that of the followers of Christ (in Protestant lands): in Europe it is steadily dwindling; in America Islam is little known; large tracts of Asia are entirely under its sway; and in Africa it is not only dominant, but shows a tendency to gain ground And if it could serve as a half-way house between paganism and Christianity, its extension might be regarded without dismay; but experience shows that there are no such half-way houses; the road from darkness to light must be unbroken, a half-way house is a bar to progress, because the force that should have lasted to the end of the journey is not there recruited, but broken and exhausted. There is this further terrible difficulty in facing Islam, that it represents itself as an advance on the Christian system."—*D. S. Margoliouth,* Laudian Professor of Arabic at Oxford.

VIII

THE PRESENT CONDITION OF THE MOSLEM WORLD

A World-wide Religion.—If we regard numbers, Islam is perhaps the mightiest of all the non-Christian religions; as regards its geographical distribution, it is the only religion beside Christianity which holds a world-empire of hearts in its grasp; and its wonderful and rapid spread proves beyond a doubt that it is a great missionary religion and aims at world-conquest. Mohammed's word has been fulfilled: "So we have made you the centre of the nations, that you should bear witness to men."[1] The old pagan pantheon at Mecca has become the religious capital and the centre of universal pilgrimage for one-seventh of the human race. Islam in its present extent embraces three continents and counts its believers from Sierra Leone, in Africa, to Canton, in China, and from Tobolsk, Siberia, to Singapore and Java. In Russia Moslems spread their prayer-carpets southward toward Mecca; at Zanzibar they look northward to the Holy City; in Khansu and Shensi, millions of Chinese Moslems pray toward the west, and in the wide Soudan they look eastward toward the Beit Allah and the Black Stone—a vast Moslem brotherhood.

[1] Surah ii, Sale's Koran, 16, note.

Arabic is the language of the Koran, but there are millions of Moslems who cannot understand a single sentence of Mohammed's book, for they speak Russian, Turkish, Persian, Pashtu, Bengali, Urdu, Chinese, Malay, Swaheli, Hausa and other languages. Around the same Kaaba diverse lands and civilization meet every year to profess one religion and repeat the same ritual. On the streets of Mecca one may see drawn together by a common faith the Turkish Effendi in Paris costume, with Constantinople etiquette; the half-naked Bedouin of the desert; the fierce Afghan mountaineer; the Russian trader from the far north, the almond-eyed Moslem from Yunnan; the Indian graduate from the Calcutta universities; Persians, Somalis, Hausas, Javanese, Soudanese, Egyptians, Berbers, Kabyles and Moors. Mecca at the time of the annual pilgrimage has a pilgrim population of about sixty thousand, and among them are representatives of every nation under heaven.[1]

Numbers.—It is manifestly impossible to obtain anything better than a careful estimate of the total Mohammedan population of the globe, for so many lands that are prevailingly Moslem have never had a census nor heard of one, and there is great uncertainty as to the total population of large districts in Africa and of the western provinces of China. On the other hand, it is needless to discredit all such statistical estimates or say with Professor Vambery: "The rumors current about the uncounted millions in the Dark Continent, in China and in Arabia deserve as much credit as the haphazard numbers of the Mohammedans of Turkey, Persia and Afghanistan; where up to the present no census has been taken and

[1] See Blunt's Table of Mecca Pilgrimage in Zwemer, "Arabia; the Cradle of Islam," 33, Hadji Khan, "With the Pilgrims to Mecca," 168, 225, 226. (John Lane: New York, 1905)

where all numerical data rest upon guesswork."[1]   The following estimates of the total Moslem population of the world at least prove that independent investigations lead to the belief that there are between two hundred and two hundred and fifty millions who are nominally Mohammedans:

"Statesman's Year Book," 1890.....................203,600,000
Brockhaus, "Convers-Lex...on," 1894................175,000,000
Hubert Jansen, "Verbreitung des Islams," 1897 259,680,672
S. M. Zwemer (*Missionary Review*), 1898...........196,491,842
Algemeine Missions Zeitschrift, 1902.. 175,290,000
H. Wichmann, in Justus Perthes' "Atlas," 1903 .... .240,000,000
William Curtis, in "Syria and Palestine," 1903..... ..300,000,000
Encyclopedia of Missions, 1904.....................193,550,000
"The Mohammedan World of To-day." (Cairo Conference, 1907)..... 232,966,170

The discrepancy in these estimates depends almost entirely on the varying estimates of the number of Moslems in the Soudan and in China.   For the rest of the world there seems to be agreement.   The most careful and detailed statistics can be found in Jansen, and the conservative results obtained in the papers prepared for the Cairo Conference are given in the accompanying table.

Geographical Distribution.—To begin with Africa, where Islam has covered the largest area in its conquest and missionary propaganda, the stronghold of Mohammedanism lies along the Mediterranean. North of twenty degrees latitude the Moslems constitute ninety-one per cent. of the total population. Thirty-six per cent. of Africa's entire population is Mohammedan, or nearly fifty-nine million souls out of the whole number, one hundred and sixty-four million. South of the equator there are already over four million Mohammedans and

[1] In an article on "Pan-Islamism," *The Nineteenth Century* for October, 1906.

in the Congo Free State there are said to be nearly two million. The situation in Africa as regards Islam is alarming, and can be summarized in the words of the Rev. Charles R. Watson, D. D.: "The missionary problem of Africa is not paganism, which fast crumbles away before the Gospel of Christ, but Islam, which resists like adamant the appeals of the herald of the cross. The Christian Church has not yet attacked this problem with the seriousness and earnestness of loving witness which the undertaking requires. When she does, her Lord will glorify His Church and Himself by crowning her efforts with success."[1] The accompanying map of Islam in Africa should be carefully studied in connection with the table of statistics. Dr. W. R. Miller, for some years a missionary in West Africa, states that "Islam seems to be spreading in Lagos, the Yoruba country, Sierra Leone, and the French Soudan; but in most of these places, as also in the Nupe country, it is of a very low order, and in the presence of a vigorous Christian propaganda it will not finally add strength to Islam. Still the number of Moslems is undoubtedly increasing rapidly. Islam and Christianity between them are spoiling heathenism and will probably divide the pagan peoples in less than fifty years."[2] But unless the Church awakes to the peril of Islam she may once more be defeated in Africa. "The spread of Islam in Africa is one of the most striking phenomena of the nineteenth century and taken in connection with the cultural revival of the Moslem world in Asia is the feature of the situation which is of the gravest import. There are three currents of Mohammedanism which are spreading in Africa,—from the Upper Nile,

[1] "The Mohammedan World of To-Day," 285.
[2] Ibid, 47.

from Zanzibar into the Congo region, and lastly up the Niger basin. Christianity, which is only a feeble plant in these regions, is likely to be overwhelmed altogether, just

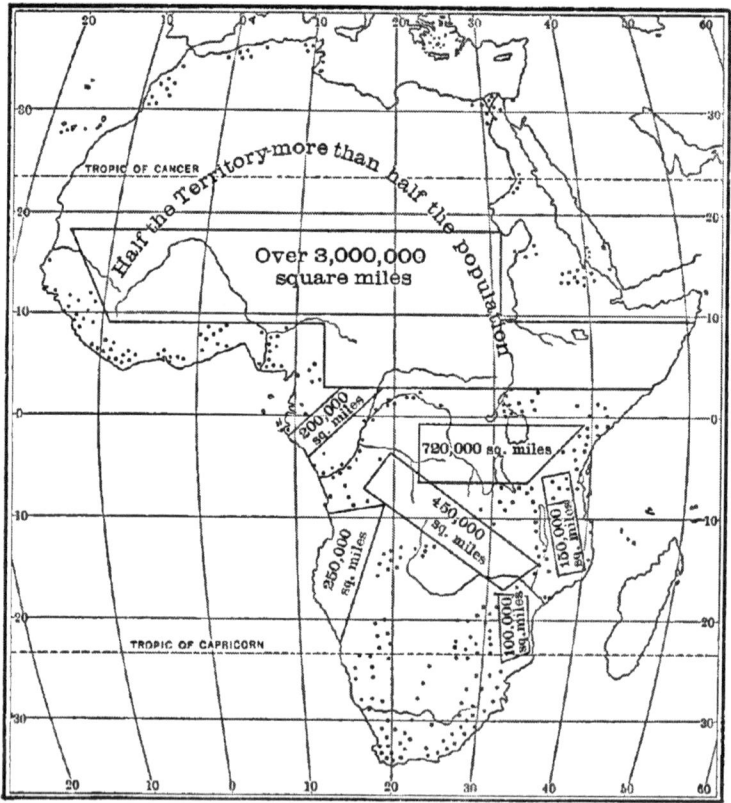

UNOCCUPIED MISSION FIELDS IN AFRICA[1]
(Dots represent mission stations)

as the flourishing North African Church was overwhelmed by the Arabs at an earlier stage of history."[2]

[1]This map was prepared by Professor Wilson S. Naylor, and appeared in *The Missionary Review of the World* for March, 1906.

[2]Archibald R. Colquhoun, in article on "Pan-Islam," *North American Review*, June, 1906, 916.

Islam in Asia and Europe.—Of the total population of
the world there are about one hundred and sixty-nine
million Moslems in Asia and about five million in Europe.
Generally speaking, one-seventh of the total population of

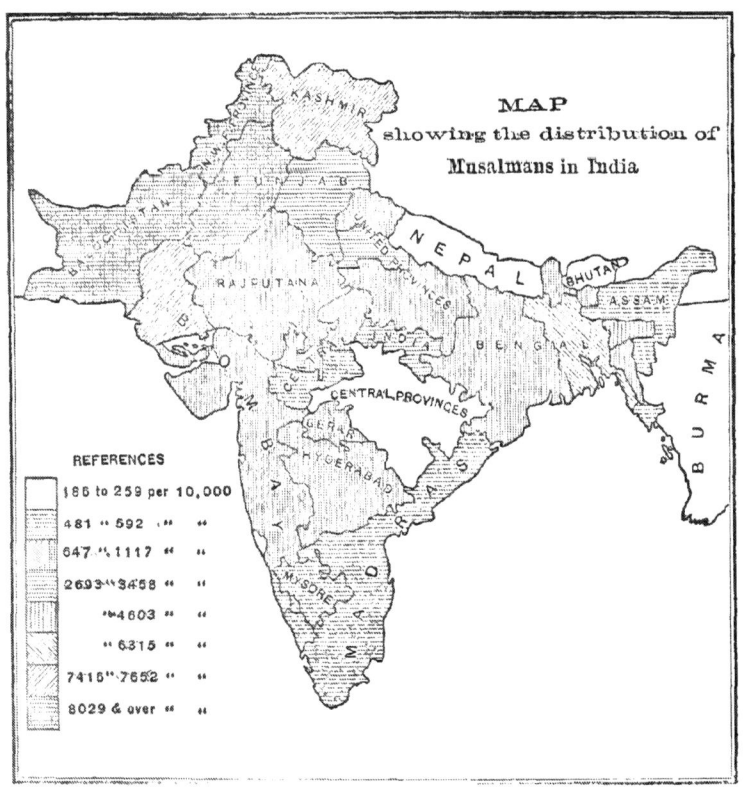

MAP SHOWING THE DISTRIBUTION OF MOSLEMS IN INDIA[1]

Asia, and of the world, is Mohammedan.   The following
countries in Asia are predominantly and some almost
wholly Moslem: Arabia, Asia Minor, Mesopotamia,
Turkestan, Bokhara, Khiva, Persia, Afghanistan, Balu-

[1]"Census of India." 1901. Vol. I., 383.

chistan, Java, Sumatra, Celebes and the Southern islands of the Philippine group.   In Syria and Armenia the non-Moslem population outnumbers that of Islam. *The chief numerical strength of the Mohammedan faith, however, is in India, which has a larger Moslem population than all Africa and far more than the total populations of Arabia, Persia, Egypt and the Turkish Empire combined.*   By the last census the number of Moslems in India is 62,458,-077.   In Bengal, including Assam, there are 27,076,643, and in the Punjaub, 12,183,345. In the Dutch East Indies there are nearly thirty million Moslems out of a total population of thirty-six millions.   The number of Moslems in China is variously given from twenty to thirty or even forty millions.[1]   The largest number is in the province of Kansu, in the extreme northwest, where 8,550,000 are reported.   Some 6,500,000 are found in Shensi, in the north, and 3,500,000 in Yunnan, in the extreme southwest.   In Peking there are 100,000 Moslems, and Canton has four mosques.

"Mohammedans in China, at least in fifteen out of the eighteen provinces, have become merged in the Chinese population and are hardly distinguishable from their neighbors.   They speak the language of the country in which they live and wear its costume; there are some physical features by which they may be differentiated, their cheek bones being generally more prominent and their noses better shaped than the majority of the Chinese, and they have a habit of clipping the mustache which the Chinese do not follow.   They do not intermarry with the Chinese, but frequently adopt native children into

[1]The latter number is far too large, but is given by Mon. E Lamairesse in his "Theologie Musulmane," viii (Carrè· Paris, 1894) "The States-man's Year Book" gives 30,000,000. The figures for India are taken from the same source (edition 1907).

their families. They make no attempt to convert their Chinese neighbors, and the religious opinions which they hold are, to a great extent, unknown to outsiders."[1]

In the Philippines there are about 300,000 Moslems; a German authority puts the number at 420,000.[2] The total number of Moslems in the Russian Empire, chiefly in Asia, is given in the "Statesman's Year Book" as 13,906,972, which equals 9.47 per cent. of the total population, while the Russian Jews number only 3.55 per cent.[3] For other lands see the map and appendix.

Distribution by Languages.—The sacred language of Islam is Arabic. Mohammed called it the language of the angels. And the Arabic Koran is to this day the text book in all Moslem schools of Turkey, Afghanistan, Java, Sumatra, New Guinea, Russia and China. Arabic is the spoken language not only of Arabia Proper, but forces the linguistic boundary of that peninsula three hundred miles north of Bagdad to Diarbekr and Mardin, and is used all over Syria, Palestine and the whole of Northern Africa. As a written language it has millions of readers in every part of the Moslem world; and yet to three-fourths of the believers Arabic is a dead language and not understood of the people. Still all public worship and all daily prayer must be in the Arabic tongue. In the Philippine Islands the first chapter of the Arabic Koran is repeated before dawn paints the sky red. The refrain is taken up in Moslem prayers at Pekin and is repeated across the whole of China. It is heard in the

[1]"The Mohammedan World of To-day" Rev. W. Gilbert Walshe, in "Islam in China," 249-264 This account conflicts, however, with that of T W Arnold, who says the Moslems form separate communities and intermarry with the Chinese See Chap. III, 70-72.

[2]Dr Ernest Faber, in *Zeitschrift des Evangelischen Protestantischen Missions Vereins.*

[3]"Statesman's Year Book" 1382 (1907.)

valleys of the Himalayas and on "The Roof of the World." A little later the Persians pronounce these Arabic words, and then across the peninsula the muezzins call the "faithful" to the same prayer. At the waters of the Nile the cry, "Allahu akbar," is again sounded forth, ever carrying the Arab speech westward across the Soudan, the Sahara and the Barbary States, until it is last heard in the mosques of Morocco and Rio de Oro. As the speech of the Moslem conquest, the influence of the Arabic language on other tongues and peoples has also been great, ever since the rise of Islam   The Persian language adopted the Arabic alphabet and a large number of Arabic words and phrases, so that, as Renan remarks,[1] in some Persian books all the words are Arabic and only the grammar remains in the vernacular   As for Hindustani, three-fourths of its vocabulary consists of Arabic words or Arabic words derived through the Persian. The Turkish language also is indebted for many words taken from the Arabic and uses the Arabic alphabet. The Malay language, through the Moslem conquest, was also touched by Arabic influence and likewise adopted its alphabet. In Africa its influence was yet more strongly felt. The language extended over all the northern half of the continent and is still growing in use to-day. The geographical nomenclature of the interior is Arabic, and Arabs preceded Livingstone, Stanley and Speke in all their journeys. The languages of the southern Soudan, the Hausa, and even those of Guinea borrowed largely from the Arabic. Europe itself did not escape the influence of the conquering Semitic tongue, as is evident in Spain and Italy. But Islam spread even more rapidly than did the language of the Koran, and in consequence

[1] Ernest Renan, "Histoire des Langues Semitiques."

the Mohammedan world of to-day is no longer of one speech, but polyglot.[1] The Mohammedans, so far from thinking, as some suppose, that the Koran is profaned by a translation, have themselves made translations, but always interlinear ones with the original text, into Persian, Urdu, Pushtu, Turkish, Javan, Malayan, and two or three other languages, but such copies of the Koran in two languages are, however, expensive and rare.

A table was prepared for the Cairo Conference, showing into which languages, spoken by Moslems as their vernaculars, the Bible has been translated in whole or in part. It shows at once the polyglot character of Islam and the splendid array of weapons prepared in God's providence for the spiritual conquest of the Moslem world.[2]

---

[1]An approximate estimate shows that 63,000,000 Moslems speak the languages of India, only 45,000,000 speak Arabic as their mother tongue; 32,-000,000 use African languages other than Arabic; 31,000,000 Moslems in China, Chinese-Turkestan and among the Chinese of Southern Asia speak Chinese, 30,000,000 the languages of the Malay Archipelago; and other millions Turkish Slavonic and Turkish, as indicated on page 166

[2]Table showing into which languages, spoken by Moslems as their vernaculars, the Bible has been translated in whole or in part.

1. Arabic whole Bible.
2. Persian whole Bible.
3. Urdu whole Bible.
4. Turkish—
   Ottoman· whole Bible
   Azarbaijani whole Bible.
   Uzbek four Gospels.
   Bashkir four Gospels.
   Jagatai: St Matthew.
   Kalmuk: New Testament.
   Karass· New Testament.
5. Pashto: whole Bible.
6. Bilochi: portions
7. Malay—
   High } portions.
   Low
8 Javanese portions.
9 Kisuaheli. whole Bible.

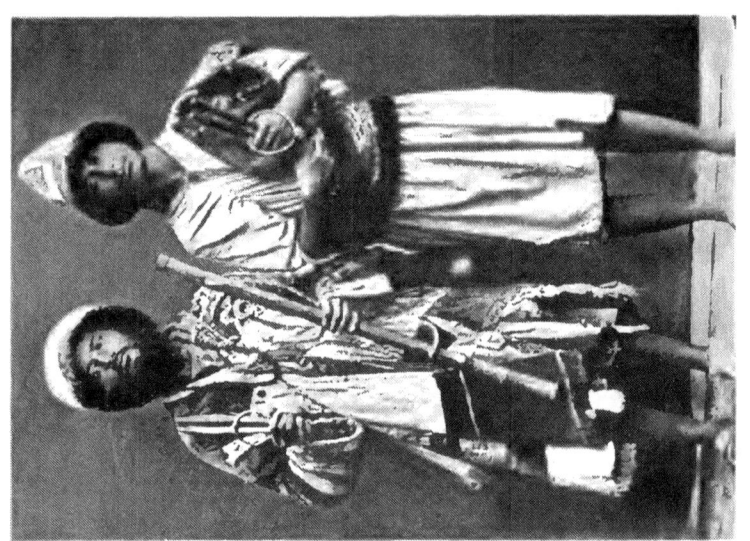

Dervishes from Bokhara

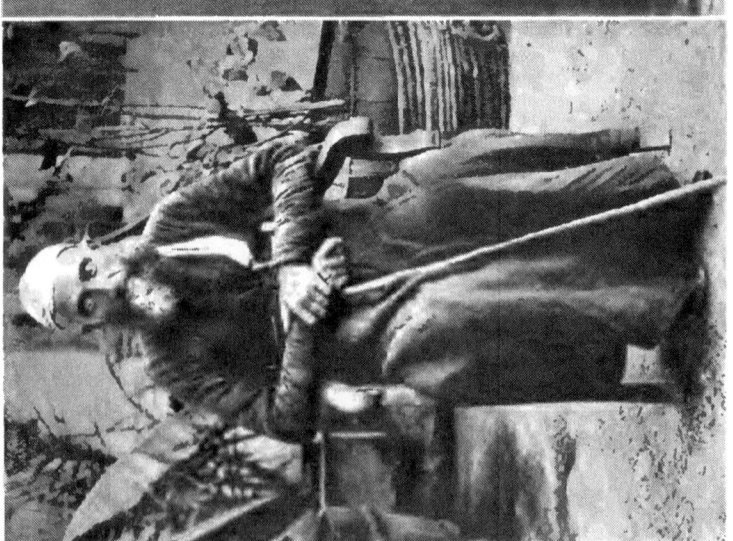

From India

The chief literary languages of Islam next to Arabic are Turkish, Persian, Urdu and Bengali. In all of these languages there is a large Moslem religious literature, dogmatic, apologetic and controversial. Even in Chinese there is a considerable amount of Mohammedan literature   Some works are published under the imprimatur of the Emperor, but a translation of the Koran is not permitted.[1]

Political Divisions.—The present political division of the Mohammedan world is a startling evidence of the finger of God in history and an unpredecented missionary challenge to the churches of Christendom. Once Moslem empire was co-extensive with Moslem faith. In 907 A. D. the Caliphate of political power included Spain, Morocco, Algiers, Tunis, Tripoli, Egypt, Asia Minor, Syria, Arabia, Persia, Turkestan, Afghanistan, Baluchistan and the region around the Caspian Sea. To-day the empire of Abdul Hamid, Caliph of all believers, has shrunk to such small proportions that it includes less than sixteen million Moslems and covers only Turkey, Asia Minor, Tripoli and one-fifth of Arabia. The following table shows the present division of the Mohammedan population of the world

10 Hausa: portions.
11 Kurdish—
     Kirmanshahi: four Gospels; also the New Testament in another dialect of Kurdish, but printed in Armenian characters.
12 Bengali (Musalmani). portions.
13. Chinese: whole Bible.
14 Ki-ganda whole Bible.
15 Berber: two Gospels
16 Kabyle New Testament.
17 Albanian New Testament.
18. Kashmiri: whole Bible (but not in Arabic character for Moslems)
19. Gujarati. whole Bible (but not in Arabic character)
20 Punjabi. Bible (parts in Arabic character and in language understood by Moslems).—"Methods of Mission Work Among Moslems," 87, 88.

[1]"The Mohammedan World of To-day " Rev. Gilbert Walshe's paper on "Islam in China," 260.

as regards governments. It was prepared prior to the Algeciras Conference, and the more recent disturbances which practically make Morocco a protected State:

MOHAMMEDAN POPULATION UNDER CHRISTIAN RULE OR PROTECTION

Great Britain in Africa	17,920,330	
Great Britain in Asia	63,633,783	
		81,554,113
France in Africa	27,849,580	
France in Asia	1,455,238	
		29,304,818
Germany in Africa		2,572,500
Italy, Portugal and Spain in Africa		722,177
The United States in Asia		300,000
The Netherlands in Asia		29,289,440
Russia in Europe and Asia		15,889,420
Other States in Europe; Greece, etc.		1,360,402
Australasia and America		68,000
Grand total		161,060,870

UNDER NON-CHRISTIAN RULERS

Africa	2,950,000
Chinese Empire[1]	30,000,000
Siam	1,000,000
Formosa	25,500
Total	33,976,500

UNDER TURKISH RULE

Europe	2,050,000
Africa	1,250,000
Asia	12,228,800
Total	15,528,800

UNDER OTHER MOSLEM RULERS

Morocco	5,600,000
Oman and Nejd, etc.	3,500,000
Afghanistan	4,500,000
Persia	8,800,000
Total	22,400,000
Grand total	71,905,300

[1]The latest estimates give 30,000,000 and not 20,000,000 for China.

STATISTICAL SURVEY OF THE MOHAMMEDAN WORLD
PREPARED FOR THE CAIRO CONFERENCE BY CHARLES R. WATSON AND SAMUEL M. ZWEMER

AFRICA	Population	Moslems
I COUNTRIES LYING NORTH OF 20° N LATITUDE		
Egypt	9 734 405	8.978 775
Tripoli	1 100 000	1 250 000
Tunis	1 900 000	1 700 000
Algeria	4 40 057	4 073 080
Morocco	6 000 000	5,000 000
Rio de Oro	130,000	130,000
Total	23 803 962	21 730 855
II COUNTRIES LYING BETWEEN THE EQUATOR AND 20° N LATITUDE		
Eretrea	274 944	102 177
French Somaliland	200 000	200,000
British Somaliland	300,000	300 000
Italian Somaliland	400 000	300,000
British E, Africa Prot	4 000 000	500 000
Uganda Protectorate	4 000 00	200 000
Abyssinia	3,500 000	350 000
Anglo Egyptian Sudan	2,000 000	1 000 000
Senegambia Niger	20,000 000	18 000,000
Rio Muni	140 000	
Kamerun	4 000 000	2 000 000
Lagos Protectorate	1 500,000	50 000
Nigeria	25 000 000	6 000 000
Dahomey	1 000 000	240 000
Togoland	1 500 000	72 500
Gold Coast Protectorate	1 486,443	35 000
Ivory Coast	2 500 000	800 000
Liberia	2 000,000	600 000
Sierra Leone	1 076 655	533 000
French Guinea	2 200 000	1,500 000
Portuguese Guinea	820 000	60 000
Gambia Protectorate	163 718	147 347
Senegal	167,828	100 000
Total	78 169 876	33,080 034

AFRICA	Population	Moslems
III COUNTRIES LYING BETWEEN THE EQUATOR AND 20° S LATITUDE		
Zanzibar Protectorate	200 000	180,000
German East Africa	6,847 000	500 000
Portuguese East Africa	3 120 000	60,000
Central African Protectorate	996 181	100,000
North East Rhodesia	346 109	
Southern Rhodesia	579 567	
North W Rhodesia	1,074 433	
Congo Independent State	25 000 000	2,000,000
French Congo	10 000 000	1 000,000
Angola	4,119 000	
Total	52 276,481	3.840 000
IV COUNTRIES SOUTH OF 20° S LATITUDE		
Transvaal Colony	1 268 710	20 000
Swaziland	85 484	1 50
Natal	1 018 787	15 000
Basutoland	348 628	
Orange River Colony	207 503	1,000
Bechuanaland	120 770	
Cape of Good Hope	2 455,352	15,000
German S W Africa	200,000	
Total	5,676,444	55 000
V ISLANDS ABOUT AFRICA		
Seychelles	20 100	52 500
Mayotte and Comoro	95,640	70 000
Madagascar	3,000 000	41 208
Mauritius	378 195	15,000
Reunion	173 312	
St Helena	9 850	
Ascension Island	450	
Fernando Po etc	21 046	
Cape Verde Islands	147 4 3	
Total	3,800 930	178 708
Total for Africa	103 736 693	58 864 087

ASIA	Population
I UNDER FOREIGN RULE BRITISH EMPIRE	
Aden Perim	11 222
Sokotra and Kuria Muria Is	12 000
Bahrein Is	60 100
British Borneo	200 000
Ceylon	3,578 333
Cyprus	237 022
Maldive Is	30 000
INDIA	
Ajmere-Merwara	476,912
Adarbans and Nicobars	24,649
Assam	6 126 113
Baluchistan	810 740
Bengal	78 493 410
Berar	2 754 019
Bombay	25,468 209
Burma	10 90 624
Central Provinces	11 873 029
Coorg	180 607
Madras	42 397 522
N W Frontier Province	2 125 480
Punjab	24 754 737
United Provinces	48 493 879
Baroda	1 052 092
Central India	8,628 781
Hyderabad	11 141 142
Kashmir	2 905 578
Mysore	5 539 399
Rajputana	9 723 301
Total for India	281 361 056
Federated Malay States (Perak etc)	678.595
Straits Settlements	572 240
Total for Asia under British Rule	
UNITED STATES OF AM	
The Philippines	7 635 420
Guam	9 100
Samoan Is	7 500
DUTCH EAST INDIES	
Java	28 746,688
Sumatra	4 188,312
Borneo	1 120,860
Celebes etc	2,955,411
Total for Dutch E Indies	36 000,000

Statesman's Year Book 19

This table shows that the balance of political power in the Mohammedan world is in the hands of England, France, Russia and the Netherlands. Each of these European powers is deeply concerned in the future of Islam, since each has more Moslem subjects than there are in the whole Turkish empire. Germany has over two and a half million Mohammedans under her flag in Africa, and she, too, is deeply concerned in the future of Islam. The total number of Mohammedans under the rule or protection of Christian powers is 161,060,870, and it does not require the gift of prophecy to see yet greater future political changes in the Levant, Arabia and Persia than have taken place in Africa during the past two decades, with the result of adding more millions to this number— and to the responsibility of Christian rulers.

Present Political Unrest.—Because of the urgent duty of *Jihad*, or warfare for the spread of Islam, the whole world came to be regarded from the days of the Caliphs, both by the propagandists of the faith and by the rulers of Moslem lands, as divided into two great portions—the *Dar-ul-Harb* and the *Dar-ul-Islam*, the territory of war and the territory of Islam. These two divisions, one of which represented the lands of infidels and darkness, the other of true believers and light, were supposed to be in a continual state of open or latent belligerency until Islam should have absorbed the lands of infidelity or made them subject. All works on Moslem law and jurisprudence treat at length of this subject and define the rights of *Zimmis*, or non-Moslem subjects, who live under a Moslem government.[1] *Islam contemplated a world-empire, political as well as spiritual.*

[1] See article "Zimmi" in Hughes, "Dictionary of Islam" Hamilton, "Hedaya," Vol. II, *passim* Shedd, "Islam and the Oriental Churches," 91-139.

But history has turned the tables, as we have seen, and three-fourths of the two hundred millions of "true believers" are now under non-Moslem rule. In proportion, therefore, as during the past century the political independence of Moslem countries was threatened or annihilated, there arose unrest, envy and open or secret rebellion against non-Moslem rule. The pilgrims meeting at Mecca from distant lands all had the same story to tell—the infidel governments were taking possession of the Mohammedan world. Fifty years ago an Arabic pamphlet was sent out by a learned theologian at Mecca, Ahmad al Barzinji al Hasaini, entitled "General Advice to the Kings and Peoples of Islam." It drew attention to the steadily increasing political power of Christian nations, to the crying wrongs and cruelties committed by them against Islam, and pointed out the only way of escape from total destruction.[1] About the year 1905 there appeared in the Cairo paper, *Ez-Zahir,* a proclamation to Indians and Egyptians to rise against England, of which the following extracts will suffice to show what Egyptian Moslems think of British rule: "It is thus that the English suck the blood of millions of Indians, and when a few years ago the cholera broke out, ravaging the country frightfully, the English, instead of using preventive measures, did nothing to stop the evil. India has become a place of pleasure-trips and sport for the Britisher. The Indian chiefs give valuable presents to the visitor, who returns richly laden to his country, parading at the same time the honesty, integrity and incorruptibility of his nation. . . . And then was it not the English Government which appointed Warren Hastings, a most ignorant, corrupt and tyrannical fellow, as ruler over the

[1] *The Nineteenth Century,* October, 1906, 548.

whole of India?   It was only after numberless complaints
of crying injustices had reached the Central Government
that he was dismissed from office.   Well, such is the
manner of acting of the famous, just, civilized and mod-
erate English.   Happily their policy of infinite treachery
and ruse is beginning to burst, and the time of revenge
against these insolent, overbearing and haughty oppres-
sors has arrived at last.   The elongated shadow of the
afternoon sun of their power will soon disappear.   When
His Majesty the King of England, in a speech from the
throne, said: 'We shall accord liberty and independence
to the people of the Transvaal, in order to facilitate their
progress and to secure their attachment to the Crown,'
the people of India may well ask, 'Why are similar concessions not accorded to India, or are the Indians less
capable and less gifted than the South Africans?'   And,
further, if the English avail themselves of such pretexts,
who is the cause of our having remained behind—we, the
quiet and obedient people, or the so-called disinterested,
magnanimous teacher?

"It is all useless to misrepresent facts, for it is patent
that there is no difference between India of to-day and
between India of the middle ages, and all high-sounding
statements about our great strides in civilization is but
grandiloquent, empty talk.   Nobody can deny that the
Indians were formerly the great owners of Central Asia;
their culture was predominant, and some of their towns
became the centre of learning and knowledge, from which
it had spread to the most distant parts of the world. Until
quite recently nobody knew scarcely anything about
Japan; but unity, coupled with the firm and resolute intention of a handful of men, has produced extraordinary
results and vanquished the once much-dreaded power of

the North. Afraid of this wonderful success, proud and haughty Albion had to condescend and to seek the friendship and alliance of Japan, which occupies to-day a foremost rank amongst the great nations of the world, whereas India, having passed one hundred and fifty years under foreign rule, is still in need of instruction and education. This is what we know as the result of British rule in India. Are we not entitled to ask what will become of Egypt under the rule of the same power ; of Egypt, known as the Beauty of the East, the trade centre of the world, and the Lord of the Seas; of Egypt, whose export has lately risen to a height never attained by India? We consequently ask: Has the time not come yet when, uniting the suppressed wailings of India with our own groans and sighs in Egypt, we should say to each other, 'Come and let us be one, following the divine words, Victory belongs to the united forces'?"[1]

The former French Minister of the Interior, M. G. Hanotaux, in a series of articles in the *Journal de Paris,* 1906, spoke of the political menace of Islam in Algiers and the French Soudan as a constant peril not only to French rule, but to Christian civilization. "Dangerous firebrands of discontent are ever smouldering under the resigned surface of these conquered races, which have been often defeated but never discouraged. The religious orders of Islam, failing a political leader for the present, are yet keeping their powder dry for the day of the great slaughter and the great victory."[2]

The same spirit of unrest obtains in Java and Sumatra, where Dutch rule, altho so favorable to Islam, seems to

[1] Quoted in full in Professor A. Vambery's article in *The Nineteenth Century,* October, 1906

[2] A synopsis of these important articles appeared in *Der Soudan Pionier,* Wiesbaden, February, 1907.

gall their pride and awaken their desire for autonomy. The editor of the official organ of the Barmen Mission, which has had so much success among the Mohammedans in Sumatra, wrote a few years ago: "We have often been forced to observe that the whole Mohammedan world is connected by secret threads, and that a defeat which Islam suffers in any part of the world, or a triumph which she can claim, either real or fictitious, has its reflex action even on the work of our missionaries in the Mohammedan part of Sumatra. Thus the recent massacres in Armenia have filled the Mohammedans in this part of Sumatra with pride. They say to the Christians: 'You see now that the Raja of Stamboul (that is, the Sultan of Constantinople) is the one whom none can withstand; and he will soon come and set Sumatra free, and then we shall do with the Christians as the Turks did with the Armenians.' And it is a fact that a considerable number of Mohammedans who were receiving instruction as candidates for baptism have gone back since the receipt of this news." A mass meeting of Indian Moslems, attended by over four thousand persons, was held in Calcutta on May 20, 1906, to protest against the action of the British Government in the matter of the Egyptian boundary dispute, and in the resolution passed "the Mohammedans of Calcutta express profound regret and dissatisfaction at the unhappy policy which has culminated in strained relations between His Imperial Majesty, the Sultan of Turkey, the spiritual head of millions of Mohammedans, and the British Government."[1]

This attitude of Moslems to-day toward Christian governments is sometimes a real danger to their civilizing

[1]Correspondence, *The New York Sun*, June 20, 1906

efforts, but is more often used by Moslems themselves as a scarecrow for political purposes. And then, through fear of Moslem fanaticism, real or invented, the Christian powers of Europe grant Islam favors and prestige in Asia and Africa which strict neutrality in matters of religion would never countenance and which are not shown to the Christian faith. Here are some striking examples of this short-sighted and un-Christian policy. In West Africa the British Government has become involved "in backing up Islam politically and inevitably religiously also. Repairing broken-down mosques, by order, subscriptions to Mohammedan feasts, forcible circumcision of heathen soldiers on enlistment, etc., etc., are some of the ways in which the general trend is indicated."[1] The British Government, while professing to be neutral, hampers Christian missions, but allows Islam freedom to proselytize. In Egypt the British Government is especially favorable to Mohammedan interests and pays undue respect to Moslem prejudices at the expense of Christians. There are glaring instances of injustice against Christians in the courts which, for example, are also open on Sundays and closed on Fridays.[2] When the Sacred Kiswa, or covering for the Kaaba at Mecca, leaves Cairo, or returns, I was told that British soldiers, as well as native infantry, are drawn up to salute it. And at the Gordon Memorial College, Khartoum, the Bible has no place, but the Koran is a required text book, and Friday is the weekly holiday. If Moslems could be won over to loyalty by such favors and favoritism, surely Java and Sumatra would be an example. The contrary is the case. "The idea of some colonial rulers that

[1]"The Mohammedan World of To-day," 46, 47.
[2]Ibid, 29, 30.

EGYPTIAN SOLDIERS ESCORTING THE MAHMAL

The picture shows some of the Moslem people at the of Cairo at the Procession of the Mahmal on trimortar camel litter, which accompanies the Kiswah, or sacred covering of the Kaaba, sent annually from Egypt.

Mohammedans can be won over to loyalty in a peaceful way has been clearly disproved in Achin. In order to please the Moslems, a splendid mosque was built in Achin by the Dutch Government, but very few Achinese ever come to it."[1] The present attitude of the Dutch Colonial Government has wisely been entirely changed. Christianity now finds protection and Islam no unfair favors. "Christian chiefs are given a share in judicial administration, so as to counteract the oppression of the Moslems, and Christian missions desiring to begin work in territories still pagan or threatened with Mohammedan propaganda are assisted by the government."[2]

Social Condition of Moslem Lands.—The present social and moral condition of Mohammedan lands and of Moslems in all lands is not such as it is in spite of, but because of, their religion. The law of cause and effect has operated for over a thousand years under every possible natural and political environment, among Semites, Negroes, Aryan races and Slavs. *The results are so sadly similar that they form a terrible and unanswerable indictment of the social and moral weakness of Islam* There is no better proof of the inadequacy of the religion of Mohammed than a study of the present intellectual, social and moral condition of Arabia. Cradled at Mecca, fostered at Medina, and reformed in the Nejd, Islam has had undisputed possession of the entire peninsula for almost thirteen centuries. In other lands, such as Syria and Egypt, it remained in contact with a more or less corrupt form of Christianity, or, as in India and in China, in conflict with cultured heathenism, and there is no doubt that in both cases there were and are mutual concessions and

[1]"The Mohammedan World of To-day," 212.
[2]Ibid., 225.

influences. But in its native Arabian soil the tree planted by the Prophet has grown with wild freedom and brought forth fruit after its kind. As regards morality, Arabia is on a low plane. Slavery and concubinage exist everywhere; while polygamy and divorce are fearfully common. Fatalism, the philosophy of the masses, has paralyzed progress, and injustice is stoically accepted. Bribery is too common to be a crime, lying is a fine art and robbery has been reduced to a science. Doughty and Palgrave, who both crossed the heart of the peninsula, have given it as their verdict that there is no hope for Arabia in Islam. It has been tried zealously for, thirteen hundred years and piteously failed.

Arabia is only typical of other Moslem lands. Social and moral conditions are no better in Persia, Afghanistan, Baluchistan, Tripoli or Morocco. The holy cities of Persia are hot-beds of immorality.[1] Polygamy and divorce are common. Marriage often takes place when the girl is seven or nine years of age, in accordance with Mohammed's example in the case of Ayesha.[1] The low moral condition of Baluchistan and Afghanistan is indescribable. Girls are put up at auction and sold to the highest bidder, while compensation for blood is often ordered paid in yet unborn female children.[2]

In the Kelat State the vilest orgies are enacted at the court of the Khan, and among the Baluchis immorality is so common among the Moslem clergy that syphilis is spoken of as the Mullah's disease.[3] One who has been a missionary for years in India testifies: "However the phenomenon may be accounted for, we, after mixing with

[1] Dr. W. St. Clair Tisdall, in "The Mohammedan World of To-day," 117.
[2] A Duncan Dixey, in Ibid., 141.
[3] "The Mohammedan World of To-day," 139, 140.

Hindus and Mohammedans for nineteen years back, have no hesitation in saying that the latter are as a whole some degrees lower in the social and moral scale than the former."[1]

Polygamy has not diminished licentiousness in any Moslem land, but everywhere increased it. "Immorality among African Mohammedans is commonly indescribable. It is worse among the Arabs of the intensely Mohammedan countries to the north than it is among the Negro races to the south."[2]

And to complete the picture of social Islam in the twentieth century, here is a sketch of the slave-market at Mecca—this open slave-market is within a stone's throw of "the house of God," at the centre of the Moslem world: "Go there and see for yourself the condition of the human chattels you purchase. You will find them, thanks to the vigilance of British cruisers, less numerous and consequently more expensive than they were in former years; but there they are, flung pell-mell in the open square. . . . The dealer, standing by, cried out: 'Come and buy; the first-fruits of the season, delicate, fresh and green; come and buy, strong and useful, faithful and honest. Come and buy.' The day of sacrifice was past and the richer pilgrims in their brightest robes gathered around. One among them singled out the girl. They entered a booth together. The mother was left behind. One word she uttered, or was it a moan of inarticulate grief? Soon after the girl came back. And the dealer, when the bargain was over, said to the purchaser: 'I sell you this property of mine, the female slave, Narcis-

<hr />

[1] J. Vaughan, in Jessup, "Mohammedan Missionary Problem," 47. The same testimony is given by other missionaries in Bengal and the Punjaub. See also Dennis, "Christian Missions and Social Progress," Vol. I, 91.

[2] Charles R. Watson, in "The Mohammedan World of To-day," 284.

sus, for the sum of forty pounds.' Thus the bargain was clinched. . . . Men slaves could be bought for sums varying from fifteen pounds to forty pounds. The children in arms were sold with their mothers, an act of mercy; but those that could feed themselves had to take their chance. More often than not they were separated from their mothers, which gave rise to scenes which many a sympathetic pilgrim would willingly forget if he could."[1]

Illiteracy.—The illiteracy of the Mohammedan world to-day is as surprising as it is appalling. One would think that a religion which almost worships its Sacred Book, and which was once mistress of science and literature, would in its onward sweep have enlightened the nations. But facts are stubborn things. Careful investigations show that seventy-five to one hundred per cent. of the Moslems in Africa are unable to read or write. In Tripoli ninety per cent. are illiterate; in Egypt, eighty-eight per cent.; in Algiers, over ninety per cent.[2] In Turkey conditions have greatly improved and illiteracy is not above forty per cent., while of women it is estimated as under sixty per cent. Among the Kurds and Circassians illiteracy is more prevalent.[3] In Arabia there has been scant intellectual progress since "the Time of Ignorance," before Mohammed, when the tribes used to gather at Okatz to compete in poetry and eloquence. The Bedouins are nearly all illiterate, and in spite of the Wahabi revival and the attempt of Turkish officials to open schools, there is little that deserves the name of edu-

[1] Hadji Khan, "With the Pilgrims to Mecca   The Great Pilgrimage of A H 1319" (A. D 1902), 306 308
[2] "The Mohammedan World of To-day," 284, and Statistical Tables also, 33
[3] "Anatolicus" in article on "Islam in Turkey," in "The Mohammedan World of To day," 57.

MOSLEM DAY SCHOOL, TUNIS

cation, even in the large towns.[1] The system of education at Mecca is typical of that in all Moslem lands not
yet influenced by Western civilization and governments.
The youth learn to read the Koran, not to understand its
meaning, but to drone it out professionally at funerals
and feasts, so many chapters for so many shekels. Modern science or history are not even mentioned, much less
taught, at even the high-schools of Mecca. Grammar,
prosody, caligraphy, Arabian history and the first elements of arithmetic, but chiefly the Koran commentaries
and traditions, traditions, traditions, form the curriculum
of the Mohammedan college. Those who desire a post-
graduate   course   devote   themselves   to   mysticism
(Tassawaf), or join an order of Derwishes, all of whom
have their representative sheikhs at Mecca. The method
of teaching in the schools of Mecca, which can be taken
as an example of the best that Arabia affords, is as follows.[2] The child of intellectual promise is first thought
his alphabet from a small wooden board on which they
are written by the teacher; slates are unknown. Then he
learns the Abjad or numerical value of each letter—a useless proceeding at present, as the Arabic notation, originally from India, is everywhere in use. After this he
learns to write down the ninety-nine names of Allah and
to read the first chapter of the Koran; then he attacks the
last two chapters, because they are short. The teacher
next urges him through the book, making the pupil read
at the top of his voice. The greatest strictness is observed as to pronunciation and pauses, but nothing whatever is said to explain the meaning of the words. Having thus finished the Koran, that is, read it through once,

[1]"The Mohammedan World of To-day," 109
[2]S. M Zwemer, "Arabia, the Cradle of Islam," 43, 44; and Snouck Hurgronje, "Mekka," Vol. II, *passim.*

the pupil takes up the elements of grammar, learning rules by rote, both of *sarf* (inflection) and *nahw* (syntax). Then follow the liberal sciences, *al-mantik* (logic), *al-hisab* (arithmetic), *al-jabr* (algebra), *al-ma'ana wa'l beyan* (rhetoric and versification), *al-fikh* (jurisprudence), *al-akaid* (scholastic theology), *at-tafsir* (exegetics) *ilm-nl-usul* (science of the sources of Koran interpretation), and lastly the very capstone of education, *al-ahadith* (Traditions). What that capstone includes we have seen in the chapter on the Faith and Practice of Islam. And in all this again Mecca is a typical city.

Persia now has a constitution, but it has no national system of education, and ninety per cent. of the population are illiterate.[1] In Baluchistan, according to the British census, only 117 per 1000 of the Mohammedan men and only 23 per 1000 among the women can read.[2] But the most surprising, and at the same time the most accurate, statistics of illiteracy are those of India. *According to the last census, the total of illiterates among the 62,458,077 Mohammedans of India is the enormous figure of 59,674,499, or about 96 per cent.!*[3] Such widespread illiteracy in all lands, and especially prevalent among Moslem women, results in every sort of superstition in the home-life and among the lower and middle classes. Even among the leaders of these blind, intellectually, modern science is despised or feared, and everything turns, on the Ptolemaic system, round the little world of the Koran. Jinn are exorcised; witches and the evileye avoided by amulets and talismans; alchemy and as-

[1]"The Mohammedan World of To-day," 118. Table, 295.
[2]Ibid., 137.
[3]The percentage of literates is given in the census as 3.27 per cent. "The Mohammedan World of To-day," 162. Table, 294.

trology are studied and patronized; and pagan practices often flourish on the soil of Moslem bigotry.[1] It is a dark world.

The Intellectual Awakening.—It has always proved impossible to put the new wine of free thought and education into the old wine-skins of Moslem orthodoxy. The history of Moslem dogma proves it. And therefore the recent intellectual awakening of those relatively few Moslems who received a liberal education in Syria, Egypt, India or Algiers, whether in government or mission schools, or of those who became enamored of Western civilization, was inevitably an intellectual revolt against the old Islam. This clash of modern life and thought with the medievalism of Al Ghazzali gave birth to the New Islam. Though called by different names in India, the Levant and Egypt, the cause and effect of the movement are the same. The leadership and initiative of the New Islam in India belong to Sir Saiyad Ahmed Khan of Aligarh. After a period of government service and visit to England in 1870, he began by editing a journal called *Tahzib ul Akhlak,* or *The Reform of Morals.* In 1878 he started an Anglo-Mohammedan College at Aligarh, which has since, through gifts of educated Moslems and government assistance, become the Mohammedan University for all India. In 1886 he began an Annual Educational Conference for the Mohammedans of India. Sir Saiyad Ahmed also wrote a Commentary on the Bible, which has doubtless helped to bring some educated Moslems to a more intelligent view of the real character and integrity of the Christian Scriptures. But the attempt to rationalize Islam and give it new life by a broad

[1]See Indian Census Reports of Bengal, "The Mohammedan World of To-day," 72, 89, 219, etc.; Hughes, "Dictionary of Islam," *Exorcism* and *Jinn;* and "Our Moslem Sisters," *passim.*

interpretation of its theology, has failed.   Competent observers in India state that "the movement has practically
lapsed into a sort of social and political reform," and that
"just at present there is a marked indication, even among
educated Moslems, mainly to drift back to the old school
of thought."[1]   The hands of the clock are put back to
midnight, altho it strikes the hour of dawn.

The institution at Aligarh, however, now contains 340
students in the college department and 364 in the preparatory school; of these eighty-eight are Hindu students and the rest Mohammedans.   But the tone of the
college is agnostic rather than Moslem and secular rather
than religious.   This was the testimony given me by the
two resident professors of Moslem theology when I visited the college in 1902, and was also my own impression
after meeting the students.

In Egypt also there is an intellectual awakening on the
part of many educated Moslems.   The late liberal-mind-
ed Mufti at Cairo attempted to reform Islam and depre-
cated the ignorance and bigotry of his co-religionists.   He
tried to bring order out of chaos in the Azhar University,
both in its material affairs and its method of instruction.
A great impetus was given to education through his efforts.   Book and tract societies were started.   He even
attempted to reform the Moslem courts of law, which are
notoriously corrupt.   But whether the measures he
initiated will be fruitful of permanent result is very
doubtful.[2]

Yet the printing-press is carrying these messages of
reform and preaching a New Islam wherever Moslem
journals of this type find readers.   And wherever Mos-

---

[1] "The New Islam," in "The Mohammedan World of To-day," 187-204.
[2] Andrew Watson, in Ibid., 32, 33.

THE MARKET PLACE OF BAMUM (KAMERUN), WEST AFRICA

This town has a population of 12,000. On the right is the mosque built for the Hausas by the still heathen King of Bamum.

lems come into touch with the non-Moslem world of the West in its politics and commerce, or through Christian missions, there follows the inevitable conflict between the old and the new in the minds of those who dare to think for themselves. Dr. William A. Shedd points out that Islam to-day must meet a new crisis in its history. "It is coming into close contact with modern thought and civilization. It must meet these changed conditions if it is to live, and the question arises whether it can do this or not. History shows that Islam is capable of great things and of flourishing under very varied conditions. It also shows that it has received into its system from the very beginning elements from outside, and it is reasonable to suppose that this process may go on. . . . However, the elements which have entered Islam from outside in the past have not been assimilated. This inability of Islam to assimilate the elements received into it has been made the reason for denying to it the claim to be a universal religion and the argument seems to be thoroughly valid."[1]

That the Mohammedans themselves are conscious of this crisis in their religious outlook is evident from the press and the platform wherever these two blessings of a Christian civilization obtain in the Mohammedan world. The following words, spoken by Mustapha Pasha Kamil of Egypt (whom Professor Vambery calls "the actual leader of the anti-English movement on the Nile") before the Pan-Islamic Society at the Criterion Restaurant, London, in July, 1906, are an illustration: "Tell the people who live the life of animals and are led like dumb driven cattle, Awake! and realize the true significance of life.

[1] Kuenen-Hibbert Lectures (1882), "Natural Religions and Universal Religions," Lecture I. Quoted in Shedd, "Islam and the Oriental Churches," 87.

Fill the earth and adorn it with results of your labors. Gentlemen, you alone can make them understand the full meaning of life ; nay, you alone can give them life. Hasten. therefore, with your medicine. O physicians, the patient is in a critical state, and delay spells death. The malady of the Moslem nations is twofold. One I have already alluded to, the other is the absurd belief of millions of people that devotion to Islam is incompatible with progress and enlightenment. They say that our death is more profitable to mankind than our life. The contemplation of this fills the heart of every educated Moslem and every cultured Oriental with sorrow. It is no use referring them to the glorious pages of our past history. It is no use pointing out to them that we owe allegiance to a liberal faith, which enjoins upon us the search of knowledge from the cradle to the grave. Our decline and fall and present degradation is living proof contradicting your assertion. You must prove it by deeds and not by mere words. The march of events and vicissitudes in the world has proved that the strong current of science and knowledge, alone can give us life and sovereign power. Those who march with the current arrive at the harbor of salvation. Those who go against it are doomed."

Will it be possible "to march with the current" and continue to hold the teaching of the Koran and the Traditions? The present condition of the Mohammedan world answers that question emphatically in the negative. And will "marching with the current of science and knowledge" after all ever give the weary, sinful, sorrowing millions of Islam spiritual peace or lift Mohammedan womanhood and manhood out of their degradation into the glorious inheritance of the Sons of God?

MISSIONS TO MOSLEMS

"Sive ergo Mahometicus error hæretico nomine deturpetur; sive gentili aut pagano infametur; agendum contra eum est, scribendum est." . . .

"Aggredior vos, non ut nostri sæpe faciunt armis, sed verbis, non vi sed ratione, non odio sed amore."—*Petrus Venerabilis,* 1157 A. D.

"The time has come for the Church of Christ seriously to consider her duty to this large fraction of our race It is not to be supposed that a church guided and inspired by an Almighty Leader will neglect a duty simply because it is difficult and calls for faith and fortitude. It is especially foreign to the spirit of American Christianity to slight a task because it is hard, or ignore a question of moral reform or religious responsibility because it looks formidable."—*Rev. James S. Dennis, D. D.*

IX

MISSIONS TO MOSLEMS

A Neglected Problem.—Islam dates from the year 622
A. D. The first missionary to the Mohammedans in the
annals of the Christian Church was Raymund Lull, who
was dragged outside the town of Bugia and stoned to
death on June 30, 1315. Before the time of Lull there
was little organized missionary effort in the Church East
or West to preach Christ to the Moslem nations. And as
far as we know, Lull had no successors, with his spirit,
until Henry Martyn's day. Had the spirit of Raymund
Lull filled the Church throughout those long centuries of
neglect, we would not now speak of more than two hundred million unevangelized Moslems.

At first the terror of the Saracen and the Turk smoth-
ered in every heart even the desire to carry them the
Gospel. And when Christendom in Europe recovered
from the shock of the Saracen invasion and that of the
Turks, its first impulse was to take the sword and by the
sword its hosts of Crusaders perished. The Crusades
were the reply of Christendom to the challenge of Islam,
but the reply was not in the spirit of the gospel. It was
Raymund Lull who wrote: "I see many knights going
to the Holy Land beyond the seas, and thinking that they
can acquire it by force of arms; but in the end all are
destroyed before they attain that which they think to

have. Whence it seems to me that the conquest of the Holy Land ought not to be attempted except in the way in which Thou and Thine apostles acquired it, namely, by love and prayers and the pouring out of tears and blood."[1] But his was a voice crying in the wilderness.

Even in the sixteenth century, devoted as were the Roman Catholic missionaries who then went forth to the pagan world, there was little to attract and less to welcome in lands under Moslem rule the men who instituted the inquisition at Goa and intrigued for political power in China and Japan.

When the modern missionary revival began in Protestant Christendom with Carey, the idea was to carry the Gospel to the *heathen* and the Mohammedans were neglected. It is true that there has been the work of illustrious pioneers, and wherever Protestant missions came in contact with Islam, whether laboring for the reformation of the Oriental churches or in heathen lands, a great work of preparation has been accomplished. But the fact remains that no part of the non-Christian world has been so long and so widely neglected as Islam. The task has either appeared so formidable, the obstacles so great or faith has been so weak that one might suppose the Church thought her great commission to evangelize the world did not apply to Mohammedans. There are to-day eighty-eight societies organized for the conversion of the Jews; but no great missionary society has yet been organized to convert Mohammedans and scarcely a dozen missions are professedly working directly among and for Moslems.[2] Many of those who write on world-wide missions or on countries where Islam is widely prevalent ig-

[1] Quoted by S. M Zwemer in "Raymund Lull," 52.
[2] Bliss, "Encyclopedia of Missions," 496, 846, 847. (Edition 1904.)

nore the Mohammedan population. Dr. Jones calls his admirable book on India, for example, "India's Problem, Krishna or Christ," and there are not two pages in the whole book on Mohammedanism, while *one-fifth* of India's population is Moslem.[1] Dr. Gustav Warneck, the missionary expert of Germany, does not include missions to Moslems in his plan for evangelization; and in a recent sumptuous volume of six hundred pages, published in Germany, on the history of Protestant missions, work for Moslems is dismissed in a single paragraph and labeled hopeless.[2]

Early Attitude of the Church.—The reason for this neglect was on the one hand the attitude of the Church toward Islam and on the other that of Islam toward the Church. "Christendom," says Keller, "accustomed itself ever since the time of the Crusades to look upon Islam as its most bitter foe and not as a prodigal son to be won back to the Father's house."[3] Centuries before the Crusades, Islam was considered a scourge of God for the sins and divisions of the Church, each party considering the Saracens as God's special avenger on their rivals.[4] There was also the greatest ignorance of the real character of Islam, and the Councils of the Church were so busy with minor matters of the faith that they ignored this gigantic heresy which was sweeping over the lands once Christian.

And there was mutual hatred. "Marvel not," wrote Marco Polo, "that the Saracens hate the Christians; for

[1] Robert E. Speer, in "The Mohammedan World of To-day," 270.

[2] Reinbold Gareis, "Geschichte der Evangelische Heidenmission" (Constance, 1901) Eleven maps and over 300 illustrations; yet see page 320 on "Islam"

[3] A. Keller, "Geisteskampf des Christentums gegen Islam bis zur zeit der Kreuzzüge" (Leipsic, 1896.)

[4] Ibid., 12.

the accursed law which Mohammed gave them commands
them to do all the mischief in their power to all other
descriptions of people and especially to Christians; to
strip such of their goods and do them all manner of evil.
In such fashion the Saracens act throughout the world."[1]
Dante voices the common opinion of the West in his day
when he puts Mohammed in the deepest hell of his Inferno and describes his fate in such dreadful language as
offends polite ears.[2] Alanus de Insulis (1114-1200)
wrote a book on Islam, in which he classes Moslems with
the Jews and Waldenses! Western Europe, according
to Keller, was for a long time ignorant even of the century in which Mohammed was born, and Hildebert, the
Archbishop of Tours, wrote a poem on Mohammed in
which he is represented as an apostate from the Orthodox
Church, and which contains these lines:

> "Plus nocet ut nostis ad cuncta domesticus hostis
> Et res ipsa docet qualiter ille nocet."

The poem closes with the words:

> "Musa manum teneat et Mahumet pereat."[3]

Such efforts surely would not arouse a missionary spirit
on behalf of Moslems!

John Damascenus and Petrus Venerabilis.—These two
names are worthy of remembrance in the history of missions to Moslems, not because they were missionaries,
but because they first studied Islam with sympathy and
employed spiritual weapons in defence of the faith against
Moslems. They were the first to take up the pen against

[1]"Marco Polo's Travels." Colonel Yule's edition, Vol. I, 69
[2]Cary's edition of Dante's "Divina Comedia," Hell, canto XXVIII, 20-39.
[3]A Keller, "Geisteskampf des Christentums gegen den Islam," 39, 40.

the sword, and with Al Kindi[1] led the long list of Christian apologists in the Mohammedan controversy throughout the centuries that followed. John of Damascus was by far the ablest theologian of the eighth century and lived in Palestine under the protection of the Saracens to escape the vengeance of the Byzantine Emperor, whom he opposed in a controversy about the worship of images. He died at Jerusalem in 760 A. D. For a considerable time he was employed in the service of the Saracens and known by the Arabic cognomen, Mansur.[2] Among his less known works is one entitled *De Haeresibus*, which, among other tractates, contains a dispute between a Moslem and a Christian. "This treatise," says Keller, who gives interesting extracts from it, "was the armory for all future controversial writings against Islam in the Eastern Church." John of Damascus shows his acquaintance with the Koran text and with the early Moslem traditions in regard to its interpretation. He admits the truths of Mohammed's teaching, points out its errors and also the blots on Mohammed's character. The dialogue is evidently intended to instruct Christians how to give "an answer for the hope that is in them."

Petrus Venerabilis, whose pregnant words at the head of this chapter show his missionary spirit, belonged to the Benedictine order of monks, and was Abbot of Clugny in the twelfth century, his death occurring in 1157 A. D. He was distinguished for his learning, liberality and kindly spirit, and was the first to translate the Koran into a language of Europe, the Latin, and to study Islam with sympathy and scholarship. He made a plea for the translation of portions of Scripture into the language of

[1] Sir William Muir, "Apology of Al Kindy", translated from the Arabic second edition, 1887. See Table opposite page 214.
[2] Kurtz, "Church History," Vol. I, 2(5.

the Saracens and in this respect antedated Henry Martyn by seven centuries.   This early champion of the Church wrote two remarkable books against Mohammedanism which have recently appeared in a German translation.[1] In them he treats at length and with keen insight two main topics, the divine character of the Koran and the question whether Mohammed was a prophet.   He shows that the Koran testifies against itself and that we admit the weakness of our Christianity *by not defending it against Mohammedan attacks and winning Moslems by our proof of its truth.*   He carefully distinguishes the true and the false in the teaching of Islam and even points out its pagan. Christian, and Jewish elements.[2] He expresses regret that he has no time to leave his books and studies and enter upon the conflict in person, but says he will not cease to use his pen.   Something must be done to stem the tide of Islam.   The Crusades, in his opinion, were a failure; so he says, "I come to meet the Moslems, not with arms but with words, not by force but by reason, not in hatred but in love."

Who shall say that these earliest literary efforts were a failure?   On the contrary, we cannot but believe, after reading the Abbot's books, that there were Moslems who accepted Christianity, though their numbers may have been few.   As circumstantial evidence we know that in the same century the Eastern Emperor erased from his creed the old anathema against "the god of Mohammed" as likely to offend those Mohammedans who had embraced or were disposed to embraced Christianity.[3]   This

[1] Joh. Thomä, "Zwei Bucher gegen den Muhammedanismus von Petrus Venerabilis" (Leipsic, 1896) Akademische Buch-handlung.

[2] A Keller, "Geisteskampf," etc , 41, 43, etc.

[3] Sir William Muir, "The Mohammedan Controversy," 4; and Kurtz, "Church History," Vol. I, 267.

concession was evidently made because there was a call for it.

Raymund Lull.—John of Damascus, Petrus Venerabilis and others tried to reach Moslems by their pen; Raymund Lull was the first to go to them in person. They offered arguments; he offered his life. Eugene Stock, formerly editorial secretary of the Church Missionary Society, declares "there is no more heroic figure in the history of Christendom than that of Raymond Lull, the first and perhaps the greatest missionary to Mohammedans."[1] "Of all the men of his century," another student of missions says, "of whom we know, Raymund Lull was most possessed by the love and life of Christ, and most eager, accordingly, to share his possession with the world. It sets forth the greatness of Lull's character the more strikingly to see how sharply he rose above the world and church of his day, anticipating by many centuries moral standards, intellectual conceptions, and missionary ambitions to which we have grown only since the Reformation."[2] Raymund Lull was born at Palma, in the Island of Majorca, in 1235, of a distinguished Catalonian family, and when of age spent several years at the court of the King of Aragon. He was a court poet, a skilled musician and a gay knight before he became a scholastic philosopher and an ardent missionary to the Mohammedans. The manner of his conversion at the age of thirty-two reminds one of the experiences of Saul on his way to Damascus, and of St. Augustine under the fig-tree at Milan. After his vision of the Christ he sold all his property, gave the money to the poor, and reserved only a scanty allowance for his wife and children. He

[1]"History of the Church Missionary Society," Vol. I
[2]Robert E. Speer, in "Introduction" to Zwemer's "Raymund Lull," xii.

entered upon a thorough course of study, mastered the
Arabic language, using a Saracen slave as teacher, and
began his life work at the age of forty. The labor to
which he felt called, and for which he gave his life with
wonderful perseverance and devotion, was threefold:
He devised a philosophical system to persuade non-
Christians, especially Moslems, of the truth of Christianity; he established missionary colleges for the
study of Oriental languages; and he himself went and
preached to the Moslems, sealing his witness with his
blood.

In his fifty-sixth year, after vain efforts to arouse
others to a missionary enterprise on behalf of the Mohammedans, he determined to set out alone and single-handed
preach Christ in North Africa. On arriving at Tunis he
invited the Moslem literati to a conference. He announced that he had studied the arguments on both sides
of the question, and was willing to submit the evidences
for Christianity and for Islam to a fair comparison. The
challenge was accepted, but the Moslems being worsted
in argument, and fanaticism being aroused, Lull was cast
into a dungeon by order of the Sultan, and narrowly
escaped death. After bitter persecutions he returned to
Europe, where he made other missionary journeys. In
1307 he was again on the shores of Africa, and at Bugia,
in the market-place, stood up boldly and preached Christ
to the Moslem populace. Once again his pleadings were
met with violence, and he was flung into a dungeon, where
he remained for six months, preaching to those few who
came, and befriended only by some merchants of Genoa
and Spain, who took pity on the aged missionary of the
Cross.

Although banished for a second time and with threats

against his life if he returned, Lull could not resist the
call of the Love that ruled his life. "He that loves not
lives not," said he, "and he that lives by The Life cannot
die." So, in 1314, the veteran of eighty years returned
to Africa and to his little band of Moslem converts. For
over ten months he dwelt in hiding, talking and pray-
ing with those who had accepted Christ, and trying to
win others. Weary of seclusion, he at length came forth
into the open market and presented himself to the people
as the man whom they had expelled. It was Elijah showing himself to a mob of Ahabs. Lull stood before them
and threatened them with God's wrath if they still per-
sisted in their errors. He pleaded with love, but spoke
the whole truth. Filled with fanatic fury at his boldness
and unable to reply to his arguments, the populace seized
him and dragged him out of the town. There, by the
command, or at least the connivance, of the Moslem ruler,
he was stoned to death on the 30th of June, 1315.[1] And
so he became the first martyr missionary to Islam. To be
stoned to death while preaching the love of Christ to Moslems was the fitting end for such a life.

Yet his was a voice crying in the wilderness and his
loneliness was the loneliness of leadership when there are
none awake to follow. "One step further," says Dr.
George Smith, "but some slight response from his church
or his age, and Raymund Lull would have anticipated
William Carey by exactly seven centuries." But there
was no response. The story of his life and abundant
labors in the dark ages is a challenge of faith for us,
who live in the light of the twentieth century, to win the
whole Mohammedan world for Christ. We have larger
opportunity, and far greater resources, and therefore can

[1] S. M Zwemer, "Raymund Lull," 143.

do it if we will.   But we, too, must go in the spirit of
Raymund Lull and in his Master's name.

Francis Xavier.—Toward the close of the sixteenth
century another champion of the faith attacked the citadel
of Islam.   The Society of the Jesuits, under the patron-
age of the King of Portugal, sent Francis Xavier from
Goa with letters of introduction to the Great Mogul.
Xavier visited Lahore, in North India, during the reign
of the Emperor Akbar, and after twelve years of resi-
dence and study finished his book on Christianity called
"A Mirror for Showing the Truth."   He presented this
apology for the faith to the Emperor Jahangir, Akbar's
successor, and held many discussions at the court with
the Moslem teachers.   From his book (which has been
preserved in the library of Queen's College, Cambridge,
and translated into English,[1] we can see that Xavier was
a man of high ability, that he knew the Mohammedan religion thoroughly, but that as a Roman Catholic con-
troversialist he is often compelled to leave the strongholds
of the Christian faith and defends the outworks of his
Church.   His skill and subtlety are engaged in arguments
to convince Moslems of the reasonableness of honoring
relics and of miracles, of prayers for the dead and the
worship of images.   The book, with all its weaknesses,
was strong enough, however, to provoke a Moslem reply
twelve years after its appearance.[2]   And there is no

[1] Rev S Lee, "Persian Controversies." (Cambridge, 1824)
[2] Sir William Muir, "The Mohammedan Controversy," 7 Wherry, in "Islam and Christianity," gives the following testimony to its character: "It
was addressed to Moslems and was dedicated to the Emperor Jahangir, the
title bearing these words, 'Address to the Shadow of God, the Asylum of
Empire, the great King of Kings, Jahangir.   May God perpetuate his kingdom and power.'
"An examination of the contents of this book, comprising 800 pages, dis-
closes the fact that the main points of contention between Christian and
Moslem, in the capital city of the Punjab three centuries ago, were prac-

doubt that such discussions and such a book stirred thought in the ranks of Islam, altho we do not read of conversions or baptisms.

Henry Martyn and Missions in India.—Again we have to make a leap of centuries in the account of pioneer effort for the evangelization of the Mohammedan world. And while the Church was neglecting the problem, Islam was spreading in all directions and taking root in new lands and among new peoples. Five centuries of inactivity and then the mantle of Raymund Lull fell upon Henry Martyn, saint and scholar, and first modern missionary to the Mohammedans. "His life," says Dr. George Smith, "is the perpetual heritage of all English-speaking Christendom and of the native churches of India, Arabia, Persia and Anatolia in all time to come.[1] Born in 1781 and graduated with the highest academical honor of senior wrangler in 1801, he was ordained in 1803, and arrived in India in 1806 as a chaplain of the East India Company, with his heart on fire to labor for the benighted peoples of the Orient. Before his arrival he had already studied Sanscrit, Persian and Arabic, and afterwards he labored unceasingly by tongue and pen, by preaching and by prayer, "to burn out for God." In 1808 he completed

tically the same as those still discussed in the bazaars and chapels of Lahore to-day. These points are: The mystery of the Holy Trinity, the Divinity of the Messiah, the Integrity of the Christian Scriptures, and the Moslem claim that the former Scriptures have been abrogated by the Koran. Excepting the portion of this book devoted to the defence of image worship and the reverence bestowed upon relics and saints, the discussions were conducted with considerable ability. On the practical aspects of the teaching of the Koran, the missionary attacked its immoral teaching in respect to marriage, polygamy and divorce, etc , and represented the facility with which Islam ministers to the desires and passions of men, as like unto the production of a cook, who studies the palate of his master, while the less attractive aspects of Christianity are like unto the bitter of a wholesome medicine."

[1]George Smith, "Henry Martyn: Saint and Scholar, First Modern Missionary to the Mohammedans, 1787-1812." (New York, 1900.)

a version of the New Testament in Hindustani, and later into other languages of India. With a special desire to reach the Mohammedans he perfected himself in Persian and began a version of the New Testament in that language. In 1811 he sailed from Calcutta to Bombay and for the Persian Gulf, partly because of his broken health, but more so, as is evident from his journals, that he might give the Mohammedans of Arabia and Persia the Word of God. On his voyage from Calcutta to Bombay he composed tracts in Arabic, spoke with the Arab sailors and studied the Koran. He stopped at Muscat on April 20th; and we can tell what his thoughts then were in regard to Arabia, for a year earlier he wrote in his diary: "If my life is spared there is no reason why the Arabic should not be done in Arabia and the Persian in Persia. . . . Arabia shall hide me till I come forth with an approved New Testament in Arabic. . . . Will the Government let me go away for three years before the time of my furlough arrives? If not, I must quit the service and I cannot devote my life to a more important work than that of preparing the Arabic Bible."[1] He reached Shiraz in June, 1811, and there revised his Persian translation, also holding frequent discussions with the Moslem mullahs. One year after entering Persia he left Shiraz and proceeded to the Shah's camp near Ispahan, to lay before him the translation he had made. Let him tell us the story in his own words:

"June 12th I attended the Vizier's levee, when there was a most intemperate and clamorous controversy kept up for an hour or two, eight or ten on one side and I on the other. The Vizier, who set us going first, joined in it latterly, and said, 'You had better say God is God, and

[1] S. M. Zwemer. "Arabia; the Cradle of Islam." 318, 319.

Mohammed is the prophet of God.' I said, 'God is God,' but added, instead of 'Mohammed is the prophet of God,' 'and Jesus is the Son of God.' They had no sooner heard this, which I had avoided bringing forward until then, than they all exclaimed in contempt and anger, 'He is neither born nor begets,' and rose up as if they would have torn me in pieces. One of them said, 'What will you say when your tongue is burned out for this blasphemy?' One of them felt for me a little, and tried to soften the severity of this speech. My book, which I had brought, expecting to present it to the King, lay before Mirza Shufi. As they all arose up, after him, to go, some to the King, and some away, I was afraid they would trample upon the book, so I went in among them to take it up, and wrapped it in a towel before them, while they looked at it and me with supreme contempt. Thus I walked away alone, to pass the rest of the day in heat and dirt. What have I done, thought I, to merit all this scorn? Nothing, thought I, but bearing testimony to Jesus. I thought over these things in prayer, and found that peace which Christ hath promised to His disciples."[1]

But his testimony was not wholly in vain, even in those early days. We read of one, at least, who accepted the truth, and, as Martyn himself said: "Even if I never should see a native converted, God may design by my patience and continuance in the word to encourage future missionaries."

Only the Last Day will reveal the extent of the influence of this man, who, with no Christian to tend or comfort him in his last illness, laid down his life at Tocat on the 16th of October, 1812. He was the first of that noble band of missionaries of the Church Missionary

[1] George Smith, "Henry Martyn," 466, 467

Society, Bishop French, Hughes, Elmslie, Wade, Clark, Hooper, Gordon, Bruce, Klein and many others who have emulated him in their endeavor to give the Gospel to the Moslems of India, Persia, Arabia, Afghanistan, Egypt and Africa.

For Mohammedan India, Martyn accomplished most. And from the time of Martyn on, many missionaries in India have done definite work for Moslems as well as for Hindus, altho not to as great an extent. Books and tracts were prepared specially to meet Mohammedan objections. Moslem pupils attended the mission-schools, the Scriptures were translated into the other languages used by Moslems, and in more recent years a few missionaries have been set apart specially for this work. The missionary societies which have been specially active are the Church Missionary Society, the Society for the Propagation of the Gospel, the London Missionary Society, the Churches of Scotland's Missions, the various American Presbyterian Missions, the American Methodist Episcopal Mission and the English and Australian Baptist Missions.[1]

Persia and Arabia.—The next laborer in Persia after Henry Martyn was Karl Gottlieb Pfander, missionary linguist and author, who left so wide and permanent an impression, not only in Persia, but throughout the Mohammedan world, through his celebrated *Mizan-ul-Hak.* This great controversial work has been translated into almost every Moslem language and has aroused more interest and discussion than any book of its character.[2] He was sent out by the Basel mission in 1826. Altho only twenty-two years old, he began the study of

[1] E. M. Wherry, "Islam and Christianity in India."
[2] For a brief description, see the Table opposite page 214.

FACSIMILE OF THE FIRST PAGE OF THE ORIGINAL GERMAN
MANUSCRIPT OF PFANDER'S "MIZAN-UL-HAK"; OR,
"BALANCE OF TRUTH"

Original in the Basel Mission Museum

three languages, Turkish, Armenian and Persian. In 1829 he went to Bagdad to learn Arabic and two years later to Ispahan. On a missionary journey to the town of Kermanshah, after a discussion with the Mullahs, he came near to winning martyrdom. But God spared his life and he labored on, first in Russia, then in India and finally in Constantinople. Everywhere his tongue and pen were mighty forces in the proclamation of the truth. He died at Richmond-on-the-Thames, Dec. 1st, 1865.[1]

In 1827 Dr. Joseph Wolff visited Persia, and as a result of his writings the American Board determined to begin work among the Nestorians. In 1834 Rev. J. L. Merrick went out under the same Board and attempted work among Moslems, but the way was not open. For many years the work of the American missionaries was entirely among the Nestorians. In 1871 this mission came under the Presbyterian Board, and in more recent years there has been work also among Moslems. Some have professed Christ openly and several have suffered martyrdom, among them Mirza Ibrahim.[2]

In 1869 the Rev. Robert Bruce, of the Church Missionary Society, visited Persia, and in 1875 that society began work in Ispahan. Their work has been largely among the Mohammedans. Three other stations, Yezd, Kirman and Shiraz, have been occupied, and the work has been fruitful in results to a remarkable degree.

The pioneer missionary to Arabia was Ion Keith-Falconer, altho there were efforts made before his time to reach Arabia with the gospel by Dr. John Wilson of Bombay and by the Bible Society.[3] The statesmanlike

[1] C F. Eppler, "Dr. Karl Gottlieb Pfander, Ein Zeuge der Wahrheit unter den Bekennern des Islam." (Basel, 1888.)
[2] See sketch of his life in Robert E. Speer, "Men Who Overcame."
[3] S. M. Zwemer, "Arabia, the Cradle of Islam," 320, 325.

explorations of the coast of Arabia and of Yemen by
Major-General F. T. Haig, and his plea for a mission,
led Keith-Falconer to decide on Arabia and called the
attention of others to this neglected peninsula. Keith-
Falconer did not live long (dying at Sheikh Othman on
May 11, 1887, after less than two years' service), but he
lived long enough to do what he purposed, *"to call attention to Arabia."* The United Free Church of Scotland has
continued his work at Aden and inland; the Danish
Church has recently sent out workers to join their number.
These, with the Mission of the Church Missionary Society
at Bagdad and the (American) Arabian Mission on the
east coast at Busrah, Bahrein and Muscat, are all working directly for Mohammedans and reaching far inland
by tours and hospital-service. Arabia has been rich in
martyrs. Beside that of Keith-Falconer, it holds as a
heritage of promise the graves of Bishop French, Peter
J. Zwemer, George E. Stone, Harry J. Wiersum, Dr.
Marion Wells Thoms and Mrs. Jessie Vail Bennett.
The Arabian Mission of the Reformed Church in America, organized in 1889, now has nineteen missionaries on
the field, with twenty native helpers, two hospitals and
three out-stations.[1]

The Turkish Empire.—The territory of the Turkish
Empire is well covered by mission societies. The Amer-
ican Board is the oldest in the field and occupies Euro-
pean Turkey, Asia Minor and Eastern Turkey. The
Presbyterian Church (North) occupies Syria. The
Methodist Episcopal Church has work in Bulgaria, the
Reformed Presbyterians in Northern Syria, and the
Church Missionary Society occupies Palestine. These

[1] S M Zwemer, "Arabia; the Cradle of Islam," 353-390, Mission Reports
and recent numbers of *Neglected Arabia*, a quarterly issued by the Arabian
Mission, 25 East 22d Street, New York City.

are the chief agencies at work and count a total of 637 foreign missionaries, yet, according to the "Encyclopedia of Missions," "the Church Missionary Society is the only one that has made a special effort to establish mission work distinctively for Mohammedans."[1]

Until recent years the difficulties of the problem and the terror of the Turk seem to have prevented direct work for Moslems, altho by printing-press, schools, colleges, and hospitals many Mohammedans were reached indirectly and sometimes even incidentally. "The missionaries have devoted a relatively small part of their time and strength to the Moslem work. In Egypt, Syria, Turkey, and Persia the greater portion of the energy of the missionaries has been devoted to work for Copts, Maronites, Greeks, Armenians, Jews, and Nestorians. Apart from the schools (and the number of Mohammedan pupils in schools in Turkey is almost inconsiderably small) comparatively little has been done. Through medical missionaries many have been accessible and some have been reached, but we do not have, and have not had for years, a systematic and aggressive though tactful and quiet campaign for the evangelization of Moslems."[2] And one needs only to study the reports of these societies to see how little the Mohammedan problem, for one reason or another, comes to the front. At the Haystack Centennial at Williamstown, Mass., in October, 1906, Dr. James L. Barton said: "This is the first time that the question of missionary work for Moslems has been openly discussed upon the platform of the American Board";[3]

[1]"The Encyclopedia of Missions," 755. (1904)
[2]Robert E. Speer, in "The Mohammedan World of To-day," 270 In some of the colleges, however, the number of Moslem students is steadily increasing.
[3]"The Haystack Centennial Volume," 289 (Boston, 1907.)

and the Jubilee volume of the same society, issued after fifty years of missionary work, has, as far as I could find, no reference to Islam in text or index. Yet the American pioneers in the Turkish Empire planned the mission with direct reference to the Moslems. "We must not calculate too closely the chances of life," wrote Mr. Smith in 1827, and he was sure that the missionary "would find a prop upon which to rest the lever that will overthrow the whole system of Mohammedan delusion." Dr. Perkins and Dr. Grant were sent to the Nestorians "to enable the Nestorian church, through the grace of God, to exert a commanding influence in the spiritual regeneration of Asia."[1] Perhaps these early ideals were lost sight of, or more probably they were crushed by the later political restrictions and persecutions in Turkey, so that direct work was not attempted or was impossible; nevertheless much has been accomplished in the face of tremendous difficulty and determined opposition for the future evangelization of Moslems. "Protestant missions have given the entire population the Bible in their own tongue; have trained hundreds of thousands of readers; published thousands of useful books; awakened a spirit of inquiry; set in motion educational institutions in all the sects of all parts of the Empire, compelling the enemies of education to become its friends, and the most conservative of Orientals to devote mosque and convent property to the founding of schools of learning. It has broken the fetters of womanhood. . . . Every evangelical church is a living epistle to the Mohammedans with regard to the true nature of original apostolic Christianity. . . . Encouraged by the spirit of reform and modern progress, even the Mohammedan doctors of Constantinople have

[1] Robert E Speer, in "The Mohammedan World of To-day," 271.

issued orders that all editions of old Mohammedan authors which recount the fabulous stories of Moslem saints and Welys are to be expurgated or suppressed and not to be reprinted."[1] As a single striking example among hundreds of this great though indirect work for the Moslem evangelization, take the Arabic version of the Scriptures by Drs. Eli Smith and Cornelius Van Dyck. This arduous task was begun in 1848 and not finally completed until 1865. The completion of this matchless version marked an epoch in missions for the Mohammedan world greater than any accession or deposition of Sultans. That Bible made modern missions to Arabia, Egypt, Tunis, Tripoli and the Arabic-speaking world possible. And it has only begun its conquests.

North Africa.—As early as 1825 the Church Missionary Society sent a band of five Basel men to Egypt, one of them the famous Samuel Gobat. There were schools and distribution of the Scripture and conversations with thoughtful Copts and Moslems, but the encouragement was small. Mohammedanism appeared unassailable.[2] The first American missionaries reached Egypt in 1854, and every student of missions knows how their mission has spread along the entire Nile Valley, like a fruitful vine, and grown in numbers, influence and results chiefly among the Copts, but also among Moslems. For example. in 1906, over three thousand Moslem pupils attended the schools of the American Mission, and for the past five years meetings for public discussion on the difference between Islam and Christianity have been held twice a week in Cairo. Special literature for Moslems has also been printed and distributed. In 1882 the Church Mis-

[1] H. H Jessup, in the "Encyclopedia of Missions," 757.
[2] Eugene Stock, "History of the Church Missionary Society," Vol. II, 149.

sionary Society resumed its work in Egypt and began work directly among Moslems, with encouraging results.

In 1880 Mr. George Pearse began investigations in Algiers which led to the formation of the North Africa Mission. At that time there was not a single Protestant missionary between Alexandria and the Atlantic coast of Morocco, nor southwards from the Mediterranean almost to the Niger and the Congo.[1] Now this mission, which works very largely among Moslems, has eighteen stations in Egypt, Tripoli, Tunis, Algiers and Morocco, manned by eighty-six missionaries. A hospital and dispensary are established at Tangier and a dispensary at Fez. There are also other smaller independent missions working in North Africa and very recently work has begun in the Soudan.

"But," says an authority on Africa, "for every missionary to the Mohammedans in Africa you can find twenty missionaries to the pagans of Africa and for every convert from Mohammedanism in Africa I think you can find one thousand converts from paganism in Africa. And if this does not prove that the real missionary problem in Africa is Mohammedanism, I scarcely see how that point could be proved at all."[2] One-third of the population of Africa is Mohammedan, and yet Mohammedan Africa, though nearest to Europe, is darkest Africa, and has by far the fewest mission stations.

Malaysia.—Sumatra and Java are the principal and the typical fields of work for Moslems in Malaysia. A Baptist missionary reached Sumatra as early as 1820, and in 1834 Munson and Lyman went out under the American Board, but were brutally murdered. The

[1]"The Gospel in North Africa," 129.
[2]Charles R. Watson, at the Nashville Student Volunteer Convention, "Students and the Modern Missionary Crusade," 458.

A MISSION HOUSE IN CAIRO

In this building are a ser... .... ay scho... a chapel
and ... ... mo... ... ... ssi... aries

Rhenish Missionary Society entered the field in 1861 and has had marvellous success. Other societies from the Netherlands also labor on the island. Dr. Schreiber, formerly inspector of the Rhenish Mission, said: "I do not know if there is any other part of the mission field, with the exception of some parts of Java, where such large numbers of Mohammedans have been won for Christ as among the Battaks of Sumatra."[1] The attitude of the

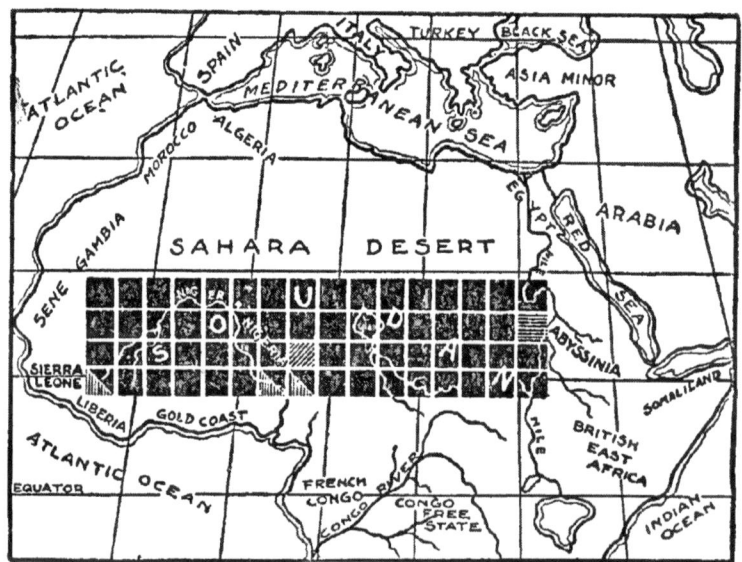

MAP OF THE SOUDAN[2]

Each black square in this map represents one million people; only the shaded squares have been touched by missions.

Dutch Government has in recent years greatly changed, and is now favorable to missions. In Sumatra the issue between Christianity and Islam was boldly faced from the

[1]Harlan P. Beach, "A Geography and Atlas of Protestant Missions," Vol. I, 193, 194.
[2]From the *Missionary Review of the World.*

outset; there was neither fear nor compromise in mission methods, and this fact, together with considerable freedom to preach, perhaps accounts for the great success in winning converts.

Java is the richest and largest of Dutch colonial possessions. Six Dutch missionary societies labor on the island, which has a dense population of 28,746,688; of these 24,270,600 are Moslems. Surely a large and difficult field. Yet by preaching, the sale of Scriptures and medical work nearly twenty thousand Mohammedans have been won over to Christianity in Java—many of them at great cost and under severe persecution. These miracles of grace should encourage the Christian Church to venture out boldly and use every method possible to gain like trophies in all Moslem lands.[1]

[1]"The Mohammedan World of To-day," 222-239.

METHODS AND RESULTS

"If these great things are to be achieved we must pay what it costs. What will be the price? Undoubtedly it involves giving ourselves to the study of missionary problems and strategy with all the thoroughness and tirelessness which have characterized the intellectual work of those men who have brought most benefit to mankind It will cost genuine self-denial. In no sphere so much as that of extending the knowledge and sway of Christ is the truth of His own word illustrated, 'Except a grain of wheat fall into the earth and die, it abideth by itself alone; but if it die, it beareth much fruit' "—*John R Mott* in "The First Two Decades of the Student Volunteer Movement."

X

METHODS AND RESULTS

How to reach Moslems.—The Mohammedan missionary problem is a challenge to our faith, for it is beset with many difficulties, and there are opinions current, as we have seen, to the effect that missions to the Moslems are fruitless, if not hopeless. Back of all methods, therefore, we need faith, such faith as dwelt in the pioneer heroes who led the attack against this citadel of error— Raymund Lull, Petrus Venerabilis, Henry Martyn, Pfander and Keith-Falconer. Such faith exhibits itself in the words of a lady missionary in Algiers, Miss I. Lilias Trotter: "Take it at its very worst. They are dead lands and dead souls, blind and cold and stiff in death as no heathen are; but we who love them see the possibilities of sacrifice, of endurance, of enthusiasm, of life, not yet effaced. Does not the Son of God, who died for them, see these possibilities, too? Do you think He says of the Mohammedan, 'There is no hope or help for him in his God'? Has He not a challenge, too, for your faith; the challenge that rolled away the stone from the grave where Lazarus lay? 'Said I not unto thee that, if thou wouldst believe, thou shouldst see the glory of God? Then took they away the stone.' To raise the spiritually dead is the work of the Son of God. But we are to believe and take away the stone from the place where the dead lay."[1]

The Bible.—The distribution of God's Word has proved the best method for beginning work in all Moslem lands. It is nearly everywhere permitted. It is strong yet inoffensive. It strikes at the root of Islam by placing the Bible over against the Koran, and the sublime story of the life of Jesus, the Christ, over against the artificial halo that surrounds the life of Mohammed. In this method of work we have immense advantage over Islam. Translations of the Koran into other Moslem languages than Arabic exist, but they are rare, expensive, and are necessarily far inferior to the original in style and force. But the Bible has been translated into nearly every Mohammedan tongue, and is the cheapest and best printed book in the Orient; nor has its beauty or power ever been lost in a good translation. The Arabic Koran is a sealed book to all non-Arabic-speaking races, but the Bible speaks the language of every cradle and every market-place in the Moslem world. Every missionary to Moslems should be a colporteur and every colporteur a missionary. Distributions should be by sale, not by free gift. We prize that which we pay for. Among Moslems there are portions of Scriptures which are especially acceptable and therefore effective, viz., Genesis, Matthew's Gospel, John's Gospel and the Psalms.

Medical Missions.—These break up the fallow ground of prejudice and fanaticism, are possible nearly everywhere, and, when conducted with evangelistic zeal, have proved fruitful in results as has no other agency. The Punjab, Persia and Egypt are examples. Hospitals and

[1]From one of her missionary leaflets, entitled "A Challenge to Faith." (London), to which the author is indebted for the sub-title of this book.

AGENT OF THE AMERICAN BIBLE SOCIETY AND COLPORTEURS IN EGYPT

dispensary clinics reach the crowded centres, but medical missionary touring is essential in sparsely settled countries like Arabia, Persia and Morocco.

Educational Institutions.—"To make wrong right, let in the light." From the kindergarten on the veranda of a mission house to the well-equipped university of India, all educational forces, great and small, help to undermine that stupendous rock of ignorance and superstition, Moslem tradition. But the work of education is only preparatory. The New Islam of India and Egypt is the revolt of the educated mind against traditionalism. We must reach the heart and conscience, or fail. Education is only a means to an end.

Preaching.—There are many ways of doing this that are more suitable to Moslems and the Orient than the pulpit or the platform. Preaching in this larger sense includes talking with men by the wayside, or in the coffee-shop, with a group of sailors on deck, or to the Mohammedan postman who brings your letters. The glorious liberty of bazaar preaching is not yet granted in many Moslem lands, nor do Moslems as yet come in large numbers to Christian churches; but that does not mean that there is no opportunity for preachers or preaching. It is well to remember the resolution of the Church Missionary Society, passed as early as 1888: "While the difficulties in the way of missionary work in lands under Mohammedan rule may well appear to the eye of sense most formidable, this meeting is firmly persuaded. that, so long as the door of access to individual Mohammedans is open, so long it is the clear and bounden duty of the Church of Christ to make use of its opportunities for delivering the Gospel message to them, in full expectation that the power of the Holy Spirit will, in God's good time, have a signal manifestation in the triumph of Christianity in those lands." There is no question about the door of access to individual Moslems being open. It is wide open everywhere for men and for women. What single lady missionaries have done and are doing in North Africa and Persia among fanatical villagers proves that there is a loud call for women to preach to their Moslem sisters the unsearchable riches of Christ.

Preaching must have for its subject the essentials of Christianity. Preach Christ crucified. Show the reasonableness of the mysteries of revelation, of the incarnation, and of the Holy Trinity; but never try to explain them by mere philosophy. The problem is to reach, not the intellect, but the heart and conscience, to arouse it from stupor, to show the grandeur of moral courage to the man who is intellectually convinced of the truth. In trying to convince the will—that citadel of man's soul—we must follow the line of least resistance. Yet compromise must not take the place of tact.

The right angle for the presentation of truth can best be learned by studying the strength and the weakness of Islam. The history of Moslem theology, for example, shows that heterodoxy has nearly always been connected with a strong desire for a mediator This natural longing for an intercessor and an atonement is fully supplied in Christ, our Savior. Again, when Moslems object to the eternal pre-existence of the Word of God as a form of polytheism, point out that orthodox Islam holds the Koran to be eternal and uncreated simply because it is the word of God. Preach to the Moslem, not as a Moslem, but as to a man—as a sinner in need of a Savior. There is no use in arousing the picket-guard by firing blank cartridges before the attack, yet controversy has its place.

The Place of Controversy.—That it has a place, and an important one, in reaching Moslems is evident from the whole history of Mohammedan missions. But the subject is a large one and perplexing, because it is hard to look at things from the Moslem viewpoint. Dr. Tisdall's "Manual of the Leading Mohammedan Objections to Christianity" is indispensable for the missionary, and is a deeply interesting book for all students of missions. Prayerful contact with the Moslem mind will teach one how to use this keen weapon to the best advantage in every special case. There is a large amount of controversial literature in many languages. The table opposite page 214 shows what there is in the Arabic language. In dealing with inquirers it is helpful to remember three facts and three texts which apply to such cases:

There are many secret believers in all Moslem lands of whom the missionary will perhaps never know. Pray for them. "Yet I have left me seven thousand in Israel, all the knees which have not bowed unto Baal, and every mouth which hath not kissed him."[1]

It is exceedingly difficult, even in countries under Christian rulers, for a Moslem to break away from Islam and confess Christ. Be tender and patient. "A bruised reed shall He not break, and smoking flax shall He not quench, till He send forth judgment unto victory."[2]

In every possible way encourage public confession of Christ. Living apostles who, freed from the yoke of Islam, preach the gospel with all boldness and are ready to die for Christ, such, and such alone, will vanquish the religion of Islam. "Whosoever, therefore, shall confess

[1] Kings xix, 18.   [2] Isaiah xlii, 3.

me before men, him will I also confess before my Father which is in heaven. But whosoever shall deny me before men, him will I also deny before my Father, which is in heaven."[1]

Some Results of Missions to Moslems.—The results of missionary effort for Moslems, or in Moslem lands, have been direct and indirect. The latter have been far greater than the former and have in God's providence prepared the way for the final assault and the victory.

The preliminary work has largely been accomplished. In the first place it is a remarkable fact that when we study the map of the Mohammedan world we see nearly every strategic Moslem centre occupied by Protestant missions. The following cities, each of which has a population of over 100,000,[2] and a very large Moslem population, are centres of missionary effort by printing-press, hospital, school or college, and in each of them, directly or indirectly, the gospel reaches Moslems:

	Population
Calcutta	1,026,987
Constantinople	1,106,000
Bombay	776,006
Cairo	570,062
Madras	509,346
Haidarabad	448,466
Alexandria	319,766
Teheran	280,000
Lucknow	264,049
Rangoon	234,881
Damascus	230,000
Delhi	208,575
Lahore	202,964
Smyrna	201,000

[1]Matthew x, 32 and 33.
[2]Figures of population taken from the "Statesman's Year Book." (1907.)

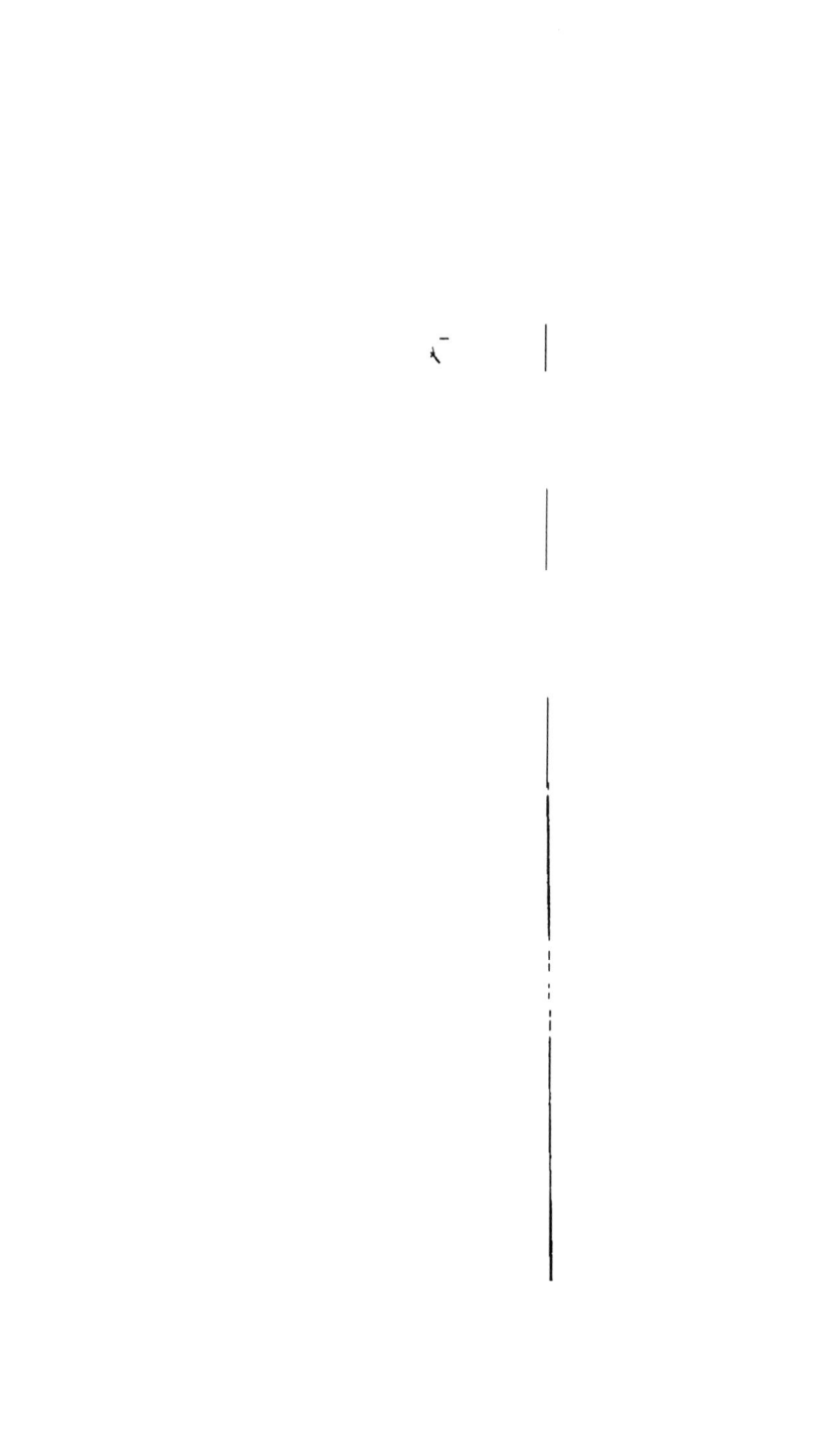

DATE.	ARABIC TITLE.	ENGLISH TITLE.	NO. OF PAGES	AUTHOR	WHERE PRINTED	
Circa 830	Essalet Abd el Messiah Ibn Ishak el Kindy.	"Al Kindy." (Translated by Sir William Muir.)	Arabic, 272. English, 122.	Abd el Messiah el Kindy a Christian at Court of Al Mamun, Bagdad.	S. P. C. K. London. 1885 and 1887.	Two letters; one from Kindy. They ar trenchant, almos tween this and F essay and listenin ments are, howev
1843	Mizan-el-Hak.	"Balance of Truth." (Translated by Rev. R. H. Weakley.)	Arabic, 260. English, 133.	Rev. C. G. Pfander. D.D. C. M. S. Missionary.	Arabic. S. P. C. K. London. English. C. M. House London 1867.	A conciliatory pref Bible and the Ko of Christianity e futes Islam and those who have l lent for inquiring
1893	Bakoorat-esh-Shahiya.	"Sweet First Fruits." (Translated by Sir William Muir.)	Arabic, 242. English, 176.	A Native Syrian Christian.	Arabic. London, Cairo. English. R. T. S. London	A story with a purp story is one of M fulness under pi nantly on the int It is eminently s preme value as more on the aton
1891	Minar-el-Hak.	"The Beacon of Truth." (Translated by Sir William Muir.)	Arabic, 136. English, 166.	A Native Syrian Christian.	Arabic. London Cairo. English. R. T. S. London, Cairo	A series of argume is pressed to the g that the Koran n not in the line of able for burned M
1898	Mabahit es Islam.	"Treatise on Islam."	Arabic, 400, English, 80.	George Sale and Cairo Arab	Cairo.	A literal translatio The former is ca of Islam. The la
1898 1901	El Hidaya, 4 vols.	"Right Guidance."	Vol. I., 320. Vol. II., 300. Vol. III., 394 Vol. IV., ——	An Egyptian Protestant Christian.	American Mission. Cairo.	Reply to Moslem a Mizan-ul-Hak. V of 110 Mistakes in lation. How We for controversy a
1885	Ithbat Sulb el Messiah.	"Proof of Death of Christ."	80.	Muir, etc.	Eng. London. C. M. S. Arab. Cairo. C. M. S.	Proof of Christ's Moslem denial.
1898	Mishah-el-Huda.	"The Torch of Guidance to Mystery of Redemption"	25.	Native.	R. T. S. London Cairo	The sacrifice of Isaa Proofs given that
1899	Dawet el Mesimeen.	"Call to Moslems to Read the Bible"	40.	Sir William Muir.	Cairo. London.	Proofs of Integrity of Scripture.
1897	Burhan el Jalil, etc.	"The Clear Proof," etc.	43.	Native.	Cairo.	Tract on Genuinenes
1898	Salamet el Injil, etc.	"Freedom of the Bible from Corruption"	13.	Native.	Cairo.	Similar to the abov
	El Kitang Je...	...		Rev. G. H.	Arabic, Cairo.	A curios. Short an

	Population
Cawnpore	197,170
Agra	188,022
Ahmadabad	185,889
Tabriz	200,000
Allahabad	172,032
Tunis	250,000
Amritsar	162,429
Howŕa	157,594
Poona	153,320
Soerabaya (Java)	146,944
Bagdad	145,000
Fez	140,000
Patna	134,785
Aleppo	127,150
Beirut	118,800
Karáchı	116,663

Many other cities of less population, but not less strategic, are also mission stations. For example, Aden, Muscat, Algiers, Jerusalem, Quetta, Peshawar, Yezd, and so forth. The efforts carried on in all these cities prove that work for Moslems is possible under all conditions and everywhere. *Yet at none of these strategic centres are the efforts to reach Moslems at all commensurate with the opportunities. All of these cities are calling for more laborers.* Each is a challenge and a vantage point for work among a large Moslem population yet unreached.

Another result which we have already mentioned is that the Bible has been translated into nearly every language spoken by Moslems. Thousands of portions of Scripture are already in use by Moslems and tens of thousands of copies are being sold to them every year by colporteurs and missionaries. The Beirut Press alone has issued over a million volumes of the Arabic Scriptures since it was founded. The demand for the vernacular

Bible in Persia, Arabia, Egypt, and the Turkish Empire is phenomenal.

Not only has the Bible been translated and widely distributed, but a large and important body of Christian literature, apologetic and educational, is ready for Moslems. This is especially true of Arabic, Persian, Turkish, Urdu, and Bengali, the chief literary languages of Islam. The weapons are ready for the conflict.[1]

And there have been unconditional surrenders. It is an old falsehood widely current even among the ignorant friends of missions, that "it is no use trying to convert Mohammedans," and that there have been no converts from Islam. The fact is, as we have seen, that there was a convert from Islam even before the death of Mohammed![2] And there have been converts ever since in all lands where the gospel was preached to Moslems, although not as many as there might have been but for our neglect.[3]

"The accessions from Islam," says Dr. Wherry, "especially in Northern India, have been continuous during all the years since the death of Henry Martyn. One here and another there has been added to the Christian Church, so that now, as one looks over the rolls of church membership, he is surprised to find so many converts from Islam, or the children and children's children of such converts. In the north, especially the Punjab, and the Northwest Frontier Province, every congregation has a representation from the Moslem ranks. Some of the churches have a majority of their membership gathered from among the Mussulmans. In a few cases there has been something like a movement among Moslems towards

[1]"Methods of Mission Work Among Moslems," 79-95   [2]See page 23.
[3]W. A. Shedd, "Islam and the Oriental Churches," 148, etc.

السرق والغرب

كلية ديِنية أدبيَّة

١٩٠٧ مارس ٢٤ ﻫ

التورية والانجيل والقرآن،

تعاليمها عن ذات الله

- - - Tourat, Injeel, Koran, - - -

Their Conception of God.

OUR task at this time is to show the elements in Jewish monotheism, (that is, in the revelation of God in the Tourât), which go beyond the idea of abstract divine transcendence and hint plainly at the Christian doctrine of God.

And this we are all the more glad to do first, because of the close connection between this subject and the Islamic doctrine of *Tauçrfa*, which we have already criticised, and, also, because some of our Readers are

نبيّنا في هذا المقال في أن نبين وجه الوحيد في التعاليم

اليهودية اي في اعلان الله في التورية وان ثبت ان تلك الوحدة او

الاعتبارات تتم الى اسمى ما يتم الله بمصب بذكر الله وتمزز

سلام بن من ،

Christianity, and a considerable number have come out at one time. But perhaps the fact which tells most clearly the story of the advance of Christianity among Moslems in India, is this, that among the native pastors and Christian preachers and teachers in North India there are at least two hundred who were once followers of Islam."[1]

The American Mission in Egypt, although its work has been chiefly among the Copts, reports one hundred and forty baptisms of adult Moslems during its history. In Persia there are Moslem converts at every station of the Church Missionary Society. Even in Arabia and in the Turkish empire there have been converts and martyrs to the faith.[2] From North Africa, the latest reports tell us that at almost all the stations there have in past years been some converts. At Fez there is a band of Christians, nine or ten of whom are employed as colporteurs; at Jemaa Sahrij there is another band, and these meet in two stone halls, one built for men and one for women. At Tangier, Alexandria, Shebin el Kom and Tunis there are also some who regularly meet with the missionaries to partake of the Lord's Supper.

During 1906 some thirty Moslems were converted at Fez, and two men and one woman were baptized. At Algiers a Kabyle young man was baptized and another converted. At Bizerta a man was baptized. At Alexandria also, a well educated man, long under instruction since his conversion, was baptized. Several young men were converted at Jemaa Sahrij. At Tripoli a convert of many years' standing died, after long proof of his trust in Christ for salvation and much quiet preaching to

[1]E. M. Wherry, "Islam and Christianity"
[2]"The Mohammedan World of To-day," 19, 36, 39, 112, 126, 170, etc.

others. At Shebin el Kom, on New Year's eve, ten out of a gathering of eighteen met around the Lord's Table at midnight, and dedicated themselves afresh to God; seven years ago there was not a single convert there.

In addition to these pronounced cases, most of whom have had to bear persecution, there are many secret disciples.[1]

In Sumatra the Rhenish mission has 6500 converted Moslems, 1150 catechumens, 80 churches, 5 pastors and 70 lay preachers, while they baptized 153 Mohammedans in 1906. In the district of Si Perok a Christian convert from Islam has become chief in place of a Mohammedan.[2]

In Java there have been still greater numerical results. According to latest statistics there are now living in Java eighteen thousand who have been converted to Christianity from Islam and the converts from Islam amount to between three hundred and four hundred adults every year.[3] In Bokhara and the Caucasus, where work has only just begun, a number of Moslems have been converted and baptized. The testimony of a Moslem professor in the high school in Bokhara, now a convert, may well close this brief summary of results. Coming from the heart of Asia and of the Mohammedan world, his word is prophetic: *"I am convinced that Jesus Christ will conquer Mohammed. There is no doubt about it, because Christ is King in heaven and on earth, and His Kingdom fills heaven now, and will soon fill the earth."*[4] How soon shall it be? Are not the results already attained a

[1] *North Africa*, March, 1907, 34.
[2] "The Mohammedan World of To-day," 222   *The Missionary Review of the World*, 1907, 395.
[3] C. Albers and J. Verhoeven at the Cairo Conference, in "The Mohammedan World of To-day," 237
[4] "The Mohammedan World of To-day," 244.

challenge to us to look forward with faith in God to far greater results? "Hitherto ye have asked nothing in My name. Ask and ye shall receive."[1]

[1] John xvi, 24.

THE PROBLEM AND THE PERIL

"Yet another force that is aggressively our enemy is Moham-medanism. We see it actively spreading over Africa, where Christianity is not progressive. It comes with the Arab-slaver and was identified with the slave traffic. It comes now with a certain racial pride and appeals to the African, because it seems to link him with a great world-empire."—*Donald Frazer in* "Stu-dents and the Modern Missionary Crusade," p 207.

"Difficulties are not without their advantages. They are not to unnerve us. They are not to be regarded simply as subjects for discussion nor as grounds for scepticism and pessimism. They are not to cause inaction, but rather to intensify activity. They were made to be overcome. Above all they are to create profound distrust in human plans and energy, and to drive us to God."—*John R. Mott* in "The Evangelization of the World in This Generation," p. 50.

XI

THE PROBLEM AND THE PERIL

The Evangelization of the Mohammedan World.— When Samuel J. Mills and his associates met under the shelter of the Haystack one hundred years ago, they were not unmindful of the difficulties of world-wide evangelization nor of the difficulties of reaching Mohammedan lands. Loomis maintained that "the time was not ripe, and such a movement was premature. If missionaries were sent they would be murdered, and what was needed was a new crusade before the gospel could be sent to the Turks and Arabs." The others replied that God was always willing to have His kingdom advanced, and that if Christian people would only do their part, God could be relied on to do His. "We can do it if we will."[1] We know now that Loomis was wrong and Mills was right. No Christian army has ever subdued Turkey or Arabia, yet both are mission fields. And surely if one hundred years ago the faith of these men of the Haystack did not stagger at the obstacles, but accepted the challenge, we can do it now if we will. The evangelization of the Mohammedan world, of which we have had glimpses in the foregoing chapters—so great in its extent, so deep in its degradation, so hopeless without the

[1]Thomas C. Richard, "Samuel J. Mills: Missionary Pathfinder, Pioneer, and Promoter," 30, 31.

gospel—is one of the grandest and most inspiring problems ever undertaken by the Church of Christ. It may
be a work of "surpassing difficulty which will require a
new baptism of apostolic wisdom and energy, faith and
love," and may "tax the intellect, the faith, the wisdom,
the zeal and the self-denial of the whole church in every
land";[1] but, unless Christ's great commission has lost its
meaning and His power is insufficient for this undertaking, the Mohammedan world must and will be evangelized. While other religions and systems of error have
fallen before Christian missions, like Dagon before the
ark of Jehovah, Islam, like mighty Goliath, defies the
armies of the living God and the progress of Christ's
kingdom. In three continents it still presents an almost
unbroken phalanx, armed with the old proud and aggressive spirit of defiance.

Only five years ago Sheikh Abd ul Hak, of Bagdad, a
Moslem of the old school, wrote an article on behalf of
the Pan-Islamic league. It appeared in a French journal
and was entitled, "The Final Word of Islam to Europe."
From this remarkable, outspoken and doubtless sincere
defiance we quote the following paragraph:

"For us in the world there are only believers and unbelievers; love, charity, fraternity toward believers; contempt, disgust, hatred and war against unbelievers.
Amongst unbelievers the most hateful and criminal are
those who, while recognizing God, attribute to Him earthly relationships, give Him a son, a mother. Learn then,
European observers, that a Christian of no matter what
position, from the simple fact that he is a Christian, is in
our eyes a blind man fallen from all human dignity. Other

[1]H. H. Jessup, "The Mohammedan Missionary Problem," 22, 23.   Cf.
"The Inaccessible Fields of Islam and How to Reach Them," Dr. James
S. Dennis, in *Missions at Home and Abroad* (Am. Tract Society, New York).

infidels have rarely been aggressive toward us. But Christians have in all times shown themselves our bitterest enemies. . . . The only excuse you offer is that you reproach us with being rebellious against your civilization. Yes, rebellious, and rebellious till death! But it is you, and you alone, who are the cause of this. Great God! are we blind enough not to see the prodigies of your progress? But know, Christian conquerors, that no calculation, no treasure, no miracle can ever reconcile us to your impious rule. Know that the mere sight of your flag here is torture to Islam's soul; your greatest benefits are so many spots sullying our conscience, and our most ardent aspiration and hope is to reach the happy day when we can efface the last vestiges of your accursed empire."[1]

In view of such an attitude on the part of some of the leaders of Islam, Christendom must answer the challenge with a new and nobler crusade than that of politics or commerce. The unselfishness of sacrificial love must be manifested in the work of missions that we may win the love of men like Abd-ul-Hak in spite of their hatred toward us. We must

"Through the promise on God's pages,
Through His work in history's stages,
Through the Cross that crowns the ages,
Show His *love* to them."

Islam as a religion is doomed to fade away in time before the advance of humanity, civilization and enlightenment; but whether its place will be taken by atheism, by some new false religion, or by the faith of Christ, depends, humanly speaking, upon the measure of our devotion to

[1]Quoted in *Der Christliche Orient*, Vol. IV, 145. (Berlin.) And also, at the time, in other papers from the French original.

our Lord and our consciousness of the Moslem's need of Him.

There are many factors in this great problem of Moslem evangelization, each of which is a challenge to faith. Whether we look at the lost opportunities because of neglect in the past or turn to the greater opportunities of to-day; whether we consider the extent of Islam or its character, the problem is so colossal that we are shut up to faith in God. All things are possible to him that believeth. "By faith the walls of Jericho fell down after they were compassed about seven days." *He* can do it if He will, and we can do it with Him.

Occupied and Unoccupied Lands.—In the previous chapters we have seen something of the work of missions, direct and indirect, in lands like Egypt, Turkey, India, Sumatra, Java, and Syria, where for many years the Moslem populations have come more or less in contact with missions. These lands and others more recently entered may in a sense be considered occupied. Yet there is not a single one of them where the total number of laborers is in any sense adequate to the work of evangelization. In Egypt, for example, only a small fraction of the Moslem population is reached in any way by the gospel. The unoccupied lands and regions are those where nothing has yet been done and where there are neither mission stations nor mission workers.

Perhaps a more distinctive though not more comprehensive classification of Moslem lands in relation to Christian missions is that given by Dr. Weitbrecht.[1] He groups them into three classes:

(1) The lands where Islam is dominant or greatly

[1] H. U. Weitbrecht, Paper on the Cairo Conference at the Anglican Church Congress. 1906

preponderant and has been long established. Such are North Africa, Arabia, Turkey, Persia, and Central Asia, including Afghanistan. In these lands the remnants of the Christian churches, where they exist at all, have been worn out by centuries of oppression, and though they have not abandoned their faith, they do not preach it to Moslems, and almost fear to admit a Moslem convert. And wherever Moslem rule obtains in these lands there is no liberty to confess Christ, and the life of each convert from Islam is in daily jeopardy. Yet educational, medical and literary work for Moslems has proved possible where it has been tried. All these forms of effort should be pushed, therefore, to their utmost and new centres rapidly occupied.

(2) The lands of ancient pagan civilization, where Islam has been modified by contact with cultured paganism and where Moslems are in the minority. Such are India and China. In India there have been many converts, and a considerable literature has been prepared for Moslems, but the unique opportunities for direct missionary effort have not been fully met. With the largest Mohammedan population of any country on the globe before them, the missions in India are vitally concerned in the Mohammedan missionary problem and should lead all lands in its solution. In China we have to confess that in view of the appalling pagan population of the Empire special work among its thirty million Moslems is nonexistent.[1]

(3) The border-marches of Islam in Africa and Malaysia. Here we have to do with masses of newly converted tribes on the pagan frontiers, where, as Pastor Würz shows, "it is often hard to tell just where paganism

[1] H. O. Dwight. "Blue Book of Missions," 86 (1905.)

ceases and Islam begins.   Those who profess Islam still worship their fetiches and cling to rum."[1]   In these lands we are face to face with one of the greatest responsibilities of the Christian Church, as we shall note later when we consider the Moslem peril in Africa.

Among the countries occupied perhaps the most notable strategic point is Egypt.   *In lower Egypt the Moslems form about ninety-eight per cent. of the population and in upper Egypt about eighty-eight per cent.*   The need of the country is therefore the need of the Moslems.[2] Egypt is under British rule and connected by regular rail and steamboat service with distant points in Africa. Cairo is the literary capital of the Mohammedan world, as Mecca is its religious and Constantinople its political capital.   "As rapidly as experts trained in Koranic lore can be educated for the reinforcement of the workers now on the ground, the Christian Church should drive a wedge into this outwork of the great stronghold."[3]

The strategic centres of Moslem population, given in the last chapter, are also many of them, because of their geographical position, commercial centres, and stand at the cross-roads of international communication between Moslem lands.   The importance of massing our spiritual forces here cannot be overestimated.   A book sold at Cairo may be read by the camp-fires of the Sahara, in the market-place of Timbuktu or under the very shadow of the Kaaba.   Were a strong mission established for the Mohammedans of Bombay, its influence would reach far along the coast of India and to the Moslem traders of Malabar and Ceylon.   These strategic centres are an appeal for immediate reinforcement and a call to come

[1]"Die Mohammedansche Gefahr in West Afrika," 18.
[2]"The Mohammedan World of To-day," 22
[3]H. O. Dwight, "Blue Book of Missions," 84.   (1905.)

STUDENTS OF THE ASSIUT TRAINING COLLEGE, EGYPT

to the help of those who, often single-handed, are fighting against fearful odds and still winning the battle inch by inch.

And what shall we say of those lands where Mohammed's rule has never yet been challenged and where vast areas are without any missionary? Surely, if anywhere in the world, here is opportunity. The very dangers, loneliness, hardships of such pioneer fields will prove an irresistible attraction to men of heroic stamp.

> "So near is grandeur to the dust,
>   So close is God to man,
> When duty whispers, 'Lo! thou must,'
>   The youth replies, 'I can.'"

Beginning with Africa, the following areas are unoccupied by missions. In the Central Soudan,[1] one of the most densely populated portions of Africa, are these States (larger some of them than New York, Wisconsin or Ohio) waiting for the gospel:

The Land	The Size of	Gov'm't	Missionaries
Kordofan	England	British	None
Darfur	France	British	None
Wadai	Italy and Ireland	French	None
Bagirmi	Switzerland Holland Belgium and Tasmania	French	None
Kanem	Greece and Denmark	French	None
Adamawa	Turkey in Europe	German and British	None
Bornu	England	British	None
Sokoto	Japan	British	5 C. M. S. workers
Gando	Scotland and Ireland	British	None
Nupe	Bulgaria	British	6 Canadian workers.

[1]"The Call of the Soudan," *Missionary Review of the World*, January, 1907.

"Taking the parallel of latitude that would touch the northern bend of the Niger as the northern limit, and that which would touch the northern bend of the Congo as the southern limit, and modifying these boundaries at either side of the continent so as to omit the mission stations on the West Coast and on the upper courses of the Nile, we find a territory about equal to that of the United States, and far more densely populated, without a single representative of the Gospel of Jesus Christ. With a mission station just established by the United Presbyterians of America on the Sobat River, of the Upper Nile basin, and with the stations opened by the Church Missionary Society and the United Soudan Mission in the Niger basin, 1500 miles to the west, *the situation presented is as if the United States, with her 85,000,000 of people, had one missionary in Maine and another in Texas, and no gospel influence between.*"[1]

And the problem in all this vast region is the problem of Islam. Hear the testimony of the Rev. J. Aitken: "When I came out in 1898, there were few Mohammedans to be seen below Iddah. Now they are everywhere, excepting below Abo, *and at the present rate of progress there will scarcely be a pagan village on the river banks by* 1910. Then we shall begin to talk of Mohammedan missions to these people, and anyone who has worked in both heathen and Mohammedan towns knows what that means."[2]

If Dr. Kumm's estimates are trustworthy, this great destitute district of the Soudan, one of the most strategic and the most important unoccupied territories in the world, has a population of at least fifty millions. And

[1] W. S Naylor, "Unoccupied Mission Fields in Africa," *Missionary Review of the World*, March, 1906 See map on page 159.
[2] "The Call of the Soudan," Ibid., January, 1907.

yet only sixteen missionaries are found in the entire area, namely, at Sokoto and Nupe. All of the other lands are destitute. Within twenty years it will be settled whether Islam or Christianity shall be dominant and triumphant. All the indications now are that Islam is fast winning the field.[1]

Turning from darkest Africa to Asia, we find in this continent a situation hardly less needy and with even greater, because more varied, opportunity. In Asia the following lands and areas of Moslem population are still wholly unreached :[2]

	Estimated Moslem Population
Afghanistan	4,000,000
Baluchistan[3]	750,000
Hejaz, Hadramaut, Nejd and Hassa (Arabia)	3,500,000
Southern Persia	2,500,000
Russia in Caucasus	2,000,000
Russia in Central Asia	3,000,000
Bokhara[4]	1,250,000
Khiva	800,000
Mindanao (Philippines)	250,000
Siberia (East and West)	6,100,000
China (unreached sections)	20,000,000
	44,150,000

These unevangelized millions in Asia, all of them under the yoke of Islam, are a challenge to faith, and in some cases a rebuke for the neglect of the church. Kafiristan, one of the five provinces of Afghanistan, is a sad example. "It was a sorrowful day for them," writes Colonel

[1] H. Karl Kumm, "The Soudan."
[2] "Statesman's Year Book," 1907; and "Blue Book of Missions," 1905.
[3] Has one mission station at Quetta.
[4] Work just begun at one station.

G. Wingate, "when by a stroke of the pen in the British Foreign Office eleven years ago their country was brought within the boundaries of Afghanistan. At last the Kafirs were the subjects of the Ameer. In consultation with Ghulam Haider, his commander-in-chief, he determined to convert them and bring them into the fold of Islam. The distasteful offices of the mullah were offered at the muzzle of the breech-loader, the rites of the Mohammedan belief were enforced upon an unwilling people, mosques took the place of temples, the Koran and the traditions of the Caliphate would be the spiritual regeneration of the pagan Kafir. Yet twenty-five years ago a message from the Kafirs of the Hindu Kush stirred the Christian Church; they asked that teachers might be sent to instruct them in the religion of Jesus Christ. It is a sad example of how an opportunity may be lost, for to-day there is imposed between the ambassador for Christ and the eager Kafir the hostile aggression of a Mohammedan power intensely jealous of the entrance of the foreigner."[1]

The Mohammedans now under the American flag in the Philippine Islands have a special claim on the American churches. And who can tell whether tactful, loving labor among them would not be rewarded with a speedy harvest of souls, as was the case among the Battaks of Sumatra? "The isles shall wait for His law." And who will take up the burden of Islam in Russia and China with a total number of Mohammedans in these two empires of over forty millions?

Lastly, there are great and effectual doors to be opened where there are many adversaries—pioneer fields that

---

[1]G. Wingate, "Unevangelized Regions in Central Asia," *The Missionary Review of the World*, May, 1907. *Kafiristan* signifies "Land of Unbelievers."

await heroic faith—in Arabia, in Persia, in Afghanistan, in Central Asia. Nothing is too hard for prayer to accomplish, and lives laid down in loving service; the things that are impossible with men are possible with God. "If neither treaties nor frontiers can exclude the pioneers of trade or the artificers of workshops, or the physician and surgeon, how much less should such barriers avail to shut out that Gospel which hath a pathway of its own across the mountain ranges into forbidden territory, moving from heart to heart, in a manner that rulers cannot restrain, and bringing to the sin-sick soul peace and to the weary rest. The Story of the Central Asia Pioneer Mission shows that God is even now leading some to attempt to reach these mid-Asian territories with the gospel."[1]

The Moslem Peril.—The problem of evangelizing the Moslem peoples of Africa and Asia is not only a vast one and one too long neglected, but an urgent one. Islam is aggressive and is to-day overrunning districts once pagan. Its numbers are increasing in Bengal, Burma, Southern India, the East Indies, West Africa, Uganda, the Congo basin, Abyssinia, and on the Red Sea littoral. On the west coast of Southern India "the Mapillas are now energetic in propagating Islam and their numbers have increased from 612,789 in 1871 to 912,920 in 1901."[2]

In West Africa and Nigeria missionaries speak of a "Mohammedan peril." They say every effort should be made to forestall the entrance of Islam into the border-

---

[1] G Wingate, "Unevangelized Regions in Central Asia"; also "Story of the Central Asia Pioneer Mission," procurable at the office of the Mission, 2 and 4 Tudor Street London, E. C.

[2] "The Mohammedan World of To-day," 179 See also article on "Islam and Christian Missions," in *The Church Missionary Review* for April, 1907.

lands before his religion renders evangelization tenfold
more difficult than it is among African pagans. In Western Africa Islam and Christianity between them are spoiling heathenism and will probably divide the pagan peoples in less than fifty years.[1] Pastor F. Wurz, secretary
of the Basel Mission, in a recent pamphlet, sounds the
alarm of this Mohammedan aggression as a peril to the
native church. He states that the situation on the Gold
Coast is alarming. In one village a native preacher, with
his entire congregation, went over to Islam. "Missions
will scarcely be able to prevent the entrance of Islam
among a single tribe, much less into large districts. Islam
is spreading with the certainty and irresistibleness of a
rising tide. The only question is whether it will still be
possible for missions to organize Christian churches like
breakwaters, able to resist the flood and outweather it,
or whether everything will be carried away headlong."[2]
(See the map opposite page 156.) The Soudan United
Mission calls the attention of Christendom to the present
crisis in Hausa-land. All the heathen populations of the
Central Soudan will go over to Islam unless the Church
awakes to its opportunity. It is now or never; it is
Islam or Christ![3] And there are other lands where the
crisis is equally acute, though not extended over as large
an area as in Africa. In regard to the district of Khelat,
in Baluchistan, the Rev. A. D. Dixey testifies that the
inhabitants are still only nominal Mohammedans and not
bigoted. "They will listen now, but in a few years they
will have become fanatical."

In Borneo there is a special call for workers among
the Dayaks, who are not yet Mohammedan, but are in

[1] "The Mohammedan World of To-day," 47.
[2] "Die Mohammedansche Gefahr in West Afrika," 24, 25. (Basel, 1904.)
[3] H. Karl Kumm, "The Soudan."

A GROUP OF HAUSA MOSLEMS AT PRAYER IN THE MARKET PLACE, KAMERUN (WEST AFRICA)

danger of speedily becoming such through the influence of Mohammedan Malays, by whom they are surrounded.[1] In India there are to-day a multitude of low-caste people, especially in Bengal, who will shortly become Moslems or Christians. Ten millions in Bengal have become Moslems.[2]

On the other hand, Islam itself is alarmed, and in many parts of the world there is a feeling that something must be done to save the faith of the Prophet. In India they are forming Societies for the Defence of Islam; they are establishing presses for the production of literature to propagate their faith; they are copying missionary methods and engaging Moslem preachers to counteract the work of Christian missions. They use the substance of infidel literature from Europe and America and articles on the higher criticism to prove that Christianity is not true and that its leaders are not agreed on the fundamentals of its teaching.[3] What will be the issue if the Mohammedan propagandists in Africa, as well as those in India, begin to use the methods of Christian missions? The situation is one full of peril to the native church. This aspect of the problem was treated in a masterly paper by Professor Carl Meinhof, of the University of Berlin, at a recent conference.[4] He shows that every mission in Africa, north of the equator, will be compelled sooner or later to do direct work for Moslems or imperil its very existence.

[1] Harlan P. Beach, "A Geography and Atlas of Protestant Missions," Vol. I, 192

[2] Bishop Warne, "Methods of Mission Work Among Moslems," 27.

[3] B R Barber, of Calcutta, in "Students and the Modern Missionary Crusade," 456.

[4] "Zwingt uns die Heidenmission Muhammedaner Mission zu treiben?" Vortrag gehalten auf der Eisenacher Gemeinschafts Konferenz am 6 Juni, 1906. (Osterwieck-Harz, 1906.)

A writer in *Uganda Notes* gives the same testimony:
"Egypt draws perceptibly nearer to Uganda. The most
northerly station of the Uganda Mission, at Gondokoro,
whither two Baganda evangelists were sent in February,
is distant only 112 miles from Bor, where the Soudan
party are settled. Lower Egypt is a stronghold of Islam,
and the followers of that religion are ever busy carrying
their creed southward through Upper Egypt towards the
confines of this Protectorate. Many of the Nile tribes
have already embraced Islam, though the tribes to the
north of our missions in Bunyoro are still heathen. If
these tribes are left to accept Mohammedanism before the
Gospel is carried to them, the difficulty of our work in
these regions will undoubtedly be seriously enhanced.
. . . As far as Uganda itself is concerned, Islam is,
of course, infinitely less a power than it once was, when
in the troublous early days of Christianity it threatened
to overwhelm the combined heathen and Christian forces
arrayed against it. But it is not only from the north
that the followers of Islam are threatening an invasion.
From the eastern side the railway has brought us into
intimate association with coast influence; Swahilis and
Arabs coming up the line leave Islamism in their wake,
for almost every Moslem is more or less of a missionary
of his faith. Would that the same might be said of
Christians! Not a few Moslems are holding important
positions in Uganda, while the larger number of those in
authority in Busoga are, or were till quite recently, also
Mohammedans. The followers of the false prophet have
a great influence among the natives, which does not
give promise of becoming less as time goes on. *There
is a distinct danger of the Eastern Province becoming
nominally Moslem before Christianity has made for*

itself a favorable impression on the minds of the people."[1]

Pan-Islamism.—Another indication of Moslem activity is the movement known as Pan-Islamism. This term is used by Moslems themselves to describe the political and social combination of all Moslems throughout the world to defy and to resist the Christian Powers. For several years back the *Malumat* and the *Servet*, two good and cheap illustrated papers published in Constantinople, have carried on a crusade against all Christian nations that rule Mohammedans. In India, in Africa, in the Malay archipelago, the faithful are exhorted to hold themselves in readiness for the coming conflict. These papers and others like them, as *El Moeyid*, at Cairo, take pains to publish all real or alleged cases of oppression practiced upon the followers of Mohammed. The Dutch Government once prohibited the *Malumat*, but thousands of copies are still smuggled into the colonies. Associations bearing the name Pan-Islamic are said to exist in London, Paris, Geneva, the United States and other foreign countries. How far their organization is developed in Moslem lands is uncertain, but there are a dozen publications devoted to their propaganda, six of these appearing in Cairo.[2]

A masterly statement of the real aims and character of Pan-Islamism is found in Lord Cromer's report for 1906.[3] After giving an account of the relation of Egyptian Nationalism to this movement he defines its character thus: "In the first place it means in

---

[1]Quoted in *The Church Missionary Gleaner*, 1906.

[2]See article on "Pan-Islam," by Archibald R. Colquhoun, in *North American Review*, June, 1906, 915

[3]"Finances, Administration and Condition of Egypt and the Soudan in 1906."

Egypt more or less complete subserviency to the Sultan. . . . In the second place, Pan-Islamism almost necessarily connotes a recrudescence of racial and religious animosity. Many of its adherents are, I do not doubt, inspired by genuine religious fervor. Others, again, whether from indifference verging on agnosticism, or from political and opportunist motives, or—as I trust may sometimes be the case—from having really assimilated modern ideas on the subject of religious toleration, would be willing, were such a course possible, to separate the political from the religious, and even possibly from the racial issues. If such are their wishes and intentions, I entertain very little doubt that they will make them impossible of execution. Unless they can convince the Moslem masses of their militant Islamism, they will fail to arrest their attention or to attract their sympathy. Appeals, either overt or covert, to racial and religious passions are thus a necessity of their existence in order to insure the furtherance of their political programme.

"In the third place, Pan-Islamism almost necessarily connotes an attempt to regenerate Islam on Islamic lines —in other words, to revivify and stereotype in the twentieth century the principles laid down more than a thousand years ago for the guidance of a primitive society. Those principles involve a recognition of slavery, laws regulating the relations of the sexes which clash with modern ideas, and, which is perhaps more important than all, that crystallization of the civil, criminal and canonical law into one immutable whole, which has so largely contributed to arrest the progress of those countries whose populations have embraced the Moslem faith."[1]

[1]Quoted in article on "Egyptian Nationalism," in *The London Times*, Thursday, April 4, 1907.

So well agreed are the statesmen of Europe in regard to the power of this movement for evil that Mr. Carl Peters, the well-known African traveler, writing on the political ascendancy of Germany, used these significant, though rash, words:

"There is one factor which might fall on our side of the balance and in the case of a world-war might be made useful to us: that factor is, Islam. As Pan-Islamism it could be played against Great Britain as well as against the French Republic; and if German policy is bold enough, it can fashion the dynamite to blow into the air the rule of the Western Powers from Cape Nun (Morocco) to Calcutta."[1]

Remembering the career of Abd ul Wahab in Arabia and of the Mahdi at Khartoum, and knowing the present activity of the Senusi Derwish orders, the Pan-Islamites must not be too sure that the spirit they are evoking in the Dark Continent among savage tribes is one that will remain under their control! Lord Cromer may be right when he says, "I am sceptical of Pan-Islamism producing any more serious results than sporadic outbursts of fanaticism."[2]   And yet there are latent forces in Islam because of its very character and historic ideals that once let loose may work in a similar way, as they did under Khalid, "The Sword of God." We must evangelize the Mohammedan world for the sake of Christendom. Lord Cromer goes on to say: "I am quite confident of the power of Europe, should the necessity arise, to deal effectively with the material, though not with the spiritual, aspects of the movement."[3]

[1]Quoted in article of Professor Vambery, *The Nineteenth Century*, October, 1906, 553.
[2]*The London Times*, April 4, 1907.
[3]Ibid.

The Church of Christ must deal with its spiritual aspects. We must meet Pan-Islamism with pan-evangelism. "It is a fight for life. We have got to conquer them or they will conquer us," so said Dr. George E. Post, of Beirut College, at the Centenary Missionary Conference. "There are unknown possibilities in that great continent. Who knows what the forces of Central Asia may yet be, stored up for the future? Hear the parable of the locusts. When the locust appears in the desert he is at home. He is contented usually with its barrenness. He lays his eggs in the sand. He hatches his young and they eat the bitter and unpalatable herbs that grow in the few moist spots of the wilderness; but, at certain times, under the influence of unknown causes which science cannot fathom, these locusts take upon them to fly over the cultivated fields and the fair provinces of the Empire. At such a time there is nothing for the farmer to do but to go out and find the places where they have laid their eggs in the soil. They dig a hole a few inches in depth and they deposit a bag containing over a hundred eggs. Every egg is a locust and every locust can produce one hundred eggs, and these locusts sweep like a devouring prairie-fire all over the country, leaving nothing but dead vegetation and wailing men behind them. *We must go down to the locust's home; we must go into Arabia; we must go into the Soudan; we must go into Central Asia; and we must Christianize these people or they will march over their deserts, and they will sweep like a fire that shall devour our Christianity and destroy it.*"[1]

[1] "Report of the Centenary Conference on the Protestant Missions of the World, held in London, 1888," Vol. I, 323.

A CHALLENGE TO FAITH

"Until the present century very little systematic effort seems to have been made. As regards the work of the present century there have been the efforts of magnificent pioneers, but we need something more."—*Report of Lambeth Conference on Work for Mohammedans* (1897).

"We should lay siege to the Port Arthurs of the non-Christian world with the undiscourageable purpose to capture them. We should not shrink or falter before such apparently impregnable fortresses as the Mohammedan world"—*John R. Mott,* in address at Student Volunteer Convention, Nashville, 1906.

"The Church must awake to her duty toward Islam. Who will wake her and keep her awake unless it be those who have heard the challenge of Islam, and who, going out against her, have found her armor decayed, her weapons antiquated and her children, though proud and reticent, still unhappy?"—*Robert E. Speer,* at the Cairo Conference.

"Perhaps the Church of God has too long tried to win the day by policy and state-craft—and perhaps a little more hammer and tongs, reckless, defiant, uncalculating faith would be consummate state-craft."—*John Van Ess,* missionary in Arabia.

XII

A CHALLENGE TO FAITH

Unprecedented Opportunities.—The problem and the peril of Islam are a twofold challenge to faith, and not a cause for discouragement. Those who have tried to reach Mohammedans with the Gospel message and who are in the forefront of the fight, do not call for retreat, but for reinforcements and advance. They know that in this mighty conflict we have nothing to fear save our own sloth and inactivity. The battle is the Lord's and the victory will be His also. The love of Jesus Christ, manifested in hospitals, in schools, in tactful preaching, and incarnated in the lives of devoted missionaries, will irresistibly win Moslems and disarm all their fanaticism. It has done so, is doing so, and will do so more and more when the church realizes and seizes her unprecedented opportunities in the Moslem world. "Altogether the situation as regards work among Mohammedans," says Dr. Rouse, the veteran missionary of Bengal, "is most interesting and encouraging. It would be much more so if I saw any sign of appreciation on the part of the Church of Christ of the special opportunities for missionary work among Mohammedans which are now to be found in all India and elsewhere. Why should we not attack vigorously when the enemy is beginning to waver?"[1]

[1] "Students and the Modern Missionary Crusade," Addresses given at Student Volunteer Convention, Nashville. 457, 458.

The present political division of the Mohammedan world is a startling challenge of opportunity. When we remember Lord Curzon's remark that "the Mohammedan conception of politics is not so much that of a state-church as of a church-state,"[1] and recall what we have read of the political power of Islam in the past, we realize how great has been the change in a single century. The map (page 56) shows us how the area of the present Caliphate has dwindled to smaller proportions than it was at the time of Mohammed's death. Over one-half of the Moslem world is now under Christian rule or protection. Christian rule has not always been favorable for the spread of Christianity, yet it means generally a free press, free speech and liberty to confess Christ. Purely Mohammedan rule means an enslaved press, no freedom of speech and death for the apostate from Islam. The keys to every gateway in the Moslem world are in the political grasp of Christian powers, with the exception of Mecca and Constantinople.

Distances and dangers have become less, so that the journey from London to Bagdad can now be accomplished with less hardship and in less time than it must have taken Lull to go from Paris to Bugia. Henry Martyn spent five long months to reach Shiraz from Calcutta; the same journey can now be made in a fortnight. And without waiting for the completion of the Mecca railway, a missionary could visit the Holy Cities as easily as Lull did Tunis, were the same spirit of martyrdom alive among us that inspired the pioneer of Palma, and were it a wise thing to do so now.

Mindful of the polyglot character of Islam and of the

[1]Persia," Vol. I, 509.

HOSPITAL AT BAHREIN

fact that we have the Bible, at least in part, in every Moslem tongue, what magnificent opportunities there are to-day to establish, enlarge and endow mission presses in the chief Moslem centres of learning and literature! Those now in existence are overtaxed with work and supported in a half-hearted fashion. They clamor for men and means to meet the demand for books on the part of Mohammedans. Who can estimate the possibilities of the Beirut press, or the Nile mission press, for the Arabic-speaking world if either one had a million dollars? In the Chinese language there is a large Mohammedan literature, but only three little pamphlets have been published so far that are specially adapted to the thirty million Moslems of China.[1] Here is a call for the man with literary tastes and talent for languages. Then there is the world-wide opportunity, even in the most difficult fields, for distribution of the Word of God among Moslems by colporteurs and missionaries. Not without reason does the Koran always speak of Christians as "the people of the Book." Ours is the opportunity to prove it by carrying *the Book* to every Moslem in the world. We can safely leave the verdict on the Book to the Moslem himself. Last year there were issued from the Christian presses at Constantinople and Beirut, in languages read by Mohammedans, over fifty million pages of Christian literature, and these books are not printed for free distribution, but for sale.[2] The demand for Christian literature is everywhere on the increase. I have myself received an order by mail at Bahrein from a Moslem at Mecca for an Arabic reference Bible and a concordance, and from the

---

[1]"Literature for Moslems," 92, in "Methods of Mission Work Among Moslems." (1907)

[2]James L. Barton, in "Students and the Modern Missionary Crusade," 442.

Beirut Press they have sent Arabic Scriptures to the Moslems of China.

The opportunities for *medical* mission work among Moslems are very great, because there is a demand for missionary physicians on the part of Moslems themselves, and of all the methods adopted by Christian missions in Moslem lands none have been more successful in breaking down prejudices and bringing large numbers of people under the sound of the Gospel. The work at Sheikh Othman, Busrah and Bahrein, in Arabia; at Quetta, in Baluchistan, and at Tanta, in Egypt, are examples. Regarding the latter place, Doctor Anna Watson reports that ninety per cent. of the cases treated are Moslem women, who come from villages scattered far and wide, untouched by any other missionary agency.[1] The medical missionary carries a passport of mercy which will gain admission for the truth everywhere. All of the vast yet unoccupied territory in the Mohammedan world is waiting for the pioneer medical missionary, man or woman.

In many Moslem lands there are unprecedented opportunities for *educational* work. The spread of the New Islam, the increase of journalism, the political ambitions of Pan-Islamism, and the march of civilization are all uniting to produce a desire for higher education. Yet while there are seven American mission colleges in the Turkish empire, not including Egypt, Persia, with a population of ten million, has not a single missionary college.[2] Mr. Jordan writes:

"For some years past the Persian Government has

---

[1] "Methods of Mission Work Among Moslems," 109.

[2] S. M. Jordan, "An Unprecedented Opportunity: Wanted, a College for Persia"; a pamphlet. (Board of Foreign Missions of the Presbyterian Church, 1906.)

THE NEW METHOD OF REFORMATION IN PERSIA

been growing liberal and is now seeking to introduce free institutions. The intelligent classes believe that constitutional government and Western education will do for Persia what they have done for Japan in the past forty years. Education has become almost a fad, and the Shah professes to be the leader in the movement. They have opened elementary schools for themselves and are seeking help from every source. Last year they brought out five French professors to teach in the Imperial College in Teheran. What that institution amounts to was well summed up by one of these teachers, who replied to my inquiry for its welfare: 'Oh, it is half a pity and half a farce.' Some time ago a son-in-law of the Shah remarked to one of our missionaries: 'Why do not you Americans build a college in Teheran where we Persians can educate our sons?'

"I believe that the world has never seen a greater opportunity to influence a nation at its very centre and help it on the upward path than is presented to us in the Persian capital. It is one of the world's strategic points. Shall we not occupy it with an institution that will be a source of light and civilization and moral uplift for the whole country?"

Persia is only a typical case. There are other Moslem lands that are struggling upward, in spite of Islam, toward a constitutional government and free institutions. The addresses made by the Ameer of Afghanistan on his recent visit in India were a plain indication of an intellectual daybreak, even beyond the Himalayas. And what an opportunity there must be in India for the ordinary day-school when the census returns tell us that ninety-five per cent. of the Mohammedans of that country are illiterate!

The disintegration of Islam and the present crisis emphasize these unprecedented opportunities. From every quarter comes the testimony that the attitude of Moslems generally toward Christianity has changed for the better in the past decade, in spite of the frantic efforts of their political and religious leaders to bring about a reaction.[1]

In India Islam has abandoned, as untenable, controversial positions which were once thought impregnable. Instead of denying the integrity of the Bible and forbidding its use, they now read it and write commentaries on it. Mighty and irresistible forces are at work in Islam itself to prepare the way for the Gospel. Thousands of Moslems have grown dissatisfied with their old faith, and of tens of thousands it is true that they are hungering for a living Mediator. The Babis, the Beha'is, the Shathalis, the Sufis, are all examples of this unconscious search for our Redeemer, whom Mohammed and the Koran have so long eclipsed.

> "Far and wide, though all unknowing,
>   Pants for Thee each human breast;
> Human tears for Thee are flowing,
>   Human hearts in Thee would rest."

The Cairo Conference.—The thought of a world's conference to discuss the problems of Moslem evangelization had, no doubt, often occurred to more than one missionary at the front; especially ever since Dr. H. H. Jessup gave the Church an outline of the problem in 1879.[2] Yet missionaries felt that at none of the great general missionary conferences since that time had Islam received such breadth of treatment and careful attention

[1] See "The Mohammedan World of To-day", also Tables on 284 and 294, column S

[2] "The Mohammedan Missionary Problem." (Philadelphia, 1879.)

as the subject and the crisis demanded. Therefore, after much consultation with missionaries in every Mohammedan land and with missionary authorities in all parts of the world, the Arabian Mission, in 1904, opened correspondence with the missions in Egypt, and steps were taken to hold a General Conference on behalf of the Mohammedan world at Cairo. The conference met from April 4th to 9th, 1906, and marked a forward step in missions. The presence of sixty-two representatives from twenty-nine missionary societies in Europe and America, with nearly an equal number of missionary visitors; the manifest unanimity of spirit in all the discussions; the printed proceedings of the conference, which for the first time in history give a survey of the field; and the deeply spiritual character of the gathering —all these lead to the hope that this conference will be used of God as a means of arousing the Christian Church to more energetic and systematic effort for the millions of Islam. The papers read at the conference were in part published under the title, "The Mohammedan World of To-day," and in part, for prudential reasons, only printed for private circulation.[1] *An appeal by the conference* was sent out to the Church at large, and is itself a challenge to faith, coming as it does from men and women who have given of their strength and their service, their love and their life, to evangelize these Mohammedan lands. It speaks for itself:

"The great needs of more than two hundred million Mohammedans and the present problems of work among them, laid upon the hearts of missionaries in several

---

[1] "Methods of Mission Work Among Moslems" Papers read at the Cairo Conference. Privately printed for the use of missionaries.

countries, led to the assembling of this conference of delegates from missions in Moslem lands, which has been sitting at Cairo from the 4th to the 9th April, 1906.

"We have been presented with a series of comprehensive reviews of the whole Mohammedan world, of its ethnic, social, religious and intellectual conditions, of missionary work thus far accomplished, and of the tasks and problems still presented by it to the Christian Church; we have considered, though too briefly, some of the chief methods of missionary work among Mohammedans, in preaching, literature, medicine, and upbuilding of converts.

"These outstanding facts as to the great needs of the Mohammedan world, the first-fruits of its evangelization, and the openings for a great advance in bringing the Gospel to Moslems, have been borne in upon us as a strong call from God to His Church in the present day. Coming from many Mohammedan and Christian lands, and dealing with varied aspects of Islam, we unitedly and urgently call upon the Christian Church, as represented by her missionary agencies, for a fresh departure in the energy and effectiveness of her work among Mohammedans. We ask that it may be strengthened and promoted (1) by setting apart more special laborers and by giving them a specialized training; (2) by organizing more efficiently the production and distribution of literature for Mohammedans; (3) by systematic common arrangements for the fresh occupation of important centres, and the more effective working of those already occupied, and for forestalling the entrance of Islam into territories so far pagan. With this view we draw the attention of the Committees and Boards to the volume under publication, embodying the surveys presented to the conference,

THE GREAT MOSQUE AT DELHI

Moslems at prayer

and we suggest that action on this basis be considered by the meetings held in each country for interdenominational missionary action.

'God wills it,
May He enable us to do His will.' "[1]

The women delegates also published an additional appeal, which reads:

"We, the women missionaries assembled at the Cairo Conference, would send this appeal on behalf of the women of Moslem lands to all our sisters in the home churches of Great Britain, America, Canada, France, Germany, Switzerland, Denmark, Norway, Sweden, Holland, Australia and New Zealand.

"While we have heard with deep thankfulness of many signs of God's blessing on the efforts already put forth, yet we have been appalled at the reports which have been sent in to the conference from all parts of the Moslem world, showing us only too clearly that as yet but a fringe of this great work has been touched. Our hearts have been wrung as we have listened to statements after statements of sin and oppression, and have realized something more of the almost unrelieved darkness which reigns in the lives of our Moslem sisters.

"First—Through her physical sufferings, such as spring from the evils of child marriage; the unre-

---

[1] The appeal was signed, on behalf of the Conference, by the executive committee, as follows:

John Giffen, D.D (U. P. of N. A); H. H. Jessup, D D (Am Pres.); Milton H. Marshall (N. Africa); Dr. J. S. Tympany (Am. Baptist), Rev. D. M. Thornton, M.A. (C M S); Bishop F. W Warne (M Episcopal, U.S.A.); E. M. Wherry, D.D. (Am Pres); H. U. Weitbrecht, Ph D , D D (C.M S.), Rev F. Wurz (Basel Ev Miss); S. M. Zwemer, D D. (Ref. Ch. in Arabia). Representing twenty-nine missionary societies.

strained power of the men of the family, whether father, brother, husband or son, to beat and abuse her; her powerlessness to escape or plead her own cause; her use of narcotics and stimulants not to be wondered at, to drown her misery.

"Second—Her mental sufferings, from ignorance and a sense of inferiority and degradation, from the continual fear of being divorced; her fear of unseen powers of evil, and of death and the hereafter; her lack of real love; the absence of true family life, which blights the home of both parents and children; and her suffering from the jealousy which is inseparable from polygamy.

"Third—Her spiritual suffering and anguish of mind, without comfort in the thought of God, Who is to her only a hard master, Whose injustice she unconsciously resents.

"We feel that an outcry against the cruelty and injustice of men is not the way to meet these evils. There is no remedy but to bring the women to the Lord Jesus, Who died to save them from the curse pronounced upon them as a punishment for sin. We must teach her by love to win her husband's love, and by deserving it to win his respect, believing that God has given to every man the capacity to love his wife.

"The number of Moslem women is so vast—not less than one hundred million—that any adequate effort to meet the need must be on a scale far wider than has ever yet been attempted.

"We do not suggest new organizations, but that every church and board of missions at present working in Moslem lands should take up their own women's branch of the work with an altogether new ideal before them, determining to reach the whole world of Moslem women in this generation. Each part of the women's work being already carried on needs to be widely extended—trained and consecrated women doctors, trained and consecrated women teachers, groups of women workers in the villages, an army of those with love in their hearts, to seek and save the lost. And with the willingness to take up this burden, so long neglected, for the salvation of Mohammedan women, even though it may prove a very Cross of Calvary to some of us, we shall hear our Master's voice afresh, with ringing words of encouragement: 'Have faith in God.' 'For verily I say unto you, that whosoever shall say unto this mountain, "Be thou removed," and "Be thou cast into the sea," and shall not doubt in his heart, but shall believe that these things which He saith shall come to pass, he shall have whatsoever he saith.' 'Nothing shall be impossible to you.'"

The Challenge.—These urgent appeals from living missionaries who form the long, thin line on the forefront of battle against Islam must not fall on deaf ears. They are a challenge to faith and to sacrifice. They are a call for immediate reinforcements, for more laborers and for more efficient preparation in those sent out. To deal effectively with a community professing the religion of the Koran and guided by its highly systematized theology, it should go without saying that we need a body of men in each mission area possessing a competent knowledge of Arabic and Moslem theology, while the rank and file should have a correct acquaintance with the doctrines, duties, facts and customary terminology of Islam.[1]

Even in India, according to the Bishop of Lahore, there is "a widespread absence of real acquaintance with

[1] H. U. Weitbrecht, in *The Church Missionary Intelligencer*, June, 1906.

the Mohammedan literature" on the part of missionaries who live and labor among Moslems. "Not infrequently during my years in Delhi," he writes, "when I wanted to refer to some tradition which I knew existed in one of the well-known collections, it was a cause of real pain to me—and, as I thought, a reproach to the missionary cause—that there was scarcely a single missionary, so far as I knew, in upper India to whom I could turn for the needed reference—not more than two or three, indeed, in the whole of India, and to them I sometimes turned in vain. Surely this reproach ought to be wiped away."[1]

For the evangelization of the Mohammedan world we need, first and most of all men, "the best men the Church can afford—men who, in the spirit of Henry Martyn, Isidor Loewenthal, Ion Keith-Falconer, Bishop French, Peter Zwemer, and many others gone to their reward, hold not their lives dear; men who carry the burden of these millions of Moslems upon their hearts, and, with Abraham of old, cry out: 'O that Ishmael might live before thee!'"[2] For in the last analysis the evangelization of the Mohammedan world depends, under God, on a band of picked volunteers prepared to do pioneer work and ready to sacrifice life itself, if need be, to enter and occupy Moslem lands. The call is for volunteers.

The missionary boards and societies are taking up the challenge of Islam;[3] will the colleges and universities furnish the men for the work to-day? The time is ripe for a world-wide spiritual crusade for the conquest of Islam. The prophetic dreams of Raymund Lull and of

[1] G. A. LeFroy, "The Preparation of Workers for Work Among Moslems," in "Methods of Mission Work Among Moslems," 223, 224.

[2] Introduction to "Islam and Christianity in India"

[3] See J. L. Barton's address at the Haystack Centennial of the American Board of Commissioners for Foreign Missions, 289-296; also Report of the Conference of Mission Boards Secretaries, 1907.

Henry Martyn await fulfillment. The new century of American foreign missions calls for a new vision of the Moslem world in its strength, its weakness, its needs, its accessibility, its promise, as well as in its antagonism, to Christ, the Son of God. "Father, the hour is come, glorify Thy Son." Christ's rightful glory has been given to Mohammed for many ages in these many lands and in millions of hearts. Surely our Saviour Himself is waiting to see of the travail of His soul for the Moslem world. God wills it. That was the battle-cry of the old Crusaders. Yet there was a thousandfold more enthusiasm in the dark ages to wrest an empty sepulchre from the Saracens than there is in our day to bring them the knowledge of a living Saviour. Shall we take up that cry in a nobler crusade with the sword of the spirit?

Where Christ was born Mohammed's name is called from minarets five times daily, but where Mohammed was born no Christian dares to enter.

America entertained perverts to Islam at a Parliament of Religions, while throughout vast regions of the Mohammedan world millions of Moslems have never so much as heard of the incarnation and the atonement of the Son of God, the Saviour of the world. The Holy Land is still in unholy hands, and all Christendom stood gazing while the sword of the Crescent was uplifted in Armenia and Crete, until the uttermost confines of the Moslem world rejoiced at her apathy and impotence.

Is this to be the measure of our consecration? Is this the extent of our loyal devotion to the cause of our King? His place occupied by a usurper and His glory given to another. Shall we not arise and win back the lost kingdom? *Missions to Moslems are the only Christian solution of the Eastern question.* God wills it. Let our rallying cry be: "Every stronghold of Islam for Christ!" Not a war of gunboats, or of diplomacy, but a Holy War with the Sword of the Spirit, which is the Word of God. Let God arise and let His enemies be scattered.

God wills it; therefore we must do it. God wills it; therefore He will accomplish it. God wills it; therefore we will ask Him to do it speedily: "Thy Kingdom come; Thy will be done," throughout the Mohammedan world.

> "Not in dumb resignation
>   We lift our hands on high,
> Not like the nerveless fatalist,
>   Content to trust and die;
> Our faith springs like the eagle
>   That soars to meet the sun,
> And cries exulting unto Thee:
>   O Lord! Thy will be done!"

If Islam is a challenge to faith, faith alone can accept the challenge, *and does*. "For whatsoever is born of God overcometh the world; and this is the victory that overcometh the world, even our faith. Who is he that overcometh the world but he that believeth that Jesus is the Son of God?"

APPENDICES

APPENDIX A

CHRONOLOGICAL TABLE OF IMPORTANT EVENTS IN THE HISTORY OF ISLAM AND OF MISSIONS TO MOSLEMS

"Facts are the fingers of God.
—*Dr. A. T. Pierson.*

A. D.	ISLAM	A. D.	MISSIONS
570	Birth of Mohammed at Mecca.		
595	Yemen passes under Persian rule		
610.	Mohammed begins his prophetic career		
622.	The Hegira, or flight of Mohammed from Mecca to Medina (A.H. 1).		
623	Battle of Bedr.		
624.	Battle of Ohod.		
628.	Reputed mission of Abu Kabsha to China		
630.	Mecca entered and conquered.		
632	Death of Mohammed. Abu Bekr, first Caliph.		
634.	Omar, Caliph, Jews and Christians expelled from Arabia		
636.	Capture of Jerusalem by the Caliph Omar.		
637.	Conquest of Syria.		
638	Kufa and Busrah founded.		
640.	Capture of Alexandria by Omar		
642.	Conquest of Persia.		
644.	Othman, Caliph.		
661.	Ali assassinated Hassan becomes Caliph.		
662-750.	Omayid caliphs at Damascus.		
710-1492.	Mohammedan rule in Spain		
711	Tarik crosses the straits from Africa to Europe, and calls the mountain Jebel Tarik = Gibraltar.		
711	Mohammed Kasim overruns Sindh (India) in the name of Walid I of Damascus.		
732.	Battle of Tours. Europe saved from Islam.		

259

A D   ISLAM   A. D.   MISSIONS

742. First mosque built in North
     China.
754. Mansur.
756-1258 Abbasid caliphs at Bag
     dad
786 Haroun er-Rashid, Caliph of
     Bagdad.
809 Amin.
813. Mamun.
833 Motasim. Islam spreads into   830. Abd el Messia Al Kindy, a
     Transoxania.   Christian, at the Court of Al
847 Mutawakkel.   Mamun, writes his apology.
889 Rise of Carmathian sect.
930 Carmathians take Mecca and
     carry away the Black Stone to
     Katif.
1000. Islam invades India from the
     North.
1005. Preaching of Sheikh Ismail at
     Lahore, India
1019 Mahmud Ghazni, champion of
     Islam in India.
1037-1300 Seljuk Turks
1055. Togrul Beg at Bagdad.
1063 Alp Arslan, Saljukian Turkish
     prince.
1077. Timbuctoo founded Islam en-   1096-1272. The Crusades.
     ters Western Soudan.
1169-1193 Saladin
1176-1206. Mohammed Ghori con-
     quers Bengal.
1276 Islam introduced into Malacca.
1299-1326. Reign of Othman, founder
     of Ottoman dynasty.
1305 Preaching and spread of Islam   1315. Raymund Lull, first mission-
     in the Deccan.   ary to Moslems, stoned to
1330. Institution of the Janissaries.   death at Bugia, Tunis.
1353. First entrance of the Turks
     into Europe.
1369-1405. Tamerlane.
1389 Islam begins to spread in Ser-
     via.
1398 Tamerlane invades India.
1414. Conversion of the King of
     Bengal
1450 Missionary activity of Islam in   1452. Perfection of art of printing
     Java begins.   by Guttenberg.
1453. Capture of Constantinople by
     Mohammed II.
1492. Discovery of America. End of
     Moslem rule in Spain by de-
     feat of Boabdil at Granada
1500. Spread of Islam in Siberia.
1507 The Portuguese take Muscat.
1517. Selim I conquers Egypt and
     wrests caliphate from Arab
     line of Koreish for Ottoman
     sultans
1525-1707. Mogul empire in India.
1538 Suleiman t h e Magnificent
     takes Aden by treachery.
1540. Beginning of Turkish rule in
     Yemen
1556. Akbar the Great rules in In-   1596. Xavier holds discussions with
     dia.   the Moslems at Lahore.

A D.   ISLAM

1603. Islam enters Celebes and New Guinea
1627. Shah Jehan, Mogul ruler in India.
1630 Arabs drive out Turks from Yemen.
1659-1707. Aurangzeb in India.
1683. Final check of Turks at the gates of Vienna by John Sobieski, King of Poland, September 12 Eastern Europe saved from Moslem rule
1691 Mohammed bin Abd ul Wahab born
1739-1761. Afghan Mohammed invasion of India, and sack of Delhi
1740-1780 Wahabi reform spreads over all Southern and Central Arabia, except Oman
1757 Battle of Plassey British empire in India
1801. Wahabis invade Bagdad vilayet and sack Kerbela
1803. Mecca taken by the Wahabis.
1805-1820 British suppress Wahabi piracy in the Persian Gulf.
1820-1847 British treaties with Moslem chiefs in Persian Gulf.
1815 Battle of Bessel Wahabis defeated.
1826. Wahabi Jihad in India against the Sikhs.

1839 Aden bombarded by British fleet and taken.

1856 End of Crimean War. Treaty of Paris

1857. Indian (Sepoy) Mutiny.
1858 Bombardment of Jiddah by British
1860. Civil war in the Lebanons.

A. D.   MISSIONS

1806. Henry Martyn reaches India.
1820 Levi Parsons and Pliny Fiske, first missionaries from America, reach Smyrna
1822 American Mission Press founded in Malta.

1826. Church Missionary Society attempts a mission in Egypt
1827 Dr Eli Smith begins translation of the Arabic Bible
1829. Missionary C. G Pfander visits Persia
1831 Constantinople occupied by American Board of Commissioners for Foreign Missions.
1833 American mission begun at Tabriz.
1836. Scriptures published in Græco-Turkish

1847 Aintab occupied by American Board of Commissioners for Foreign Missions
1851 Church Missionary Society begins mission in Palestine
1856. Hatti Sherif, or charter of religious freedom, obtained for Turkey.
1857 Harpoot occupied.
1858. Mardin occupied.

1860 Dr. Van Dyck's translation of Arabic New Testament issued.
1862 The Rhenish mission enters Sumatra
1863. Syrian Protestant College founded at Beirut.
1866. First Girls' Boarding-school, Cairo
1868. Imad-ud-Din ordained at Amritsar.

A D.	ISLAM	A. D.	MISSIONS
		1869.	Cornerstone laid of Robert College at Constantinople.
		1869	Rev. Robert Bruce visits Ispahan, Persia.
1870.	Second Turkish invasion of Yemen.		
		1871.	Bible House built at Constantinople.
		1872	Teheran occupied by the Presbyterian Mission
		1875	Church Missionary Society begins mission work in Persia.
		1876.	Euphrates College established at Harpoot.
		1876.	Church Missionary Society opens mission at Ispahan, Persia.
1878.	Treaty of Berlin Independence of Bulgaria. England occupies Cyprus Reforms promised for Turkey.		
1879	Royal Niger Company founded (Britain in Africa).		
1881.	Rise of the Mahdi near Khartum.	1881	North Africa Mission organized
1882.	Massacre of Europeans at Alexandria.	1882	Church Missionary Society begins work in Egypt
1882.	British occupation of Egypt		
1883.	D e f e a t of Anglo-Egyptian forces by the Mahdi.	1883.	Mission work begun at Bagdad by the Church Missionary Society.
1885	Fall of Khartum. Murder of Gordon.	1885.	Keith-Falconer begins work at Aden
1889.	Mahdi invasion of Egypt	1889.	The (American) Arabian Mission organized
1890.	Anglo-French protectorate declared over Sahara.	1890	James Cautine, first American missionary to Arabia, sails for the field
		1891	Bishop French died at Muscat, May 14
1892.	French annex Dahomey and conquer Timbuctoo.	1893	Mirza Ibrahim martyred in Persia.
1894	Anglo-French-German delimitation of Soudan		
1895	Rebellion of Arabs against the Turks in Yemen		
1894-1896	Great Armenian massacres.		
1896	Massacre at Harpoot		
1898	Fall of the Mahdi Occupation of the Soudan.		
1900.	British protectorate declared over Nigeria and Hansa-Land		
1906.	The Algeciras Conference regarding Morocco.	1906	American Board of Commissioners for Foreign Missions opens work for Moslems at Mindanao, P. I
		1906	The first general Missionary Conference on behalf of the Mohammedan world held at Cairo.
1907.	The French Army enters Morocco. (Casablanca)	1907	The Foreign Mission Board, Methodist Episcopal Church, begins work in Algiers.

APPENDIX B

WILLIAM GIFFORD PALGRAVE'S CHARAC-
TERIZATION OF ALLAH

"There is no god but God—are words simply tantamount in English to the negation of any deity, save one alone, and thus much they certainly mean in Arabic, but they imply much more also Their full sense is not only to deny absolutely and unreservedly all plurality, whether of nature or of person in the Supreme Being, not only to establish the unity of the Unbegetting and the Unbegot, in all its simple and uncommunicable Oneness, but besides this the words in Arabic and among the Arabs imply that this one Supreme Being is also the only Agent, the only Force, and the only Act existing throughout the universe, and leaves to all beings else. matter or spirit, instinct or intelligence, physical or moral, nothing but pure unconditional passiveness alike in movement or in quiescence, in action or in captivity. The sole power, the sole motor, movement, energy and deed is God; the rest is downright inertia and mere instrumentality, from the highest archangel down to the simplest atom of creation. Hence, in this one sentence, 'La ilaha illa Allah,' is summed up a system which, for want of a better name, I may be permitted to call the Pantheism of Force, or of Act, thus exclusively assigned to God, who absorbs it all, exercises it all, and to Whom alone it can be ascribed, whether for preserving or for destroying, for relative evil or for equally relative good I say *relative*, because it is clear that, in such a theology, no place is left for absolute good or evil, reason or extravagance; all is abridged in the autocratical will of the one great Agent: 'sic volo, sic jubeo, stet pro ratione voluntas'; or, more significantly still, in Arabic: 'Kama yesha,' 'as He wills it,' to quote the constantly recurring expression of the Koran

"Thus immeasurably and eternally exalted above, and dissimilar from, all creatures which lie leveled before Him on one common plane of instrumentality and inertness, God is One in the totality of omnipotent and omnipresent action, which acknowledges no rule, standard or limit, save His own sole and absolute will He communicates nothing to His creatures; for their seeming power and act ever remain His alone, and in return He receives nothing from them; for whatever they may be, that they are in Him, by Him and from Him only. And secondly, no superiority, no distinction, no preëminence can be lawfully claimed by one creature over another in the utter equalization of their unexceptional servitude and abasement; all are alike tools of the one solitary Force, which employs them to crush or to benefit, to truth or to error, to honor or shame, to happiness or misery, quite independently of their individual fitness, deserts or advantage, and simply because He wills it and as He wills it.

"One might. at first sight, think that this tremendous Autocrat, this uncontrolled and unsympathizing Power would be far above anything like passions, desires or inclinations. Yet such is not the case, for He has, with respect to His creatures, one main feeling and source of action, namely, jealousy of them, lest they should perchance attribute to themselves something of what is His alone, and thus encroach on His all-engrossing kingdom. Hence He is ever more ready to punish than to reward, to inflict pain than to bestow pleasure, to ruin than to build. It is His singular satisfaction to make created beings continually feel that they are nothing else than His slaves, His tools, and contemptible tools also, that thus they may the better acknowledge His superiority, and know His power to be above their power, His cunning above their cunning, His will above their will, His pride above their pride: or, rather, that there is no power, cunning, will or pride save His own. But He Himself, sterile in His inaccessible height, neither loving nor enjoying aught save His own and self-measured decree, without son, companion or counselor, is no less barren for Himself than for His creatures; and His own barrenness and lone egoism in Himself is the cause and rule of His indifferent and unregarding despotism around. The first note is the key of the whole tune, and the primal idea of God runs through and modifies the whole system and creed that centres in Him.

"That the notion here given of the Deity, monstrous and blasphemous as it may appear, is exactly and literally that which the Koran conveys, or intends to convey, I at present take for granted But that it indeed is so, no one who has attentively perused and thought over the Arabic text (for there cursory reading, especially in a translation, will not suffice) can hesitate to allow. In fact, every phrase of the preceding sentences, every touch in this odious portrait has been taken, to the best of my ability, word for word, or, at least. meaning for meaning, from 'the Book,' the truest mirror of the mind and scope of its writer. And that such was in reality Mahomet's mind and idea is fully confirmed by the witness-tongue of contemporary tradition. Of this we have many authentic samples · the Saheeh, the commentaries of Beidhawi, the Mishkat-el-Misabih, and fifty similar works, afford ample testimony on this point."—Quoted in Zwemer, *Moslem Doctrine of God.* pp. 65-69 top; Palgrave, *Narrative of a Year's Journey through Arabia.*

APPENDIX C

THOMAS PATRICK HUGHES' CHARACTERIZATION OF MOHAMMED

"The character of Muhammad is a historic problem, and many have been the conjectures as to his motives and designs. Was he an impostor, a fanatic, or an honest man—'a very prophet of God'? And the problem might have forever remained unsolved had not the prophet himself appealed to the Old and New Testaments in proof of his mission. This is the crucial test, established by the prophet himself. He claims to be weighed in the balance with the divine Jesus

"Objection has often been made to the manner in which Christian divines have attacked the private character of Muhammad Why reject the prophetic mission of Muhammad on account of his private vices, when you receive as inspired the sayings of a Balaam, a David, or a Solomon? Missionaries should not, as a rule, attack the character of Muhammad in dealing with Islam; it rouses opposition, and is an offensive line of argument. Still, in forming an estimate of his prophetic claims, we maintain that the character of Muhammad is an important consideration. We readily admit that bad men have sometimes been, like Balaam and others, the divinely appointed organs of inspiration, but in the case of Muhammad, his professed inspiration sanctioned and encouraged his own vices That which ought to have been the fountain of purity was, in fact, the cover of the prophet's depravity. But how different it is in the case of the true prophet—David—where, in the words of inspiration, he lays bare to public gaze the enormity of his own crimes. The deep contrition of his inmost soul is manifest in every line—'I acknowledge my transgression, and my sin is ever before me: against Thee, Thee only, have I sinned, and done this evil in Thy sight'

"The best defenders of the Arabian prophet are obliged to admit that the matter of Zainab, the wife of Zaid, and again of Mary, the Coptic slave, are 'an indelible stain' upon his memory; that 'he is once or twice untrue to the kind and forgiving disposition of his best nature; that he is once or twice unrelenting in the punishment of his personal enemies; and that he is

guilty even more than once of conniving at the assassination of
inveterate opponents'; *but they give no satisfactory explanation
or apology for all this being done under the supposed sanction
of God in the Qur'ān*

"In forming an estimate of Muhammad's prophetical preten-
sions, it must be remembered that he did not claim to be the
founder of a new religion, but merely of a new covenant. He
is the last and greatest of all God's prophets. He is sent to convert the world to the one true religion which God had before
revealed to the five great law-givers—Adam, Noah, Abraham,
Moses and Jesus ! The creed of Muhammad, therefore, claims
to supersede that of the Lord Jesus. And it is here that we take
our stand. We give Muhammad credit as a warrior, as a legislator, as a poet, as a man of uncommon genius raising himself,
amidst great opposition, to the pinnacle of renown; we admit that
he is, without doubt, one of the greatest heroes the world has
ever seen; but when we consider his claim to *supersede* the mission of the divine Jesus, we strip him of his borrowed plumes,
and reduce him to the condition of an impostor ! For whilst he
has adopted and avowed his belief in the sacred books of the
Jew, and the Christian, and has given them all the stamp and
currency which his authority and influence could impart, he has
attempted to rob Christianity of every distinctive truth which it
possesses—its Divine Saviour, its Heavenly Comforter, its two
Sacraments, its pure code of social morals, its spirit of love and
truth—and has written his own refutation and condemnation with
his own hand, by professing to confirm the divine oracles which
sap the very foundations of his religious system. We follow the
prophet in his self-asserted mission from the cave of Hira' to
the closing scene, when he dies in the midst of the lamentations
of his harim and the contentions of his friends; the visions of
Gabriel, the period of mental depression, the contemplated suicide, the assumption of the prophetic office, his struggles with
Makkan unbelief, his flight to al-Madinah, his triumphant entry
into Makkah —and, whilst we wonder at the genius of the hero,
we pause at every stage and inquire. 'Is this the apostle of God,
whose mission is to claim universal dominion, to the suppression
not merely of idolatry, but of Christianity itself?' Then it is
that the divine and holy character of Jesus rises to our view,
and the inquiring mind sickens at the thought of the beloved, the
pure, the lowly Jesus giving place to that of the ambitious, the
sensual, the *time-serving* hero of Arabia In the study of Islam,
the character of Muhammad needs an apology or a defence at
every stage; but in the contemplation of the Christian system,
whilst we everywhere read of Jesus, and see the reflection of His
image in everything we read, the heart revels in the contemplation, the inner pulsations of our spiritual life bound within us
at the study of a character so divine, so pure.

"We are not insensible to the beauties of the Qur'an as a literary production (although they have, without doubt, been over-rated), but, as we admire its conceptions of the Divine nature, its deep and fervent trust in the power of God, its frequent deep moral earnestness, and its sententious wisdom, we would gladly rid ourselves of our recollections of the prophet, his licentious harim, his sanguinary battlefields, his ambitious schemes; whilst as we peruse the Christian Scriptures we find the grand central charm in the divine character of its Founder It is the divine character of Jesus which gives fragrance to His words, it is the divine form of Jesus which shines through all He says or does; it is the divine life of Jesus which is the great central point in Gospel history. How, then, we ask, can the creed of Muhammad, the son of 'Abdu'llah, supersede and abrogate that of Jesus, the Son of God? And it is a remarkable coincidence that, whilst the founder of Islam died feeling that he had but imperfectly fulfilled his mission, the Founder of Christianity died in the full consciousness that His work was done—'it is finished' It was in professing to produce a revelation which should supersede that of Jesus that Muhammad set the seal of his own refutation "—Hughes, *Notes on Muhammadanism,* p. 2; Hughes, *Dictionary of Islam,* pp. 398 and 399.

APPENDIX D

LIST OF MISSIONARY SOCIETIES

THE PRINCIPAL MISSIONARY SOCIETIES AND BOARDS WORK-
ING IN MOSLEM LANDS OR AMONG MOSLEMS, DIRECTLY
OR INDIRECTLY, ARE AS FOLLOWS:

American Bible Society (organized, 1816), New York; periodical, *Bible Society Record;* field, The Levant, Arabia.

American Board of Commissioners for Foreign Missions (organized, 1810),
Boston, Mass.; periodical, *Missionary Herald,* field, Turkish Empire,
India.

Arabian Mission (organized, 1889), New York; periodicals, *Mission Field,
Neglected Arabia;* field, Arabia.

Basel Evangelical Missionary Society (1815), Basel, Switzerland, periodical,
Der Evangelische Heidenbote; field, West Africa.

Bible Lands Missions' Aid Society (1856), London, England, periodical,
Star in the East, field, Egypt, Levant, Arabia.

Board of Foreign Missions, Methodist Episcopal Church (1889), New York;
periodical, *World-Wide Missions;* field, India, Algiers

Board of Foreign Missions of the Presbyterian Church in the U. S. A.
(1837), New York; periodical, *Assembly Herald,* field, Syria, Persia,
India.

Board of Foreign Missions of the United Presbyterian Church of North
America (1859), Philadelphia, Pa., periodical, *United Presbyterian Church
Record;* field, Egypt, India.

British and Foreign Bible Society (1804), London, England, periodical, *Bible
Society Reporter;* field, North Africa, Persia, India, etc

Cambridge Mission to Delhi (1867), Cambridge, England; field, India.

Central Morocco Medical Mission (1894), Dennistown, Glasgow, Scotland;
field, Morocco.

China Inland Mission (1865), Mildmay, London, England; periodical,
China's Millions; field, Yunnan Shensi.

Christian and Missionary Alliance (1887), New York; periodical, *Christian
and Missionary Alliance,* field, Palestine

Church Missionary Society (1799), Salisbury Square, London, England; pe-
riodicals, *Church Missionary Gleaner, Mercy and Truth, Church Missionary
Review;* field, Egypt, Uganda, Persia, Palestine, India, Arabia, East
Africa.

Church of England Zenana Missionary Society, 27 Chancery Lane, London, England; periodical, *India's Women;* field, India.

Deutsche Orient Mission, near Berlin, Germany; periodical, *Der Christliche
Orient;* field, Bulgaria, Persia

Egypt General Mission (1898), Belfast, Ireland; periodical, *Egypt General
Mission News;* field, Lower Egypt.

Foreign Missions of the United Free Church of Scotland (1900), Edinburgh,
Scotland; periodical, *United Free Church Record;* field, Arabia.

Java Comité (1855), Amsterdam, Holland; periodical, *Geillustrurd Zendings-blad;* field, Java

Netherlands Missionary Society (1797), Rotterdam, Holland; periodical, *Maandberichten, Madedeelingen;* field, Java

Netherlands Union for the Propagation of the Gospel in Egypt (1886), Amsterdam, Holland; field, Egypt.

North Africa Mission (1881), London, E C., England; periodical, *North Africa;* field, Egypt, Tunis, Tripoli, Morocco.

Rhenish Missionary Society, Barmen, Germany; periodical, *Missionsblatt Barmen;* field, Sumatra.

Society for the Propagation of the Gospel in Foreign Parts (1701), London, England, periodicals, *The Mission Field, The East and the West;* field, East Africa.

Southern Morocco Mission (1888), Glasgow, Scotland; periodical, *The Reaper,* field, Morocco.

Soudan Pioneer Mission (1900), Wiesbaden, Germany; periodical, *Der Soudan Pionier;* field, Assuan.

Universities Mission to Central Africa (1858), London, England; field, Central Africa.

United Soudan Mission (——), Germantown, Pennsylvania; field, ——.

APPENDIX E

SELECT BIBLIOGRAPHY FOR REFERENCE AND FURTHER STUDY

CHAPTER I

On Arabia Before Islam

CAUSSIN DE PERCEVAL, A. P.—Essai sur l'Histoire des Arabes avant l'Islamisme, pendant l'Epoque de Mahomet, et jusqua la Reduction de toutes les Tribus sous la Loi Musulmaine 3 vols. Paris, 1902.
This is a reprint of the original edition of 1847, and is a mine of information on the subject; generally reliable and authoritative.

WELLHAUSEN, J.—Reste Arabischen Heidentums. Second edition. Berlin, 1897.
Critical essays on the idols, the Haj, and the ancient cult of the Arabs, with reference to their literature and the origin of Islam.

GRIMME, HUBERT.—Die Weltgeschichtliche Bedeutung Arabiens: Mohammed Munich, 1904.
Gives an account of the Sabean civilization, and shows how much Islam owes to South Arabian monotheism. The map is excellent; there are sixty illustrations.

GOLDZIHER, IGNAZ.—Mohammedanische Studien. 2 vols. Halle. 1890
Critical essays on the relation between Arabian paganism and Islam, and on Mohammedan tradition. Invaluable to the student, but not easy reading.

SALE, GEORGE.—Preliminary Discourse to the Koran.
Printed as Introduction in most editions of Sale's Koran A brief account and, for the most part, reliable.

MUIR, SIR WILLIAM.—Introduction to his Life of Mahomet.
Excellent.

ZWEMER, S. M.—Arabia; Cradle of Islam.
Chapters XVI and XXIX

On the Sources of Islam

HUGHES, T. P—Dictionary of Islam. New York and London, 1885

A reference book of the greatest value for the whole subject, altho written from an Indian standpoint For this chapter see articles on *Jews, Christianity,* and *Mecca.*

GEIGER, RABBI—Was hat Mohammed aus das Judentum aufgenommen? Wiesbaden, 1833. Translation of the same: Judaism and Islam Madras, 1898.

A prize essay, and full of information on the parallels between the Talmud and the Koran.

TISDALL, W ST CLAIR—The Original Sources of the Qur'ân. S P.C.K London, 1905.

The result of many years of study, and the best book on the whole subject. Intensely interesting, and in compact form.

PAUTZ, OTTO.—Mohammed's Lehre von der Offenbarung Leipzig, 1898.

Contains much new material, and gives references to Moslem writers. Chapter III, on the relation of Islam to ancient paganism and Arabian Christianity, is especially important.

For further references, see the footnotes of Pautz.

CHAPTER II

KOELLE, S. W.—Mohammed and Mohammedanism Critically Considered. London, 1888.

By far the best brief biography, and from a missionary standpoint. The book gives a threefold view of Mohammed as seen in the daylight of history, in the moonshine of tradition and in contrast with Jesus Christ, our Saviour.

MUIR, SIR WILLIAM—Life of Mahomet. 4 vols. London, 1858. Reprinted in abridged form; London, 1897.

The best authority in the English language. Exhaustive

SMITH, R. BOSWORTH.—Mohammed and Mohammedanism London, 1876.

A strong apology for the prophet, and written in attractive style, but very one-sided. Read with Koelle's book.

SPRENGER, ALOYS.—Das Leben und die Lehre des Mohammed. 3 vols. Berlin, 1865 Also, Life of Mohammed from original sources Allahabad, 1851.

WEIL, GUSTAV—Das Leben Mohammed 2 vols. Stuttgart, 1864.

Based on the earliest Moslem biography by Ibn Ishak, as found in Ibn Hisham.

AMEER, ALI.—The Spirit of Islam; or, The Life and Teachings of Mohammed   Calcutta, 1902.
Written by an Indian Moslem, Judge of the High Court in Bengal. Of
considerable literary merit, and perhaps the most clever, though unhistori-
cal, apology that could be written by a follower of the New Islam.

MARGOLIOUTH, D. S.—Mohammed and the Rise of Islam. London, 1905.
Written by an Oxford professor for the "Heroes of the Nations" series.
Neither an apology nor an indictment, but a scholarly and yet popular
biography of Mohammed as founder of the Arabian Empire. Well illustrated, and with good bibliography.

The following biographies of Mohammed can also be consulted
with profit; nor is the list complete:

SIR WALTER RALEIGH.—The Life and Death of Mahomet. 1637.

GIBBON'S chapter in his Decline and Fall of the Roman Empire.

WELLHAUSEN, in Das Arabische Reich und sein Sturz.

L. KREHL (1884).—Mohammed.

H. GRIMME (1892).—Mohammed.

THOMAS CARLYLE.—The Hero as Prophet (in Heroes and Hero-
Worship.)

WASHINGTON IRVING (1850).—The Life of Mahomet.

GEORGE BUSH (1844.)—The Life of Mahomet.

MARCUS DODS, in Mohammed, Buddha, and Christ. 1878.

P. DE LACY JOHNSTONE.—Muhammad and His Power.   1901.

A. N. WOLLASTON.—The Sword of Islam   1905.

CHAPTER III

ARNOLD, T. W.—The Preaching of Islam: A history of the
Propagation of the Muslim Faith. Westminster, 1896.
The fullest and best account of the spread of Islam from the earliest
times until to-day. The author, however, is an apologist for Islam, and
tries to show that the sword was not used to any large extent in the
propagation of this faith. His arguments are often fallacious Exhaustive
bibliography of nearly three hundred books in many languages.

HAINES, C. R.—Islam as a Missionary Religion. 1889.
A good brief account of the rise and spread of Islam, giving causes of
its success Not quite up to date.

OSBORN, MAJOR —Islam under the Arabs. London, 1876.

OSBORN, MAJOR —Islam under the Khalifs of Bagdad. 1878
These books state the case against Mohammed and Islam very strongly
Good corrective for those who have read Arnold's book.

BONET-MAURY, G.—L'Islamisme et le Christianisme en Afrique.
Paris, 1906.
A splendid monograph on the conflict between Christianity and Islam
in Africa from 630 A. D to the present. Good map

MULLER, DR. A.—Der Islam im Morgen und Abendland 2
vols. With many maps and beautiful illustrations. Berlin,
1885.
The standard work on the history of Arab empire in the East and the
West. Indispensable to the student of Moslem history.

MUIR, SIR WILLIAM —The Caliphate; Its Rise, Decline and
Fall London, 1897.
Best book on the first period of Moslem conquest.

HUNTER, SIR W. W.—Our Indian Mussulmans. London, 1871.

WHERRY, E M —Islam and Christianity in India and the Far
East. New York: Fleming H. Revell Co., 1907.
A splendid piece of work; authoritative and up to date. Containing valu-
able appendix on the work of the missionary as a preacher to Moslems

DE THIERSANT, P. D'ABRY —La Mahometisme en Chine. 2 vols.
Paris, 1878.
The authoritative book on Islam in China.

SHEDD, W. A —Islam and the Oriental Churches: Their historical relations Philadelphia, 1904.
Covers the period 600-1500 A D., but deals chiefly with Persia. Important contribution to the history of Moslem propagandism.

WOLLASTON, ARTHUR N.—The Sword of Islam. New York,
1905.
A popular account of Islam and the early caliphate. Illustrated.

CHAPTER IV

On the Whole Chapter

KLEIN, F. A.—The Religion of Islam. London: Trubner & Co ,
1906.
A scholarly book which gives all the references in the original Arabic.
Facts without deductions Best for missionaries.

SELL, E —The Faith of Islam. Chapter IV. London: Trubner
& Co., 1896.
Minute and thorough. Valuable for reference.

TISDALL, W. ST. CLAIR.—The Original Sources of the Qur'ân. S.P.C K. London, 1905.
Traces Moslem beliefs to the original heathen, Zoroastrian, and Jewish sources. Invaluable and compact handbook.

On the Moslem Idea of God

ZWEMER, S. M.—The Moslem Doctrine of God. A.T.S. New York, 1905.
A monograph, from a missionary standpoint.

HAURI.—Der Islam in seinem Einfluss auf das Leben seiner Bekenner. Leyden, 1882
Scholarly and unanswerable arguments.

PALGRAVE, W. G.—Narrative of a Year's Journey through Arabia. Vol. I, pp. 365-367.
His famous characterization of Allah   A full-length portrait of the God of the Wahabi sect of Islam

CLARKE, J. F.—Ten Great Religions. Vol II, p. 68, etc.

NOBLE, F. P.—The Redemption of Africa   Vol I, p. 73.

On Angels and Jinn

The Arabian Nights   (LANE's or BURTON's edition)

HUGHES, T. P.—Dictionary of Islam. Art. Genii, Angels, etc.

LANE—Manners and Customs of Modern Egyptians. 2 vols. London.

On the Koran

SALE's Translation for the Introduction; PALMER's for the text;

RODWELL's for chronological order of the chapters.

MUIR, SIR WILLIAM —The Coran: Its Composition and Teaching S.P C K London, 1878.
A valuable compendium; accurate and brief.

WHERRY, E. M.—A Comprehensive Commentary on the Qur'ân. London, 1882.
Very valuable for reference, and has a complete index

On Mohammed

(See Bibliography of Chapter II.)

On Jesus Christ

HUGHES.—Dictionary of Islam. Pp. 229-235.

ZWEMER, S. M.—Moslem Doctrine of God   Pp. 83-89.

GEROCK, C F—Christologie des Koran. Hamburg, 1839.

On Eschatology of Islam

Read Chapter X, on the Hell of Islam, in STANLEY LANE-POOLE'S
Studies in a Mosque.

KLEIN describes the Moslem paradise, and quotes authorities.

AMEER ALI, in The Spirit of Islam. Pp. 227-240 Calcutta, 1902.
Gives an apology and attempts to spiritualize or rationalize the orthodox
literalism.

On Predestination

DE VLIEGER, A.—La Predestination dans la Theologie Musulmane.
Leyden, 1902.

DE BOER, T. J.—History of Philosophy in Islam. London:
Luzac & Co., 1903
Gives history of the conflict between the orthodox and rationalistic par-
ties in Islam.

CHAPTER V

On the Whole Chapter

Same as for Chapter IV. Also SALE'S Preliminary Discourse
to his translation of the Koran.

AMEER, ALI —The Spirit of Islam. Part II. Calcutta, 1902.
This book explains the practical duties from the standpoint of the New
Islam.

LANE-POOLE.—Studies in a Mosque. London, 1883.
Very interesting and reliable account of outward observances

On Tradition

MUIR, SIR WILLIAM.—Life of Mahomet. Introduction.

KOELLE, S. W.—Mohammed and Mohammedanism. London,
1894.
Best account extant.

PAUTZ, OTTO —Muhammeds Lehre von der Offenbarung quellen-massig untersucht Leipzig, 1898.
Scientific, and full of references to original authorities.

On Prayer

HUGHES.—Dictionary of Islam. (Art. Prayer)

HAMID SNOW.—The Prayer-book for Moslems. Lahore: Is-lamia Press, 1893 Prayer-book of the New Islam.

On Legal Alms

BAILLE, N. B. E —Mohammedan Law. London, 1869

On the Pilgrimage

BURCKHARDT, J. L.—Travels in Arabia. 2 vols. London, 1830.

BURTON, R —Personal Narrative of a Pilgrimage to El Medina and Mecca. London, 1857 and later.
As interesting as a novel; accurate and illustrated. To be found in every good library

HURGRONJE, SNOUCK.—Mekka, mit bilder Atlas. 2 vols. The Hague, 1888.
Encyclopedic Beautiful quarto photographs of scenes in Mecca

HURGRONJE, SNOUCK.—Het Mekkaansche Feest. Leyden, 1880.
A philosophical prize paper on the origin of the Pilgrimage ceremonies.

On Jihad

SPEER, R. E.—Missions and Modern History. Vol II, pp. 441-384. Revell & Co., 1904.
An account of the Armenian massacres.

COLQUHOUN, ARCHIBALD R.—Pan-Islam (in *North American Review* for June, 1906).

Also the literature on the Mahdi in the Soudan, in Somali-land, and the present agitation in Morocco.

CHAPTER VI

On the Whole Chapter

SPEER, ROBERT E —Missionary Principles and Practice. Chapter XXIV. New York: Revell & Co
Gives a picture of conditions in Persia

The Mohammedan World of To-day. Chapters II, VI, VII, IX and XIII. New York: Revell & Co.

HAURI, JOHANNES —Der Islam in seinem Einfluss auf das Leben seiner Bekenner. Leyden, 1880.
Authoritative and philosophical.

JESSUP, H. H.—The Mohammedan Missionary Problem. Philadelphia, 1889.
Succinct and strong.

HAMILTON, C.—The Hedaya: A Commentary on Moslem Law. Translated. Edited by Grady. London, 1890.
The best text-book on the subject Gives details of laws on marriage, divorce, slave-trade, usury, and the whole subject of criminal and civil law.

On Mohammed as an Ideal

(See Bibliography of Chapter II.)

On Islam and the Decalogue

KELLOGG'S Handbook of Comparative Religion. Pp. 116-124.

On Polygamy, Divorce and the Degradation of Women

Our Moslem Sisters· An account of the conditions of womanhood in all Moslem lands; written by missionaries. New York: Fleming H Revell Company, 1907.

PERRON —Femmes Arabs avant et depuis l'Islamisme. Paris, 1858.
Excellent.

JESSUP, H. H.—Women of the Arabs New York, 1874
Interesting, and not yet out of date.

DE REGLA, PAUL —Theologie Musulmane. El Kitab des lois secretes de l'Amour. Translated from the Arabic. Paris, 1906.
Reveals all "the hidden depths of Satan" in Mohammedan morals Anyone who doubts the moral degradation of Islam and its Prophet is referred to books such as this.

On Slavery

BLYDEN, E. W.—Christianity, Islam and the Negro Race. London, 1888
A strong plea for the superiority of Islam in its treatment of the negro.

Missionary Review of the World, June, 1899. Article on The Present Centre of the Slave Trade

HUGHES.—Dictionary of Islam. Article on Slavery.

CHAPTER VII

On the Whole Chapter

SELL —The Faith of Islam. Chapter III.

HUGHES.—Dictionary of Islam. Articles on Sects and on the various sects by name.

DE BOER, T J —History of Philosophy in Islam. Translated by E R. Jones. London : Luzac & Co , 1903
Best book on the subject, and very interesting reading

On the Sunnis

(All works on Islam, when not specified, describe the teaching of this, the orthodox sect)

On the Shiahs

MALCOLM —History of Persia. 2 vols 1815.

MERRICK, JAMES L.—The Life and Religion of Mohammed. Boston, 1850.
A translation of the Shiah Traditions. Unique and reliable, but rare

On Sufiism

WHINFIELD, E. H.—Masnavi-i-Manavi, the Spiritual Couplets of Jalal-ud-din. Translated and abridged. London : Trubner & Co., 1898.
A compendium of Sufi lore and teaching, full of interesting anecdotes and clever stories.

A Mohammedan Brought to Christ: Autobiography of the late Rev. Imad-ud-Din, D.D. Twenty-two pages. C M.S. London, 1900
A remarkable human document.

The Derwish Orders

BROWN, JOHN P.—The Derwishes, or Oriental Spiritualism. London : Trubner & Co , 1868.
The standard work on the subject in English, especially on ritual.

PETIT, R. P. LOUIS.—Les Confrèries Musulmanes. Paris Librairie, B Bloud, 1902.
An interesting and brief account; up to date, and with good bibliography.

JANSEN, HUBERT —Verbreitung des Islams Berlin, 1897
Gives statistics and location of all the various orders of Derwishes.

On the Babis

SPEER, R. E.—Missions and Modern History. Vol. I, pp 118-182. Fleming H. Revell Company, 1904.
A full and fair account, with references and very valuable notes by other authorities

(See also SELL's Faith of Islam.)

On the Wahabis

ZWEMER.—Arabia, pp. 190-200. Also, The Wahabis: Their Origin, History, Tenets and Influence in *Victoria Institute Journal;* volume for 1901.
Gives complete bibliography and a chronology of Wahabi Empire.

CHAPTER VIII

On the Whole Chapter

The Mohammedan World of To-day. Being papers read at the First Missionary Conference on behalf of the Mohammedan world, held in Cairo April 4 to 9, 1906. New York: Fleming H. Revell Company, 1906

Our Moslem Sisters: A cry from lands of darkness; interpreted by those that heard it. Edited by ANNIE VAN SOMMER and SAMUEL M. ZWEMER. Fleming H. Revell Company, 1907.
A series of papers, by missionaries, on the condition of women in every Moslem land.

Islam and Christianity in India and the Far East.—By Rev. E. M. WHERRY, D D. Lectures delivered before theological seminaries. Fleming H. Revell Company, 1907.
Scholarly and up-to-date account of Islam in India, China, and Malaysia. Valuable historical material. Very readable.

Statistics of Population and Distribution of Mohammedans.

JANSEN, HUBERT.—Verbreitung des Islams. Lithographed and issued in pamphlet form. Berlin, 1897.
The statistics are exhaustive and, in most cases, reliable. Bibliography is excellent.

Government Census Reports of India.

The Statesman's Year Book.

Encyclopedia of Missions.

The Statistical Tables in the Mohammedan World of To-day. See Appendix.

CHAPTERS IX, X, XI AND XII

Before Raymund Lull

KELLER, A —Der Geisteskampf des Christentums gegen den Islam bis zur zeit der Kreuzzüge Leipzig, 1896.
An account of the attitude of the Christian church toward Islam and the early controversial writings up to the time of the Crusades. Valuable bibliography

THOMÁ, JOHANNES.—Zwei Bucher gegen den Muhammedanismus von Petrus Venerabilis. Leipzig, 1896.
A translation of the controversial tracts of Petrus Venerabilis from the Latin, with introduction.

STEINSCHEEIDER, MORITZ.—Polemische und Apologetische Literateur in Arabischer Sprache Zwischen Muslimen Christen und Juden. Leipzig, 1877.
A history of Moslem and Christian controversial writings from the earliest times.

On Raymund Lull

BARBER, W T. A.—Raymond Lull, the Illuminated Doctor. A study in medieval missions. London, 1903

ZWEMER, SAMUEL M —Raymund Lull, First Missionary to the Moslems. (Full bibliography.) New York, 1902.

ANDRE, MARIUS —Le Bienheureux Raymund Lulle. Paris, 1900.
These three biographies, appearing almost simultaneously, give a threefold portrait of Lull the first of the philosopher, the second of the missionary, and the third of the Roman Catholic saint and martyr.

Other Biographies

SMITH, GEORGE.—Henry Martyn, Saint and Scholar, First Modern Missionary to the Mohammedans. 1781-1812 New York (no date).
The best life of Henry Martyn.

EPPLER, CHRISTOFF F.—Dr. Karl Gottlieb Pfander ein Zeuge der Wahrheit unter den Bekennern des Islam. Basel, 1900.
A brief biography of Pfander, with portrait.

SINKER, ROBERT.—Memorials of the Hon. Ion Keith-Falmoner, M A., Lake Lord Almoner's professor of Arabic in the University of Cambridge and missionary to the Mohammedans of Southern Arabia. Sixth edition. Cambridge, 1890.

BIRKS, HERBERT.—Life and Correspondence of Bishop Thomas Valpy French. 2 vols. London, 1895.

JESSUP, H. H.—The Setting of the Crescent and the Rising of the Cross; or, Kamıl Abdul Messiah   Philadelphia, 1898.
The story of a Syrian convert who became a missionary in Arabia   This interesting volume has been translated into German, Daı.ish, and Dutch.

AWETARANIAN, JOHANNES —Geschichte eines Muhammedaners der Christ Wurde. Deutsche Orient Mission, Berlin, 1905.
Autobiography of a Turkish convert now a missionary to Moslems

IMAD-UD-DIN —A Mohammedan Brought to Christ: An autobiography translated from the Hindustani by the late Rev. R. Clark; with appendix and notes. London: Church Missionary Society, 1900.

Organized Missionary Work

RUTHERFORD, J. and GLENNY, EDWARD H.—The Gospel in North Africa. Story of the North Africa Mission. London, 1900

WATSON, ANDREW.—The American Mission in Egypt. 1854-1896. Pittsburg, 1898.

WATSON, CHARLES R.—Egypt and the Christian Crusade. Philadelphia, 1907.

HAMLIN, CYRUS.—Among the Turks.

PRIME, E. D. G.—Forty Years in the Turkish Empire.

STOCK, EUGENE.—History of the Church Missionary Society.

ZWEMER, SAMUEL M.—Arabia, the Cradle of Islam   New York, 1900
Chapters XXX to XXXVI give the history of missions in Arabia.

BARTON, JAMES L, D.D., and others.—The Mohammedan World of To-day. Being papers read at the First Missionary Conference, on behalf of the Mohammedan world, held at Cairo April 4 to 9, 1906. New York, 1906
A symposium on the present conditions and outlook

For further information on these four chapters, consult the general histories of missions and the reports and periodicals of the societies given in the Appendix.

INDEX

INDEX

A

Abadiyah, 141.
Abbas, 112.
Abbe Huc, quoted, 20.
Abd Allah, 13
Abd ul Hak, Sheikh, 224, 225.
Abdul Hamid, 165
Abd ul Kader, quoted on sects in Islam, 136, strives to recall Arabs of North Africa, 64
Abd ul Kasim, 147.
Abdullah, father of Mohammed, 29; invades Tripoli, 62
Abd ul Muttalib, 9, 29, 33
Abd ul Wahab, 239; quoted, 151.
Abd ur Rahman ibn Ausajah, 100.
Abraha, leads expedition to Mecca, builds cathedral at Sanaa, 20, defeated at Koreish, 20, 32
Abraham, 16, 17, 89, 92, 114; first Hanif, 23; place of, 110
Abu Bekr, convert to Mohammed, 34, 59, 70, 138, proclaimed Caliph, 58; quoted, 60.
Abu Daood, 8, 100
Abu el Hassan, 147
Abu el Kasim, 139, 147.
Abu Hanifa, 137.
Abü Huraira, 104.
Abu Ishak, 100
Abu Kabsha, 70.
Abu Kuraib, 100
Abu Soofian, 9
Abu Talib, uncle of Mohammed, 34.
Abu Ubaiha, 14.
Abyssinia, 63
Achin, 173
Adam, 89, 91, 111, 122
Aden, 200, 215
Adi bin Zaid, 8.
Æsop, 91, 92
Afghans, 74, 156.
Afghanistan, 57, 68, 141, 156, 160, 162, 165, 174, 198, 227, 232, 233, 247; estimated Moslem population of, 231.
Africa, 58, 61, 155, 156, 161, 192, 193, 198, 228, 229, 231, 237; map of unoccupied mission fields, 159, Mohammedan population of, 157, 205; Moslem situation in, 158, north, 1, 57, 138, 227, spread of Islam in, 158, 159; west, 233
Agra, population of, 215
Ahmad al Barzinji al Hasaini, 168.

Ahmadabad, population of, 215.
Ahmed, Sir Saiyad, Khan of Aligarh, 179
Aisha, 31, 32.
Aitken, Rev. J., quoted, 230.
Akaba, 36.
Akba, words of, 56, penetrates Mauritania, 62.
Akbar, 75; Emperor, 194.
Akka, 148
Alanus de Insulis, 188.
Albion, 170.
Alchemy, 178.
Aleppo visited by Mohammed, 35; population of, 215.
Alexander the Great, 91, 92
Alexandria, 217; population of, 214; taken, 62
Alfarabi, 137.
Alfred, 132
Al Ghazzali, 179; philosopher of Sunnis, 137, quoted, 94, 95
Algeciras Conference, 166
Algemeine Missions Zeitschrift, 157.
Algeria, 65.
Algiers, 56, 165, 170, 176, 204, 209, 215, 217
Al Hajaj sends expedition to Daibul, 73
Al Harith, 8.
Ali, 31, 132, 135, 138, 140; convert of Mohammed, 34
Al Kindi, quoted, 59, 189.
Allah, 50, 57, 60, 61, 111, 150; not bound by our standard of justice, 122; occurs frequently in pre-Islamic poetry, 12, place and worship of, 14; speculation on attributes of, 141; superior position of, 13; winks at sins of his favorites, 122, word not invented by Mohammed, 13
Allahabad, population of, 215.
Allahu akbar, 163
Alms, legal, 108; to whom given, 109
A Lo Shan, 70.
Ameer, 232, 247.
America, 249, 251.
American Board, 200
Amina, mother of Mohammed, 29; death of, 34
Amritsar, population of, 215.
Amru bin Kulsum, 8.

285

Lightning Source UK Ltd.
Milton Keynes UK
UKHW020834150819
348022UK00004B/370/P